DATE DUE

APR 2 8 1994		
APR 2 4 1994		
DEC 1 5 1996		

GAYLORD   PRINTED IN U.S.A.

Social Policy
and
Social Services

SECOND EDITION

Social Policy and Social Services

SECOND EDITION

▶▶▶▶▶▶▶▶▶▶ **Alfred J. Kahn**

Columbia University School of Social Work

Random House   New York

Second Edition
98765·
Copyright © 1973, 1979 by Random House, Inc.

All rights reserved under International and Pan-American Copyright Conventions.
No part of this book may be reproduced in any form or by any means, electronic or
mechanical, including photocopying, without permission in writing from the pub-
lisher. All inquiries should be addressed to Random House, Inc., 201 East 50th
Street, New York, N.Y. 10022. Published in the United States by Random House,
Inc., and simultaneously in Canada by Random House of Canada Limited,
Toronto.

Library of Congress Cataloging in Publication Data

Kahn, Alfred J   1919–
   Social policy and social services.
   Bibliography: p.
   Includes index.
   1. Social service—United States.   2. United States
—Social policy.   I. Title.
HV91.K3 1979   361'.973   78-16620

ISBN: 0-394-32229-0

Manufactured in the United States of America

Book design by Judith Allan

▶▶▶▶▶▶ Foreword

This book supplants chaos with order. The social services have been a jumbled, controversial area — attacked as having ineffective methods and subsequently defended against such assaults; confused about their purposes; beset by difficult choices among contrasting principles; and disturbed over issues of appropriate organizational form. Alfred J. Kahn has charted a way through this swamp, not by a fixed line of advocacy of a staked-out position but by codifying and clarifying conflicting positions, weighing the evidence where there is any, indicating needed research, and reconciling the reconcilable and isolating the irreconcilable. And, yet, he has managed to convey his vision of what the field should be like.

Why have the social services been in chaos since the 1960s? This period of the war on poverty was both the health of the social services, since these personal services grew enormously and rapidly, and the disease of the social services, since the growth was fragmented and tumultuous. In the war on poverty the social services were assigned an enormous role, for they operated as the major strategy (or, more accurately, chance) for improving the situation of the poor. Too much was asked of the social services, because they could not compensate for the absence of programs to provide adequate cash support for individuals outside the labor market and of national economic actions to provide decent quality employment for those in the labor market. The swiftly emerging desire of minorities for autonomy and power made participation in the operation of social services a cardinal issue. The social services became enmeshed in the political-analytical research argument about the relative importance of individual defects and characteristics (often misleadingly presented as "the culture of poverty") or external constraints (unemployment, poor housing, inadequate welfare payments) as causes of poverty. Utilitarianism and rationalism were sweeping away the older concerns with decent standards of life for people, even if a better life did not improve their ability to get a job. They also combated pragmatism and empiricism in judging the effectiveness of programs whose consequences were inherently difficult to measure and in choosing among alternative ways of accomplishing goals. The methods of the economist were threatening the values of the social worker and humanitarian.

Political resistance to selective emphasis on blacks grew as the economy inflated and then was deflated and as welfare expenditure increases made effectiveness and cost prime issues in the social services. The very purposes of the services were attacked — for should they not be declining rather than expanding with rising income levels in the nation as a whole? The continuing existence of poverty amid affluence, as public money was being spent on the poor, made suspect those programs aimed at aiding the poor.

Why are the social services in chaos in the 1970s? Both the Left and the Right converged in their distrust of professionals and professionalism. The Left was concerned with coercion and the handmaiden role of social services for monopoly capitalism: legitimating the negative features of capitalism by symbolically providing minimal services; exploiting the ideology of humanitarian community care, when in fact the motives were willful "dumping" of mental patients into the community as a way of saving state costs for institutional care, and so forth. The Right joined with a different set of criticisms: the heavy burden that social service expenditures placed upon the economy; distortion of economic functions that took place with the expansion in public expenditures; and the general ineffectiveness of social services in pursuing what were considered to be, or should have been, their goals.

Clearly then, the context in which social services operate has changed considerably. But it is a mistake to think of a context as being completely of one texture or another. There are always mixtures of beliefs, desires, ideology, and morality, as well as economics, in any given context. The admixture shifts, and the balance of influence changes from one period to another. What is striking, however, is that various elements are always there even if one particular set of elements seems to dominate for the moment. At the moment there is evidence of de-professionalization, distrust of professionals and the use of managers to oversee their activities;

an enormous preoccupation with cost and a relative neglect of access; and a growing loss of faith in practice, that is, a split between beliefs that are grounded in faith but cannot be translated to action and action that is feasible but devoid of meaning. At the same time, with all the talk about overload, in fact participation rates and the level of expenditures have increased, although the rate of increase may have slowed down somewhat. And the level of welfare benefits has, at least for short periods, outpaced the rate of increase of wages.

Historically and currently, policy makers in the social services have been ambivalent and their ambivalence is caught in a set of policy dichotomies that become the recurrent issues and dilemmas of the social services. Alfred Kahn has indicated some of these: universality versus selectivity, rights versus discretion, poverty versus inequality, consumption versus investment, cash versus in-kind benefits to mention but a few. The debate revolves around specific issues that frequently do not uncover the underlying conflict of principles and purposes.

The critique of social services in recent years has revealed several major issues. 1) The great uncertainty and unsureness about the effectiveness of the means employed in the social services. To what extent can they effectively produce the kinds of results that are desired? What technology works, under what conditions? Partly this is an issue of what kinds of goals are envisioned. 2) Programs are adopted that frequently have unforeseen consequences, as the legislative and administrative history in the social services shows. 3) A small, neglected clause in a law can have a vast effect upon who is eligible and how many people acquire what level of services at what cost. The double indexing of social security, recently corrected, is a case in point.

The social services are faced with great uncertainties of principle, context, means, and results. It is important to recognize the swiftly changing circumstances or context in which social policy operates and at the same time to be aware of the basic underlying principles that recur in the policy debates. The unsureness about linking means to purposes and the complexities of legislation and administration make the results of social services very difficult to assess.

This book is particularly notable because it brings together the available evidence of what is known about various social services. It is one of those very few attempts to probe lessons from experience and translate them into general principles for action. In a period when there is a great deal of agitation and disturbance about the social services and relatively little learning about how to make them more effective, this book provides an important beacon.

Kahn has made the analysis of the social services a microcosm of many of the basic questions now facing American society. He has taken the social services from an enclave position within the vast social welfare network and shown how their future will be shaped by the American future. In doing so, he reveals many of the choice points for all of American society.

June 1978

S. M. Miller
Martin Rein

▶▶▶▶▶▶▶ Contents

I
▶▶▶▶▶Introduction

The Need to Think About Social Services ◀◀◀◀ 1

This book is about social services — what they are and what questions must be answered in deciding what they will become. The goal is to inform citizens about issues and to guide students and scholars in pursuing them — not to advocate a comprehensive viewpoint.

The United States faces major issues of social service policy. For all its rhetoric and subsequent innovation, the American antipoverty war of the 1960s began as a social service strategy. The emphasis shifted from the social services usually employed to "rehabilitate" the poor — traditional family and child welfare, probation, and clinical services — to education, job counseling, and training; but the approach was nonetheless historically continuous with earlier "service" responses to social problems. By increasing skills and motivation and eliminating or decreasing difficulties in personal functioning, society would help people improve their situations.

In subsequent years[1] this orientation came under attack. On the one side were those who urged substitution of an "incomes strategy" instead. Their proposals, which had only limited impact, culminated in the appearance of the Report of the President's Commission on Income Maintenance Programs[2] and the Nixon Family Assistance Plan. More successful were those who preferred emphasis on political activation of the poor, especially poor blacks, on the assumption that only a shift in political power would eventually produce adequate resource redistribution to abolish poverty. Theirs was the path of "maximum feasible participation," for which income as well as service strategies were vehicles, not ends.

Social services continued, of course, as new approaches were enacted or proposed, and some — day care, Head Start, family planning, specialized employment programs, services to the aged — expanded considerably. But for a while they were in eclipse among antipoverty warriors and reformers and were held in contempt by self-styled "rev-olutionaries." A policy judgment had been made.[3]

However, despite this history, advocates of improved and expanded social services were not and are not by any means all opponents of other social strategies. Late in 1968, a federal task force report on social ser-vices urged that services not be considered as a substitute for cash and called for large-scale consumer involvement in policy development, pro-gramming, and the rendering of services.[4] At the same time the report illustrated the complexity of the policy and programming issues that must be faced by those who would expand and improve social services even in a context that posits satisfactory income maintenance and consumer participation. Issues of universalism or selectivity, of service type and priority, of delivery system and staffing, of coordination and administration all need to be faced. And the existence of significant need for social services on the American scene left little doubt that such expansion and improvement were, indeed, essential.[5]

By the early 1970s, new federal and state initiatives for the disabled, for abused and neglected children, for the aged, and for alienated adoles-cents provided evidence that social service strategies had not been abandoned. Then, after a period of confusion, Title XX, amending the Social Security Act and effective on October 1, 1975, as P.L. 93-647, offered an opportunity—but not a mandate—for some coherence in state and local social service planning. Such ongoing planning, in turn, served once again to highlight questions of concept, policy, and program strategy. By 1976, long before the answers were in, public social service expenditures had more than doubled over those of 1960.

I employ the term "social service" in these early paragraphs as though there were universal clarity as to what is meant. The fact is that social services are difficult to define because the concept carries ideological baggage and because social services are in transition. The problem of definition is discussed more fully in Chapter 1. For present purposes, social services may be seen as communal provision to promote individual and group well-being and development and to aid those in difficulty. Thus, broadly defined, social services encompass health, education, and public housing, as well as such programs as family and child welfare, services to the aging, and the various counseling and assistance programs in schools, hospitals, and similar facilities. In the present context, however, the larger, separately institutionalized systems — particularly health, income supports, housing, public employment services, and education — are excluded, and the analysis focuses on the developmental, helping, and access services that remain. The British refer to these as "personal social services." They are also occasionally referred to by me as "general social services."

This book offers an introduction for those who are preparing for work in the field, as well as for the citizens, officials, and professionals concerned with the organization, improvement, and expansion of personal social services. It begins by clarifying concepts and then turns to questions of scale, cost, and effectiveness. The major focus is on issues of social policy inherent in all major considerations about social services in the more constricted sense. While no effort is made to "sell" a perspective, my general orientation is apparent in the posing of issues and the guidance offered for their resolution. The final section, concentrating as it does on problems of social service organization and delivery, deals with current administrative, staffing, and practice questions and with specific efforts at innovation. It seeks to illustrate the relationship of policy to program, and the complexity of achieving "payoff" even after a policy decision. Inevitably, while the specific program and substantive focus is on personal social services, the broader policy and planning orientation is relevant to all social services in the international meaning of the term.

What, then, is the problem addressed? Why is there concern with social service policy and practice? Although vocabularies and explanatory concepts vary, there is an astonishing range of agreement that social services are in need of major reform in the United States (and, for that matter, in many other countries as well) and that the reform, to be relevant, must not ignore certain basic issues.[6]

In this country, social services are often and justifiably characterized as inadequate in amount, range, and quality. A listing of service categories in any community may seem reasonably comprehensive, but a counting of quantity or an analysis of users is likely to reveal even less than tokenism. For example: an inquiry about provision for homemakers discloses that there are "some" in almost every city. But twelve or fifty or even one hundred homemakers in a city of one million is meaningless, as is one small group residence for adolescents or three family service agencies employing twenty caseworkers. In another field — and it could have been any one of many — the Gerontological Society reported in 1968 as follows: "To date, no community in the United States has developed a comprehensive network of services for the aging and the aged." Services, the Society stated, are inadequate in volume and range and, where they exist, are often inaccessible.[7] Perhaps, a decade later, the conclusions would be a little less sweeping, but we are still far from significant coverage.

Similarly, there is little depth or diversity in the social service repertoire, where circumstance calls for flexibility and options. Child welfare may mean foster homes or institutional care only, but not the generally conceded needed diversity of support to help families stay together. Probation may connote supervision of delinquents and monitoring of their activities, but not the required range of community interventions to assure their reintegration as full-fledged participants. For the aging there may be a senior citizens' center or a nursing home, but not the help for a productive postretirement role, suited to individual circumstance.

Nor do available services necessarily reflect the high-quality models of the professional journals or the Sunday supplements. Users may confront drab waiting rooms, uninterested staffs, poorly trained personnel, insensitive treatment teams, ambiguous helping strategies. An agency's client may lose confidence in his family counselor; a child may refuse to confide in his foster care worker. The community center group leader may be perceived as insensitive to the needs of the senior citizens with whom he works, and so on. I cannot report a quality "batting average" for each type of social service, but there is evidence that users and potential users, community observers, friends and relatives, and accrediting or licensing bodies often have good reason to be concerned about the quality of the personal help rendered to people in trouble.

Despite these limitations, many more people apparently would make use of social programs if they knew about them or, if knowing, they could gain entry.

Finally, there are the elusive matters of "imagery" and "stigma" that attach to social programs. Services, which employ the language of "helping," often seem to emphasize control of populations and problems rather than genuine assistance. They often seem to reflect moral attitudes and social evaluations that may be characterized as "blaming the victims." Simultaneously, through a process that may appear illogical but apparently has social psychological validity, the persons who staff such services are also stigmatized and even attacked, as though they have engendered the problems or deviance they have been assigned to cure or to control. Even modern industrial societies would execute the messengers who convey bad tidings.

In short, only the most naïve of proponents believes that improvement of social services hinges solely on quantitative expansion. However, the raising of standards that apply to currently available services and the improvement of access will not be a sufficient response to the present state of the general social service system.

The manifest task also goes beyond assurance of equality for and equal responsiveness to all categories of potential users. The social scene is changing rapidly in ways especially relevant for social service planners. New concepts of rights and social priorities emerge, along with new recognition of and definitions of human need. There are monumental demographic, family structural, and life cycle changes under way which have major impact on normal development, as well as on helping processes. Self-organized citizens increasingly raise questions about the responsiveness of services in type and form of organization to changing needs and differential needs among populations. Such questions arise as: What are current standards of urban amenity? What types of social services will best assist disadvantaged citizens to become fully participating community members? What are the service requirements and priorities of above-poverty citizens, of middle-class suburbanites; or should the community invest in services for such people at all? What, basically, is a proper governmental-familial division of tasks at this time?

He who would act with reference to service quantity, quality, relevance, or access also soon discovers that no single agency can proceed alone. Services are, or are said to be, interdependent, relating in many instances to others in an apparently logical interventive sequence (wherever they are located physically) and interacting with programs in their geographic proximity as well. Since social services are largely publicly supported, whether through direct or indirect financing, proposals for improvement often stress program and policy coordination.[8] However, students of social service organization also have asked whether the creation of large and controlling coordinating structures, or what Roland Warren, in an industrial analogy, calls "cartelization," is necessarily the path of social service reform and have explored competition and other market mechanisms as the route to improved social service provision and delivery. Still other analysts have argued that, although social services cannot succeed unless they are part of an organized network, a variety of approaches to achievement of a network that protects local options appear viable. Perhaps tight coordination meets the needs of administrators more than those of service users or front-line staff. The issue in any case is not simple.

Consideration of the expansion and improvement of social services also leads to questions of resources, knowledge, and skill: What can the society afford? How much do we know? What do we know how to do? What are the requirements inherent in the doing? And, underlying any social strategy, questions of value, priority, and social thrust are equally urgent, or even more important. Strategy, direction, and posture ultimately emerge as *policy* — the wedding of reality assessment and choice, of empiricism and preference — and it is policy that is the focus of this book. I conceive of policy as the explicit or implicit core of principles, or the continuing line of decisions and constraints, behind specific programs, legislation, administrative practices, or priorities. This work concentrates on major policy options facing personal social services and on the connections between the choice of specific options and the programming and implementation strategies that follow. The discussion begins with some foundations of definition and fact.*

Notes

1. For detail, see Alfred J. Kahn, *Studies in Social Policy and Planning* (New York: Russell Sage Foundation, 1969), Chapter 2.
2. *Poverty Amid Plenty* (Washington, D.C.: Government Printing Office, 1969). Also, Robert H. Haveman (ed.), *A Decade of Federal Antipoverty Programs* (New York: Academic Press, 1977).
3. Alfred J. Kahn, with the research assistance of Ruth A. Teitelbaum, "Do Social Services Have a Future in New York?," constituting the *City Almanac* (New York: New School for Social Research, February 1971).
4. *Services for People,* Report of the Task Force on Organization of Social Services (Washington, D.C.: Department of Health, Education, and Welfare, 1968).
5. Ibid.
6. For an overview, see Sheila B. Kamerman and Alfred J. Kahn, *Social Services in the United States* (Philadelphia: Temple University Press, 1976). Also, Alfred J. Kahn, *Studies in Social Policy and Planning* (New York: Russell Sage Foundation, 1969), Chapter 6, and *Theory and Practice of Social Planning* (New York: Russell Sage Foundation, 1969), Chapter 10; Elaine Cumming, *Systems of Social Regulation* (New York: Atherton, 1968); Robert Perlman and David Jones, *Neighborhood Service Centers* (Washington, D.C.:

*Of necessity, policy questions of great importance to society, but not specific to personal social services or of great direct impact upon them, must be bypassed. Nor is this a volume about method in policy development, for which the reader is referred to the following, which, in turn, contain extensive bibliographies: Alfred J. Kahn, *Theory and Practice of Social Planning,* (New York: Russell Sage Foundation, 1969); Raymond A. Bauer and Kenneth J. Gergen (eds.), *The Study of Policy Formation* (New York: Free Press, 1968); Robert A. Dahl and Charles E. Lindblom, *Politics, Economics, and Welfare* (New York: Harper Torchbooks, 1963); Ira Sharkansky (ed.), *Policy Analysis and Political Science* (Chicago: Markham Publishing Co., 1970); Yehezkel Dror, *Public Policy Making Reexamined* (San Francisco: Chandler Publishing Co., 1968), see especially bibliographic essay, pp. 327–356; Martin Rein, *Social Policy: Issues of Choice and Change* (New York: Random House, 1970); and Neil Gilbert and Harry Specht, *Dimensions of Social Welfare Policy* (Englewood Cliffs, N.J.: Prentice Hall, 1974).

Government Printing Office, 1967); *Report of the Committee on Local Authority and Allied Personal Social Services* (Seebohm Report, Cmnd. 3703) (London: Her Majesty's Stationery Office, 1968); Gilbert Y. Steiner, *The State of Welfare* (Washington, D.C.: The Brookings Institution, 1971); William Ryan, *Blaming the Victim* (New York: Pantheon, 1971); William A. Robson and Bernard Crick (eds.), *The Future of the Social Services* (Baltimore: Penguin, 1970); "Social Services," policy statements on personal social services, the aging, children and youth, American Public Welfare Association, *Public Welfare,* 35, 2 (Spring 1977), 30–47; and "The Future for Social Services in the United States," Task Force Report, National Conference on Social Welfare (Washington, D.C.: 1977).

7. *Encyclopedia of Social Work, Sixteenth Issue* (New York: National Association of Social Workers, 1971), Vol. 1, pp. 67–68.

8 The Seebohm Report offers a recent example. An earlier effort is illustrated by Alfred J. Kahn, *Planning Community Services for Children in Trouble* (New York: Columbia University Press, 1963).

The Terrain: Personal Social Services ◄◄◄◄ 2

Such terms as "social services," "social welfare," and "social work" tend to take on somewhat different meanings in different political and cultural contexts. They are also variously employed depending upon a country's stage of economic development. Given these differences, and in the interest of clarity, we must arrive at some definitions that will serve this presentation.

What, then, are social services in the sense of the present book? Let us begin with an illustrative case situation:

The Carlicks are a low-income working-class family. Mr. Carlick is a semiskilled worker in a lumber yard. His wife, a housewife, devotes her days to their four children, ranging in age from eighteen months to five years. The oldest attends kindergarten. Not long ago, on a Saturday morning, Mrs. Carlick was not well. After a few hours she sent the five-year-old to knock at a neighbor's door. By the time Mr. Carlick got home his wife was in bed, with the children in the next room, the neighbor having helped as much as possible, given her own large family. Mr. Carlick phoned the doctor. His wife needed an appendectomy. Arrangements were made for emergency hospitalization.

Mr. Carlick would care for the children on Sunday, a free day. He had no choice about Monday, even though he lost a day's pay, but his employer told him that he had to be at work on Tuesday. What could he do? In this instance, recalling a sister's experience, he telephoned her and subsequently went to a voluntary sectarian family service agency. A homemaker was provided for child care and homemaking for the duration of the hospitalization. Mr. Carlick thus had access to a so-called preventive social service, the homemaker, where others must often place children in temporary shelters (another social service) under similar circumstances.

The experience actually opened yet another social service contact for this family. In a conversation with the hospital medical social worker, as she began to recover, Mrs. Carlick asked for some advice about the second-oldest child, who seemed in many ways "slow." The social worker arranged for a clinic visit for assessment at a later point, after Mrs. Carlick returned home.

This is not a very gripping story, but it is more typical than the occasionally dramatic case that might be offered. For the particular family, of course, the services were of great importance.* Picture the difference between the experiences of four young children with the homemaker and the alternative of living in a large custodial shelter for two weeks, away from family and probably separated from one another, not understanding what it meant or whether family life would be resumed again. Consider the difference for the mother in the hospital — not fully relaxed, with a strange woman in charge, she nevertheless had far more peace of mind to concentrate on her own medical treatment than if the family had had to be broken up to permit the operation. In fact, it is unlikely that this father would have permitted the temporary placement of his young children. His job, therefore in jeopardy, was saved by the homemaker.

Nor should one underestimate the potential value of the diagnostic assessment of the mildly retarded child, an assessment initiated through the medical social work contacts.

In a relatively narrow sense, the term "social services," as often employed in the United States and as referred to in this book, includes such activities as the following:

1. Day care and similar child development and child care programs (Head Start, family day care, group care for infants or for 3- to 5-year-olds in centers, after-school care, and so on)
2. Homemaker, home help, and chore services
3. Personal and family guidance and counseling, including marital counseling
4. Child welfare activities such as foster home care, adoption, and protective services for neglected or abused children

*Of no small significance , too, is the fact that the homemaker was far less expensive for the community than almost all the alternatives.

5. Assessments for courts, schools, or camps of parental relationships (are parents neglectful? with which member of a separated couple should a child reside?) or of a child's personality and capacities (is he capable of adjusting to a normal group?)
6. Big Brother, Big Sister, and related volunteer helping and guidance efforts
7. Family planning services (advice, counseling, referral, etc.)
8. Community centers for the aged, for youth, for families
9. "Meals on wheels," nutrition, "senior citizen" programs, transportation, and special protective programs for the aged
10. A diversity of such group programs as therapeutic group work with adolescents, organization of tenants in a housing project, organization of the parents of retarded children
11. Home management counseling and educational activity, as well as home improvement services
12. Rural welfare programs and special programs for migrant laborers
13. Special programs to counsel potential migrants or immigrants and help them cope with new surroundings
14. Assistance to residents of poverty areas or members of underprivileged population groups, so that they may come together for mutual aid activity
15. Information, advice, referral, complaint, and advocacy services of many kinds
16. Institutional programs for the neglected, dependent, disturbed, or frail (state training schools, homes for the aged, adult homes, residential treatment for children, and so on)
17. Counseling, therapeutic, rehabilitation, and education services for drug addicts and alcoholics
18. Social services in schools, hospitals, clinics, churches, industrial establishments, and other settings

This is a disparate listing from several vantage points. Before examining more formal definitions or attempting to classify such services by types, some historical and social perspectives may be helpful. It will not otherwise be clear why and in what sense the above listing may constitute a field and why there are both broader and narrower listings that are also employed. Nor will the derivation of some of the policy questions subsequently introduced be understood without such background.

Social Services in Industrial and Postindustrial Societies

Social services appear everywhere in the modern world. They continue to exist and even expand, as productivity increases and as average standards of living are raised. Indeed, they are seen as part of the improved standards. Thus, quite contrary to the assumptions of a laissez-faire social ethic, social services are hardly marginal or transitional programs. To comprehend this fully, it is useful to discuss the *manifest,* the apparent, the conscious functions of social services as well as the *latent,* less visible, hidden functions.

If the point of departure is the agrarian life of the preindustrial society, the task of the social services in an urban and industrial world is to contribute to personal and group development and socialization, as a substitute for what the community as a whole or the extended family once did. Families in the rural economy were tightly knit units for production, protection, distribution, consumption, socialization, and control, which turned to outside institutions only to settle matters among them, and between them and their God, for defense against outsiders, and for the minimum of essential trade.

The specialization of modern life gives the family a much more circumscribed role, a subject to which many scholars have devoted considerable attention. The family as an economic unit has given way to specialized, usually large, organizations, in which any given individual has a limited assignment. Distribution and personal services, the activities of a few in an agrarian world, become major economic roles in the society because, as a significant unit of consumption, the family does not by itself produce goods or services, nor has it access to the productivity of others. Increasingly, this state of affairs prevails even for those in agriculture. Large farm-factories relate a worker only to one crop, often one he cannot consume. He frequently lacks the traditional small holding for the raising of produce for his own family, the agricultural worker's wage supplement in transitional periods.

The complex requirements of modern productivity and citizenship demand a level of education well beyond the family's capacity to offer. Specialized institutions take over. Progress in science removes the primary group control over cure of illness. Similarly, the interdependence of modern urban life makes it dangerous for families to take the law into their own hands. Much of the internal protection and social control is socialized and becomes a responsibility of organized society. Some families desert the church in its role in guiding motivation and defining the desirable. Major affectional, child-rearing, socialization assignments are retained in the family, but even some of these give way, as mothers of young children choose to or must work, marriages are broken by desertion or divorce, and adolescents pull away from family influence at young ages.

In an earlier day, intimate neighbors, as well as grandparents and other relatives, were ever present to transmit norms and tradition, to guide and educate, to control. Now, given the physical mobility concomitant with industrialization, they may not be anywhere nearby. Even if close, they are less likely to be in the household — or, if there, are far less influential.

Husbands and wives themselves take advantage of formal educational and self-improvement activity or of the less formal, but commercially or socially organized, recreational-cultural activities that include bowling leagues, bridge and golf clubs, and garden clubs. Some devote time and effort to a diversity of civic activities. At the same time the usual neighborhood informal social activities may exist.

The above paragraphs are written as though there were only two family types today: remnants of the old type of extended families or kinship networks and modern, small, two-adult nuclear families. The 1970 White House Conference on Children reminded its participants that modern society is actually characterized by a diversity of family types: nuclear family, dyadic-nuclear family (childless, with at least one working), dual-work family (well over half the two-parent families in the United States), single-parent family, three-generation family, middle-aged or old-aged couple, kin network, second-career family, and institutional family. Emerging experimental and deviant structures include the monogamous commune family, the group-marriage commune family, the unmarried-couple-and-child family, and homosexual couples with adopted children.

Some of these are prevalent types, some relatively rare. Some are disapproved, others held up as models. But variations in family type are more common than the earlier ethic might have recognized. Children can and do flourish in many contexts — especially where there are social supports.[1]

What are the implications of all this: the decrease of familial functions in production, distribution, education, control, and so on; the multiplication of family "types" in the modern world; the elaboration of specialized functions in extrafamilial institutions, often large and remote; the rare appearance of an extended family as a living unit;* the assignment of some affectional primary group behavior to other institutions, while certain major responsibilities continue to belong to the family? Clearly, the answer is that, unless the needs have disappeared — and they apparently have not — society must in the normal course of industrialization guarantee and institutionalize the means to assure that essential old functions are discharged in new ways and that new functions are recognized as a legitimate response to new circumstances.

---

*Modern historical and demographic research indicates that the extended family probably has never been the typical residential unit in the United States or most West European countries. See Peter Laslett (ed.), *Household and Family in Past Time* (London: Cambridge University Press, 1972; or Michael Gordon and Tamara Hareven (eds.), *New Social History of the Family,* special issue, *Journal of Marriage and the Family,* 35, 3 (August 1973), 393–495.

These, then, are the tasks of the personal social services:

1   To strengthen and repair family and individual functioning with refer-
    ence to ongoing roles
2. To provide new institutional outlets for socialization, development,
    and assistance, roles that once were — but are no longer — fully
    discharged by the nuclear or extended family, neighbors, or the kin
    network
3. To develop institutional forms for new activities, essential to individu-
    als, families, and groups in the complex urban society even though
    unknown in a simple society

In other words, social services do not merely replace or seek to correct
the family or earlier social forms. *They are also new responses to new
social situations.* They are social inventions that seek to meet the needs
of modern man in his interrelationships and roles, much as technical
innovation is a response to the physical requirements of modern living.

Latent Functions

To consider social services in this way is to recognize how inadequate is
the view that personal social services will no longer be needed as
societies abolish poverty, increase equity, and cope with their current
problems. Indeed, the very facts of economic growth and technological
change depend upon and, in turn, stimulate major social changes. Such
changes, we have seen, demand new institutional provision for meeting
the affectional, socialization, and developmental — as well as rehabilitative — needs of people. The very success of the economic growth
process requires further institutional response. This is part of the purpose
of social services. In short, the very process of implementation of concepts of fairness or equality requires institutional vehicles. The attack on
old or new social problems — and new prosperity or economic forms do
create new problems — also demands appropriate instruments.

Critics, particularly in countries that combine strong Puritan and
pioneering strains with individualism (and this may include "socialist"
states), attack the users of social services as in some way morally inadequate and as exploiters of the larger society. However correct this
may be for the occasional malingerer, a universal if minority social role, it
hardly characterizes the typical social service user in modern times. Indeed, "citizen" and "social service consumer" become synonymous
terms in the industrial and postindustrial world.

There are others, often on the political left, who question personal
social services as the "opium of the masses," a diversion from the "real

problems" of achieving social equality and money and power redistribution. These social services, they allege, are "Band-Aids." The position has logical merit, but only from an anarchist's perspective. If society does not respond to change, does not adjust institutions to new needs, does not find new ways to enrich the lives of the young and the old — as old forms are outgrown — there may build up a pressure for social upheaval. He who believes that the continuation of adverse conditions is the road to social progress opposes social services. Others will agree that well-designed and effectively delivered social services may meet needs and may even create satisfactions. This is hardly a state of affairs to be avoided. Indeed, social services, on a substantial scale and of fundamental character, may signify and implement large-scale social change and societal enrichment. They may be the instruments for redistributional policy.

Even so, it remains true that at a given time or place one may discern that the latent intent of a particular proposal or program is to create a smoke screen, offer an illusion of solutions, divert political pressure. This kind of misuse is not rare in the political world: circuses rather than bread. A youth training program is advertised with great fanfare to divert attention from the need for jobs. A major series of delinquency programs is launched to cover up the lack of an approach to adolescents who are at loose ends. A campaign is undertaken to train mothers to work and offer day care to their children as a way to obscure the refusal to develop an adequate income maintenance program for fatherless families. A request to fund a specialized counseling and group care program for blacks is approved as a way to avoid racial integration in a similar program nearby.

In short, there is no question that in the modern world social services perform essential, recognizable, even expanding functions. Their validity is unquestionable. Yet, proposals for a *given* service at a *given* time, and programs for implementing services in a specific way, merit scrutiny. The latent intent — usually relating to political strategies but sometimes otherwise motivated — may also be discerned and may shed light on issues of timing, focus, and program.

Not all latent functions reflect "plots" to divert and distort. In all public policy and action there is a multitude of motives and goals, as actors join to promote or compromise on programs. With many unknowns in the equation, participants are often unable to anticipate fully what they have wrought or to perceive the functions discharged. Thus, some aspects of the Community Action Program, under the 1964 antipoverty war, may have been intended, by some of the designers, to "universalize" or "integrate" the civil rights movement or to substitute a sociotherapeutic program strategy for a political approach. What occurred in some places, however, was different. An institutional base was offered and jobs became available more systematically to organize political and protest activity within the black community. On the other hand, paraprofessional jobs and money had the latent consequence of giving some people a stake in the status quo and co-opting them. The doctrine of participation spilled over into Model Cities and health programs, with still other results, and launched other programs.[2]

Creating Social Integration

The approach up to this point would appear excessively utilitarian to some students of social policy. Whether they approach the matter from the tradition of religiously based charity or anthropologically informed social justice, there are observers who feel that it is not accurate to overemphasize the practical values of social services. To stress concrete socialization, care, support, and help — to the exclusion of all else — is to justify economizing and market approaches to policy choice, subjects that we discuss at a later point.

In an extraordinarily strong and dramatic statement, Richard M. Titmuss, the British social policy theoretician, argues that social policy is distinguished from economic policy because of its focus on institutions that "create integration and discourage alienation." Social services are involved in those areas of "personal behavior and relationships that lie outside the reciprocal rights and obligations of family and kinship in modern society." Social services encourage "anonymous helpfulness" and obligations that derive from one's own character, not from contracts. Whether latent or manifest, altruism becomes a major function of social services in this sense — serving the donor as well as the recipient. To which Robert Pinker adds that welfare state programs depend for their successful implementation on strengthened, not declining, altruism.[3]

The Scope of Social Services in Differing Societies

It is useful to distinguish (a) those social services that become so elaborate and comprehensive as to achieve independent identity, and which in the United States are seldom thought of as social services (education, public [cash] assistance, medical care, public employment activities, and public housing, especially), from (b) the remaining social services, encompassing a field with changing boundaries and including some "free-standing" programs (child welfare or family service agencies) and some that are located in other institutions (school social work, medical social service, social services in public housing, industrial social welfare programs, and so on).

The latter programs are the subject of this book. They will be described as "personal social services." These personal, or general, social services are programs that protect or restore family life, help individuals cope with external or internalized problems, enhance development, and facilitate access through information, guidance, advocacy, and concrete help of several kinds.

To elaborate initially in a broader frame, a social service listing in a developing country might consider such personal social services as those listed above to belong to a subcategory called "social *welfare* services," insofar as they focus on assistance to individuals and families where there is a problem of adjustment and functioning or some deprivation to be remedied. A more inclusive "social service" list in such countries, addressing all population elements, would also include

1. Income maintenance (including social security as well as what Americans call public assistance or "relief")
2. Health programs (all those that are not private medicine)
3. Public education
4. All public housing activities
5. Employment programs

Varying with the country, the full social service list might or could include other activities, ranging from recreational and cultural activity to public transportation, from area rehabilitation efforts to mass indoctrination as preparation for modernization.

Most industrialized countries yield social service listings whose scopes range between the United States illustrations presented above and the more inclusive listings of developing countries.* The main criterion seems to be the social decision to guarantee a program, a facility, a right because it is part of a communally conceived minimum or is believed to fulfill a broader public purpose so important that individual access should not be determined by adequacy of one's personal income and decisions made in the marketplace. While not rejecting these views, Titmuss also notes the job market derivations of some services by describing them as

*Recent British literature refers to the "personal" social services as "the fifth social service," as distinguished from education, health, housing, income maintenance. See Peter Townsend, et al., *The Fifth Social Service* (London: Fabian Society, 1970). I add nonmarket employment programs, a sixth service system.

Britain's relevant cabinet post, covering the Department of Health and Social Security, has jurisdiction over most general social services in our sense as well as over income transfers and health. It tends to concentrate a larger proportion of personal social services than does our own Department of Health, Education, and Welfare, which shares jurisdiction with a larger group of administrations, bureaus, and departments, despite its primary role. The responsible cabinet officer is known as the Secretary of State for Social Services.

compensation for socially caused diswelfare or as a substitute for salaries (occupational welfare).[4]

Definitions often refer to scope, purpose, or characteristics of the social services — or all three. For example, in the United Nations,

social service is defined as an organized activity that aims at helping toward a mutual adjustment of individuals and their social environment. This objective is achieved through the use of techniques and methods that are designed to enable individuals, groups, and communities to meet their needs and solve their problems of adjustment to a changing pattern of society, and through cooperative action to improve economic and social conditions.[5]

This, clearly, is close to the general, or personal, social service concept.

A British report is somewhat similar in its perspective:

The social services cover a wide range of provisions to promote the health and well-being of the people of Britain and to improve the surroundings in which they live. The underlying motive is the recognition that the community as a whole has a responsibility to help its weaker and less fortunate members and to seek to secure for all its citizens those services which they cannot provide for themselves as individuals.[6]

In general, social services tend to be targeted on individuals, groups, and communities and to involve the rendering of help, the supplying of resources, and the implementation of benefits. The mutual aid and group targeting on broader social or economic conditions, described in the last phrase of the U.N. definition, is widely accepted conceptually but is actually not the common social service practice.

A United States task force suggested this:

Social services [our "personal social services"] are those services rendered to individuals and families under societal auspices, excluding the major independent fields of service [that is, excluding health, education, housing, income maintenance].[7]

The following definition, again referring to all six systems, focuses on purposes:

Social services may be interpreted . . . as consisting of programs made available by other than market criteria to assure a basic level of health-education-welfare provision, to enhance communal living and individual functioning, to facilitate access to services and institutions generally, and to assist those in difficulty and need.[8]

The "other than market criteria" in this definition is important. It conveys a societal obligation or conviction about the importance of access to the benefit. Society has decided that an individual's inability to command a service in the marketplace — that is, his inability to pay for it out of earnings or wealth — should nonetheless not deprive him of it. Kenneth Boulding calls this a unilateral or nonreciprocated benefit, in the sense that the provider offers the service or goods whether or not the recipient is able to pay.[9]

Inevitably the range, quantity, and accessibility of social services will vary with a country's stage of development and wealth, and with the sociocultural and political factors that determine the priority accorded these claims upon national income. In the post–World War II period, for example, developing countries tended to give priority to those social services that might prepare people to assume employment in new industrial settings and to live in urban areas (literacy training and health services, for instance).

As social services become more universally available and are more generally employed, for this is the tendency, there is a decreasing inclination to describe them as social *welfare* services, that is, services for those in need of *special* help and protection. On the other hand, these circumstances also create an increasing tendency to give subgroups of services independent institutional identities (health, education, housing, employment counseling, income maintenance) and not to refer to them as social services at all. It remains to be seen whether such processes will continue here, as the separation of most personal social services from public financial aid (a subject to be discussed subsequently) becomes common practice in the United States, and as there is further recognition of the applicability of services, not to the poor alone, but to all population elements.

For the present, Willard Richan's summary is useful. He notes that social services may be seen as involving:

a direct benefit, which is standardized for an identifiable population; it is socially sponsored, therefore accountable to the general society, and is exempted from (some of?) the rules of the marketplace.[10]

And we would add: Although traditionally reserved for the disadvantaged and the troublesome, and thus describable as belonging to the class of social control mechanisms addressed to deviant groups, social services are increasingly recognized as applicable to the total population — or, more accurately, *some* social services are.

Human Services, Social Services, Social Welfare

Why is it that such fields as education or health may be included in a social services listing in one country and omitted in another? A historical hypothesis may be offered.

Social work is a twentieth-century profession. However, since the breakup of feudalism there have existed rudimentary, often punitive, programs of care and control for the able-bodied poor, the elderly, dependent children, the handicapped, the mentally ill or retarded, the antisocial. They were long undifferentiated. The idea that the diverse kinds of programs we have listed be considered as components of a *system* of social services has developed within the past three or four decades. Much earlier the most industrialized and urbanized parts of the world had established extensive systems of public education and public health. These engendered their own professional hierarchies and their own organizational structures. They could not in fact be included in governmental administrative structures as components of a system that comprised child welfare, social (cash) assistance, family welfare, delinquency, and mental illness. They dwarfed these latter and refused to be associated with their stigma. For, the fact that early social services had "poor law" derivations, and often implemented the controlling, punitive, or rehabilitative aspects of "last resort" public provision of funds for the families in dire economic need,[11] is part of the general social service legacy even today.

The notion that all who receive financial relief may be assumed to require personal guidance and rehabilitation has died hard. Nor has there been easy and immediate acceptance of the view that social services may have something to offer people who are not poor. Yet anyone could see that public education activities are valid for all — and many viewed public health services in the same way.

Small wonder then that, in the United States, education and health were not termed "social services" and that other countries introduced the concept "social *welfare* services" specifically to identify programs for the needy and those in need of "help" rather than "service" — that is, those who were the objects of control or reform.

Great Britain and some other highly industrialized countries generally made the shift to a broad view after World War II, as "labor," "socialist," or "social justice" concepts led them to see the relationships among the components: health, education, housing, employment services, child welfare, and so on. Developing countries, beginning almost from scratch and with limited resources, had no choice but to plan a relatively extensive system with mutually supportive components — even if distinguishing those elements that were provided for all citizens from programs for the needy and sick. In the United States we — and we are not alone — are not quite ready either to see the whole or to ignore interrelationships completely. Rather, we tend to develop new euphemisms to convey the concepts implied in a broad view of social services. Increasingly, therefore, one hears talk of "human services," which are, in effect, social services covering both universal services (services for all citizens) and those for groups in special need. Reference is also made to "human resource programs," a less satisfactory term, since it conveys the market-oriented notion of social services that seek to prepare or rehabilitate people for employment (see pages 101ff. re services as "investment") and does not encompass other social service functions ("consumption").

What then is social *welfare?** Social welfare as an institution comprises all those policies and programs by which government guarantees a defined minimum of social services, money, and consumption rights, through the employment of access or distribution criteria other than those of the marketplace. All modern societies have considerable social welfare commitment and increasingly interweave social welfare policies with economic, physical, tax, tariff, transportation, and even broad political policies. It would therefore be conceptually accurate to describe the institution as "social welfare," the services as "social services." For the reasons given, however, we may expect to confront for some time a distinction between social services and social *welfare* services — and, perhaps, to discover a preference for some new term, such as "human services."

In short, "human services" is a term now used to describe the American equivalent of "social services" as used elsewhere in the world, covering six systems. Income transfers, education, health, housing, and employment are recognized. The personal social services, our special focus here, may thus be thought of as the emerging *sixth* human service or social service system.

Many professions and semiprofessions[12] are involved in social services such as medicine, education, public recreation, physical and vocational rehabilitation, nutrition, psychology, employment counseling, and social work. Within the field that we have called "personal social services" (nonmedical, noneducational, and so on), social work is the dominant, host profession. In recognition, general social services are now organized in Scotland through local authority social work departments, whereas the term "local authority personal social services" is preferred elsewhere in Britain. *Social work services* may thus be said to be those social services in which social work has a central role. They are sometimes rendered in agencies where social workers are the major group (family services or child welfare) and are sometimes adjunctive activities in schools, hospitals, residential institutions, or community agencies in which the social work service is less central to the main function. Historically, the majority of such services have been addressed to the poor, the troubled, the

---

*In the United States, when the term "welfare" is used alone, it generally refers to public (social) assistance programs (means-tested relief).

deviant; but services are increasingly being valued for broader population groups as well.

Socialist societies have tended to view social services in a somewhat different context. The concept of "public consumption" or "collective consumption" is employed to describe those goods and services that are, in other countries, both human services, in the above sense, and market-purchased items. The productivity and profit that might comprise the "wage pool" is deliberately divided on a policy basis, as between wages and public consumption. Reports note, for example, that several years ago public consumption in Romania represented an addition of 15.7 percent to real wages, whereas the U.S.S.R. stated that the increase was about one-third. (These estimates are probably outdated, but the concept is of interest.) The listing covers social services in the broadest sense as well as recreational and cultural items. The counseling-guidance-access service components are not very visible. The U.S.S.R. listing includes education, cultural activity, medical service, rest and convalescence, physical culture and sports, social insurance, social assistance, special programs for women, maternal and child care, aid to mothers of large families and to unmarried mothers, and housing (consumers pay only 4 to 5 percent of salaries for rent). Wages are paid according to labor force factors, but public consumption goods are distributed regardless of the quality-quantity of an individual's work (what are called "nonmarket criteria").[13]

The British have employed the concept of "social wage" in recent years as their way of highlighting public consumption through social services (all human services), as contrasted with personal consumption paid for out of income or capital.

It has become quite clear that, as East European "socialist" countries urbanize and industrialize, they recognize the significance of social policy as an independent domain and begin to develop personal social services not unlike those in the West.[14] Nonetheless, because the socialist ideological and economic frameworks generate some policy issues of their own, this book will be relevant to those countries only insofar as issues and programming problems are shared by capitalist, mixed, and socialist societies. Indeed, since even within this field selection is essential for present purposes, the criterion of relevance to the U.S. *urban* scene will be applied constantly. For the most part, reference to other countries will be made only where it clarifies elements germane to the primary focus.*

*There is considerable evidence of shared and parallel preoccupation with reference to social services in many countries. The records of the United Nations, UNICEF, and a number of other international bodies offer documentation, too, of shared endeavors pointed toward developing answers with some general validity.

Can Social Services Expand?

This section introduces very briefly a subject that will appear on many agenda.

It had long been assumed that the postindustrial society, allocating increasing proportions of its labor force to the service — rather than the industry or agriculture — sections of the economy, would continue to expand social (nonmarket) services. During the late 1970s this assumption has been questioned in both Europe and the United States on the ground of costs. In simplified form, the new analysis goes as follows: Salaries and real income have continued to rise in both the private and the public sectors. In industry and agriculture the rationale has been a marked increase in productivity. (In fact, wage increases often are geared to productivity.)

However, salary increases in the public sector and in private social services have reflected unionization, political pressure, and concern for equity. The increased costs of services, coming at a time when citizens want more service and in the absence of an equivalent of increased productivity, have placed severe strains on government and on philanthropy. In some social service fields (hospital care) and in other parts of the public sector (sanitation), there is an all-out search for increased productivity. Elsewhere (counseling, advice, education, and so on), there is dispute as to the applicability of the concept. For the first time in some decades, even the most enthusiastic proponents of the social services have expressed uncertainty about future expansion.[15] For one thing, in the absence of rapid new economic growth, government will lack the funds. Or, if it taxes industries excessively, they will raise prices and suffer in the international trade competition. For another, given the choice, consumers may prefer lower taxes and durable goods purchased in the market.

The debate about economic growth, more generally, may also be relevant here. If the most pessimistic prophets of ecological disaster are right — we are writing in the midst of an unresolved debate — society must do more than curb its birth rate. Resources must be conserved and production must be decreased; otherwise, resource depletion, pollution, and overpopulation will overcome us. Planning under such circumstances will require considerable redistribution of resources in accord with social policy. But it will surely also be premised on decreased consumption generally, as on a degree of service contraction or on careful selection of priorities and mix among social services. In either case, the specifics of social service policy will be of great importance.

And, if the forecasts are wrong because new technology will correct pollution and substitute for depleted resources, the social and technological changes will create circumstances of great significance for the social services. Whatever response is given, it will need to be informed and considerable.

Typologies

Social services have been — and may be — classified in diverse ways, depending on the purpose of the classification. For example, a United Nations publication concerned with the strategy of development planning considers the following to encompass the *functions* of social services:

1. The progressive improvement of the living conditions of people
2. The development of human resources
3. The orientation of people to social change and adjustment
4. The mobilization and creation of community resources for development purposes
5. The provision of institutional structures for the functioning of other organized services.[16]

Apparent overlapping would appear to preclude use of such a listing for operational planning purposes.

Richard M. Titmuss, examining the manifest *functions* of social service from the perspective of the society, lists the following, which we have paraphrased, rearranged, and illustrated:

1. Services or benefits designed to *add to the welfare* of individuals, families, or groups, immediately, or in the long run (a day care program)
2. Services or benefits designed to *protect* society (probation)
3. Services or benefits designed as an *investment* in people essential to achievement of social goals (a job-training program)
4. Services or benefits designed "as *compensation* for socially caused disservices," where responsibility cannot be otherwise assigned (industrial accident compensation, compensatory programs where there has been racial or sex discrimination)[17]

Of course one may also classify social services by *program focus:* occupational welfare, community service, school service, health-based service, institutional facilities, and so on.

As already noted, some countries distinguish between social services, the collective resources deemed essential for all citizens, and social *welfare* services, the programs designed for the needy and the unfortunate.

Martin Rein and S. M. Miller list the following as the major current conceptions of the *functions* of social services: amenity, access, aid at transition points, and specialized alleviation. While these authors tend to highlight differences among these several views of the functions of social services, we would argue that social services do have a series of important social functions that need not be seen as being in contradiction or conflict — even though different views are accented in competition for resources. For purposes of examining social services policy issues and problems related to the delivery of social services, the following *classification of social service functions* (which is illustrated in the sections that follow) is helpful and will be *employed in this volume:*

1. Socialization and development
2. Therapy, help and rehabilitation (including social protection and substitute care)
3. Access, information, and advice

One might assume that these would always be identifiable, mutually exclusive functions, so that at any given moment all social services, such as those listed illustratively on pages 12–13, would be easily classifiable, This is not the situation, however. From what has already been said, and from much yet to be introduced, it may be noted that social services are at the heart of a society's value debates and political philosophies. How much and what should be guaranteed to all citizens? To what extent should a society urge citizens to rely on communal provision in contrast to individual initiative? What is the goal or emphasis of a given program? Are social services solely or largely for the unfortunate and the antisocial — or should there, under any circumstances, be a segregated system for such people? Should there be priorities for the poor, the deprived?

In this context, a given social service program may have different functions and different target populations within a given city, or under varied auspices. Sometimes a program form has varied possibilities and lends itself to sound use for different purposes; whether programs serving diverse groups and different objectives should be administratively separated or unified is a programming issue. Day care is generally a child development, socialization resource. However, a specialized day care program may be therapeutically focused on a particular group of emotionally disturbed children. Or day care may be set up so that mothers can be compelled to work.

Similarly, homemakers may be a resource for all "normal" retired elderly in one place, or they may be employed to implement a rehabilitative program in another. Access or advocacy programs may be organized for universal usage or to help the very poor and deprived, who are often closed out by many programs.

Despite these difficulties in subsuming ongoing programs under one category, and one category only, all the time, it will be useful for many of the purposes of the present undertaking to employ our threefold classification.* Further elaboration and illustration is therefore in order.

Social Services for Socialization and Development

In a major sense, social services exist to protect, to change, or to innovate with respect to many of the educational, child-rearing, value-imparting, and social induction activities once assumed by the family, the neighborhood, and relatives. The goal is socialization into communal values, transmittal of goals and motivation, and enhancement of personal development. Cognitive and emotional aspects of learning are encompassed. The means are formal, semiformal, and informal.

Among the relevant social services, even in countries that do not think of formal educational machinery and the activities of church groups as social services, are such things as:

1. Day care or child development programs
2. Youth centers and hostels
3. Summer camps
4. Family planning
5. Lunch and breakfast programs in schools and churches
6. Centers for senior citizens
7. Home-delivered hot meals
8. Parent groups
9. Family vacation programs

Social Services for Therapy, Help, Rehabilitation, and Social Protection

The phrase "substitute care" belongs in this title as well. Sometimes services seek to help individuals with problems by supplementing or substituting for the primary group supports, as in the instance of a Big Brother program or adoption. Often the focus is on brief or intensive personal help with environmental, situational, interpersonal, or intrapsychic programs. Frequently the goal is restoration of as much normal functioning as possible, where there is no real cure but the possibility of reasonable readjustment of relations between an individual or group and their social environment. Often the assignment is that of assuming societal control over "dangerous" or unacceptable deviance while help is rendered, if it can be.

*For many other purposes, as will be noted subsequently, a twofold classification also is helpful: social utilities and case services. See pages 73–76.

Included in this category are such services as:

1. Family casework services
2. Child welfare programs, particularly foster home care and adoption, as well as child protection
3. Juvenile probation and parole
4. Group therapy
5. Friendly visiting of the handicapped or the aged
6. Therapeutic camps
7. Institutions for delinquents and other children considered to need supervison; also, community-based residences
8. Programs that focus help on the coping problems or adjustment needs of migrants or immigrants
9. School social work with troubled or troublesome children
10. Medical social work
11. Child guidance programs
12. Protective services for the aged

Access Services

The need for social services focused on the access function has four sources: (1) modern bureaucratic complexity, (2) variations among citizens in knowledge and understanding of rights or in appreciation of the values of certain resources, benefits, or entitlements, (3) discrimination, and (4) geographic distance between people and services.

The incremental development of social services, the mixed motivations of their framers at various moments of history, and the sheer size of caseloads and staffs make it increasingly urgent that provision for access be made. Social workers — as liaison personnel, "social brokers," "child advocates," *assistantes sociales* — often devote their major efforts to spreading knowledge and creating linkages so that programs may be reached and used. In fact, the U.N.'s Third International Survey of Social Work Education reported widespread acceptance of the following notion, one of the few universal characteristics of social work: "It is a liaison activity, through which disadvantaged individuals, families, and groups may tap all of the resources in the community available to meet their unsatisfied needs."[18]

The task of assuring access has become most urgent in recent decades, as program proliferation and increase of entitlement have not necessarily been followed by organizational realignment. Only an extremely well-informed citizen understands fully his rights and entitlements and the organizational machinery to be dealt with in gaining access to them.

Because the educated and the more affluent are more likely to know about or to have the ability to find out about services, there are those who would give priority to access services for the very poor. Others cite universal need. The question soon becomes enmeshed in all the issues relating to the universalism-selectivity policy, addressed in a later section. One specific form of the issue refers to the creation of special services for blacks, Indians, Puerto Ricans, Mexican Americans, and others who have suffered particular discrimination.

Access does not necessarily follow from provision of information alone. Access services may include information, advice, referral, complaints, case advocacy, class advocacy, and legal services, all on both individual and group bases. Included are such programs as neighborhood information centers, citizens' advice bureaus, neighborhood legal services, "hot lines," ombudsman and complaint machinery, consumer education or self-protection groups, and radio and newspaper information services.*

Brief mention may be made of an additional function sometimes attributed to social services: facilitating *participation.* A society faced by a history of exclusion and alienation may try to rectify long injustice and enhance local democracy by creating social services that encourage participation in community decision making by the excluded. The Community Action Program under the U.S. antipoverty program, as launched in 1964, emphasized participation, as did the subsequent Model Cities Program. In fact, the community organization method in social work, before it became increasingly preoccupied with formal planning, advocacy, and technical expertise in the late 1960s, was devoted overwhelmingly to facilitating citizen participation as volunteer direct service personnel, planners, fund raisers, and interpreters of programs. In the earlier period, however, the subjects of such programs were middle- and upper-middle-class Americans.

Recent participation programs have given special attention to the poor and to members of minority groups. Stress is placed on bringing citizens "indigenous" to a neighborhood into participation on all levels. The goal is variously seen as sociotherapeutic ("to reduce alienation"), individually therapeutic ("to instill a sense of confidence"), service reform ("to make programs more relevant"), or political ("to redistribute resources and power").

Programs in this category include tenant organizations, special-interest action groups (welfare mothers), and volunteer recruitment services. More recently they have been joined by self-help and mutual aid groups in many fields, ranging from single and divorced parents to ex–drug addicts to former child-abusing parents. Among their activities is

---

*Organizational alternatives for access services are discussed in Chapter 8.

"consumer" monitoring of service bureaucracies and a degree of advocacy.

I have not included participation in the preferred typology, not out of failure to recognize the significance of participation as a goal but because, in effect, it tends to overlap excessively with the other three categories. It represents a somewhat different classification perspective. Participation may be a *consequence* of how programs are organized, conducted and staffed — whether the primary or manifest objective is developmental, therapeutic, or the improvement of access.

Participation, in short, is sometimes means and sometimes goal, in my view. Nonetheless, I recognize contrary perspectives. Kramer, for example, while quite realistic about limited successes and undesirable, unanticipated consequences, considers participation a category on a par with service. In fact, his well-documented case studies suggest that "participation" and "service" could be two functions in tension and that choices must be made. In his words, the choice may have to be "the competent community or the competent program."[19] At least a given program may find it difficult simultaneously to promote both.

Nor have I suggested other possible principles of classification that, however valid, seem less fundamental than the distinctions among the three major service categories. For example, (1) there are services targeted at individuals, at groups, and at institutions; (2) there are services that would control, change, or stabilize the deviant; and (3) there are "concrete" aids (food, shelter) and relationship-oriented assistance. Much will be said about these later in a broader context, where they may be related to certain basic policy options.

Notes

1. For this view, see the report of Forum 14, *Report to the President, White House Conference on Children, 1970* (Washington, D.C.: Government Printing Office, 1971).
2. See articles by Sherry Arnstein, Melvin Mogulof, and Roland Warren in special section, "Planning and Citizen Participation," *Journal of the American Institute of Planners,* 35, 4 (July 1969).
3. Richard M. Titmuss, *The Blood Relationship* (New York: Pantheon, 1971), p. 212. The first phrase quoted is from Kenneth Boulding, "The Boundaries of Social Policy," *Social Work,* 12, 1 (January 1971), 7. Also, Robert Pinker, *The Idea of Welfare,* publication pending.
4. William A. Robson and Bernard Crick (eds.), *The Future of the Social Services* (Baltimore: Penguin, 1970), p. 15; and Richard M. Titmuss, *Essays on*

"The Welfare State" (New Haven: Yale University Press, 1959), p. 50.

5. The Development of National Social Service Programmes, Report by a group of experts, sales no. 60.IV.1 (New York: United Nations Social Commission, 1959), p. 6.

6. Quoted from Social Services in Britain in United Nations, Department of Economic and Social Affairs, Organization and Administration of Social Welfare Programmes: The United Kingdom of Great Britain and Northern Ireland, sales no. 67.IV.6 (New York: United Nations: 1967), p. 1.

7. Services for People, U.S. Department of Health, Education, and Welfare (Washington, D.C.: The Department, 1968).

8. Alfred J. Kahn, Theory and Practice of Social Planning (New York: Russell Sage Foundation, 1969), p. 179.

9. Boulding, "The Boundaries of Social Policy," pp. 3–12.

10. Willard Richan, "The Responsibilities of the Social Work Profession in the Delivery of Social Services," mimeographed (New York: National Association of Social Workers, 1968).

11. Blanche D. Coll, Perspectives in Public Welfare (Washington, D.C.: Government Printing Office, 1968); and Karl de Schweinitz, England's Road to Social Security, Perpetua ed. (New York: A. S. Barnes, 1961).

12. Amitai Etzioni (ed.), The Semi-Professions and Their Organization (New York: Free Press, 1969).

13. United Nations, Department of Economic and Social Affairs, Organization and Administration of Social Welfare Programmes: The Union of Soviet Socialist Republics, sales no. 67.IV.20 (New York: United Nations, 1967). Also, United Nations, Department of Economic and Social Affairs, Organization and Administration of Social Welfare Programmes: Romania, sales no. 67.IV.10 (New York: United Nations, 1967). The latter source, particularly, clarifies the notion that the services are expected to help individuals make a maximum contribution to productivity and, at the same time, to benefit from it. See pp. 1–4.

14. Alfred J. Kahn and Sheila B. Kamerman, Social Services in International Perspective (Washington, D.C.: Government Printing Office, 1977).

15. Daniel Bell, "The Public Household," The Public Interest, No. 37 (Fall 1974), 29–68; Theodore Levitt, "Management and the 'Post-Industrial' Society," The Public Interest, No. 44 (Summer 1976), 69–103; and Morris Janowitz, Social Control of the Welfare State (Chicago: University of Chicago Press, 1977).

16. United Nations, Economic Bulletin for Latin America, 11, 1 (April 1966), 79.

17. Richard M. Titmuss, "The Practical Case Against the Means-Test State," New Statesman, 74, 1905 (September 15, 1967), 308–310; and Vera Shlakman, "The Safety-Net Function in Public Assistance: A Cross National Exploration," Social Services Review, 46, 2 (June 1972).

18. United Nations, Department of Economic and Social Affairs, Training for Social Work, Third International Survey (New York: United Nations, 1958), p. 60.

19. Ralph M. Kramer, Participation of the Poor (Englewood Cliffs, N.J.: Prentice-Hall, 1969), p. 203.

What Services, at What Costs? ◄◄◄◄ 3

Expenditures for personal (or general) social services under the narrow definition here employed are very modest: probably about 1–2 percent of the gross national product (GNP), probably between $10–15 billion per year (1976), probably under $70 per capita. A full appreciation of policy choices in this field requires some explanation of what is included in these estimates and of the difficulty of accurate calculation. Such review also permits contrasting the investment in these programs with expenditures for income maintenance, medical care, education, and so on, and identification of choices that may be involved in future allocations among programs.

Voluntary community fund raising for social welfare purposes in the United States, by "community chests," "united funds," or the like, often employs as a slogan some version of the following: "Everybody Benefits — Everybody Gives."

The literal accuracy of the first part of the slogan will vary with a number of factors. It is much more true if the social service listing includes developmental and socialization services (community centers, Boy Scouts, and so on) than if limited to therapeutic or "helping" programs. It is far more true if one refers to public (statutory) programs such as elementary and secondary education, than if consideration is limited to programs operated by voluntary (private, nonstatutory) agencies and funded by the campaigns alone. It is far more accurate if the intent is — and it generally is — to include health programs (since considerable United Way funds are allocated to voluntary hospitals serving entire communities) than if limited to social services in the more common U.S. usage. In short, United Way campaigns, while not necessarily using the term, imply a broad, "European" definition of social services that includes health, recreation, and socialization (but not education or most employment programs).

We may generalize loosely, but variations in definitions and administrative auspices tend to complicate any effort to specify statistically the participation in and utilization of programs or their specific costs. The task is confounded further by the fragmentation of responsibility within the public sector among departments, among local, state, and federal governments, and — within the voluntary sector — among many sectarian and nonsectarian bodies. Even where the social bookkeeping may be competently organized and adequately backed, aggregated data are not easily subdivided, and fragmented data can seldom be aggregated to yield useful totals and rates. Under these circumstances it is difficult to talk about caseloads and costs in satisfactory fashion. Nor is it possible to report either expenditures or users under categories resembling our personal social services subclassifications: development-socialization, help-treatment, access.

Were we to limit our social services definition to social insurance and related programs, generalization about users and price would be easy: virtually all people currently in the labor force are participating, before long almost all persons will have some entitlement at the point of retirement, and almost all dependent survivors of deceased people will have some benefits. Similarly, elementary and secondary public schooling or acceptable private alternatives are universal, and there are known rates for college attendance. Costs are reported. Health statistics, referring both to outpatient medical care and to hospitalization, are more difficult to aggregate; but useful surveys exist. Public and some private costs are known. However, as indicated, our focus — following U.S. practice — is upon personal social services *excluding* income security, health, education, housing, and general employment services.

What are the costs? What part of *all social service* costs (broad definition) are allocated to *personal* (or *general*) *social services* (in our sense)? And how many Americans are service utilizers in various programs?

Costs

The comprehensive survey, *Social Welfare Expenditures Under Public Programs in the United States, 1929–66,*[1] defines social welfare very broadly. As modified in recent years, this data series permits identification of four categories relevant to a focus on social services narrowly defined: two of the headings appear under public aid, "social services" and "other"; one appears as a subcategory of veteran programs, "welfare and other"; and there is a major item entitled "other social welfare." Public assistance social services involve state-level expenditures that may not be limited to personal social services. (Thus our totals may be high.) We have attempted to estimate which of the "other" public aid social services are not employment-related, since most of this category refers to the Comprehensive Employment and Training Act (CETA). The veteran item is excessive but not readily subdivided here. The "other social welfare" item for vocational rehabilitation needs to be reduced to exclude straight

Table 3.1 Public and Voluntary Personal Social Services Expenditures, Fiscal 1976 (approximations, in millions)

Public assistance–related social services	2,968.6*
Public aid–related "other" social services (surplus food, repatriate aid, refugee assistance, certain Economic Opportunity Act programs) (est.)	434.2
Veteran programs: "welfare and other"	733.9*
"Other social welfare":	
Vocational rehabilitation excluding medical (est.)	859.4
Institutional care	299.9
Child nutrition	2,825.7*
Child welfare	640.0
Special OEO and Action programs	621.5
Not elsewhere classified (aging, delinquency, Indian welfare, some manpower and human development programs, many state and local personal social services, services to many categories of handicapped people, etc.)	2,601.1
Estimated Public Total (Max)	11,984.3
Estimated Voluntary Total	2,500.0+
Estimated Total (Max)	15,000.0
As percentage of 1976 GNP ($1,611.8 billion)	~1%

*Includes significant sums not allocated to personal social services.

SOURCES: See note 1. Here, we rely heavily on Alfred M. Skolnik and Sophie R. Dales, "Social Welfare Expenditures, Fiscal Year 1976," *Social Security Bulletin*, 40, 1 (January 1977), especially pp. 5–7 and footnotes. We probably have included some items more properly classified as medical, educational, or employment services but not readily separated out.

medical costs, here estimated at 20 percent of the total. The remainder of the "other social welfare" items are relatively straightforward.

In fiscal 1976, the public social welfare expenditure total was 20.6 percent of the gross national product, or $331.4 billion (social insurance and other public income maintenance accounted for $195.5 billion of this total, and education for $86.4 billion), in a year when the GNP was $1,611.8 billion. The $331.4 billion constituted almost 60 percent of all American governmental expenditures. The private social welfare expenditure total for 1976 was $111.6 billion, contributing to a grand total of $443 billion for social welfare (social services broadly defined), or 27.5 percent of the GNP.

General social services in the *narrower* sense of this book, insofar as they are identifiable under the subcategories listed above and separable from administrative costs, probably accounted for at least $10 billion and maybe as much as $15 billion of public plus voluntary expenditures in 1976, of which 82 percent were public (see Table 3.1, page 35).

The major personal social services in the public category are the diversity of state-programmed efforts under Title XX of the Social Security Act (public assistance social services), especially day care, other child welfare, community services to the aged, as well as special nutrition and feeding programs, work-oriented rehabilitation efforts, and a variety of special service programs oriented to deprived groups (Indians, refugees, the poor) or to special problems (delinquency, addiction, etc.).*

The private "welfare and other services" category, including settlement houses, family service agencies, child welfare, programs for the aged, institutional care of many kinds, church social services, and so on, is

*Title XX, "Grants to States for Services" (P.L. 93–647) became effective October 1, 1975, and replaced Titles IV-A and XVI. For the political backdrop, see Martha Dertheck, *Uncontrollable Spending for Social Service Grants* (Washington, D.C.: The Brookings Institution, 1975). The original Social Security Act had no special social service title but an insistence that states study their cases and that state plans provide for service was present from the beginning. Costs were reimbursed as "administration" at 50 percent. By 1956 the principle of providing service (to get people off the relief rolls or help them become self-sufficient) was established. The 50:50 match became 75:25 in 1962, in an effort to upgrade service, on the mistaken assumption it would cut the assistance rolls. "Former and potential" recipients could be served, and service money could be used by the state to purchase care by other public agencies. By 1967 as part of a major thrust to create a work incentive (WIN), the rules required a "single state agency" for all services and permitted purchase of service from voluntary agencies as well. What occurred in effect was that voluntary funds became state "match" funds and the federal grants were now often returned to the voluntary sector. A period of major abuse followed, as documented by Dertheck. The purchase of social services with Social Security Act service funds from both public and private agencies as well as the open-ended eligibility categories and the failure to define eligible services led to considerable refinancing of state and voluntary services in this fashion and to a cost explosion. Title XX created a cost ceiling ($2.5 billion) and a state planning process, in a compromise reform effort.

estimated at between $1.5 and $2.5 billion. Since much private expenditure, especially through the United Way, is used as local match for public Title XX funds, it may duplicate some of the public expenditure totals.

The $10–15 billion overall expenditure, perhaps an overstatement, particularly as regards private totals, is also seen in perspective if recognized as constituting slightly less than 1 percent of the GNP. Personal social services obviously is not the social service component (using the broader definition) now representing the major U.S. investment.

Table 3.2 All Social Welfare Expenditures as Percentage of U.S. Gross National Product, Fiscal 1976

Income maintenance	11.1
Health	8.6
Education	6.6
Welfare and other services	1.7
TOTAL	27.5

SOURCE: Alfred M. Skolnik and Sophie R. Dales, "Social Welfare Expenditures, Fiscal Year 1976," *Social Security Bulletin*, 40, 1 (January 1977), Table 10, p. 17. My estimate uses a narrower definition of personal social services than is here covered in "welfare and other services."

As will be noted in Table 3.2, personal social services have less claim on the GNP than the major systems (although housing and employment are in the same modest categories). The increase in recent years is noteworthy; overall expenditure for the categories in Table 3.2 grew by 26 percent between 1970 and 1976, whereas "welfare and other services" increased by between 50 and 70 percent.

Is about 1.0 or even 1.5 percent of GNP a significant figure for general social services? The annual per capita figure (about $70 at most) is, of course, comparatively high as an absolute sum, given our high national income compared with that of other countries. However, while relatively, but not precisely, comparable categories of service apparently command a smaller percentage of GNP in some of the industrial countries of Western and Northern Europe, and slightly higher percentages in others, only a major new international effort could produce truly comparable computations for detailed analyses. For present purposes we note that, whatever the relative size of the investment, it is small in absolute terms. It may cost a voluntary family agency $10–15 per staff member per client "contact" hour, and fee-paying clients may pay an average of $25 per hour. Other illustrative average costs are homemakers–home health aides, $5.09 per hour; training schools for delinquents, $74.78 per day (New York); diagnostic-reception centers, $55–60 per day (New York); modest day care,

$2,000 per child per year, and so on.* At such rates the service budget does not go as far as the totals might suggest.

We could add to these totals $10 billion in 1977 for federal employment and training programs (the issue is debatable, but the case is good), all vocational-technical training and adult education (which would seem to belong with education), and the medically oriented rehabilitation items. However, our focus is on personal social services, for which some notion of scale is suggested by the rough total of over $10 billion but less than $15 billion, for the items we have included, a per capita annual expenditure of some $70 for 1976, and the evidence of very substantial growth even in comparison with much else in social welfare in recent years.

In the "public assistance–related social services," a major element in the expenditure picture, the federal part, was 75 percent in 1976 and the state/local share was 25 percent. Under the large "other social welfare" item (and allowing for imprecision as to the medical share of vocational rehabilitation), the overall federal share was about 47 percent. The federal share of the latter especially has grown in the past two decades. The federal cost shares under "other social welfare" are highest for child nutrition, special OEO programs, and vocational rehabilitation, in that order.

The state expenditure patterns under "public assistance–related social services" are quite varied, so that generalizations are not possible. Historically, states have carried a heavy child welfare service burden (foster care, adoption, protective services), but much of this may now be "refinanced" under Title XX.

Relevant veteran and other public aid expenditures for social services are largely federal.

When health, education, income maintenance, and the more narrowly defined personal social services are combined, the public-private ratio is 73:27. The federal-state/local ratio is 60:40. Private expenditures are most important in health (about 57.8 percent of the total) and are small in all other social welfare categories, including general social services (under 14 percent each in income maintenance, education, welfare, and other services).

This public-voluntary distribution is changed at the point of service

---

*Late in 1976, New York City, a high cost area, had established these per child maximums: foster parent, $4,964 per year ($13.60 per capita per diem); agency boarding home, $9,125 ($25.00 per diem); group home or residence ($36.00 per diem); institutional care, $13,468 ($36.90 per diem). A 1974 national survey produced these foster home rates: child aged two, maximum $187, minimum $65; child aged seven, maximum $187, minimum $65; child aged thirteen, maximum $263, minimum $65. A New York State detention center was budgeted at $157.48 per day in late 1977. In 1977 these per diem costs were computed for Iowa: detention, $45.60; state hospital, $43.71. Monthly foster home payments were $210–295.

delivery, since public funds are increasingly expended through nonstatutory or semipublic programs. The federal government expended at the rate of almost $2.5 billion for social services under the Social Security Act in 1976. Of the sum, 30 percent (a rough approximation) was for purchase of care through the voluntary sector.

A different sense of scale and scope may be conveyed by putting aside the expenditures report for a moment and turning to the HEW organization chart. HEW does not have one line agency for personal social services. However, one such potential unit, the Office of Human Development Services, established under reorganization in 1977, is budgeted at about $5 billion for expenditures that are largely personal social services, as follows:

· Administration for Children, Youth, and Families (Head Start, Children's Bureau, Child Welfare Services, Child Abuse and Neglect, Youth Development, related research and demonstration) — approximately $500 million
· Administration on Aging (Older Americans Act and related programs) — approximately $400 million
· Administration for Handicapped Individuals (Rehabilitation Services, Developmental Disabilities, Mental Retardation, related research, demonstration, technical assistance, and enforcement activity) — approximately $1 billion
· Administration for Public Services (Title XX, WIN, training, research, and demonstration) — approximately $3 billion
· Administration for Native Americans — approximately $33 million[2]

Programs and Users

A relatively organized personal social services network is to be found in very few communities in the United States. It may take the form of a county social services system or of a multiservice voluntary agency, sectarian or nonsectarian. Even then it will not be completely comprehensive and will certainly not enjoy a monopoly of its fields. Related services will be under other auspices.

The more typical local picture involves several problem- or age-categorical service systems and many one-service agencies (aged, children, youth, families, etc.) organized in parallel and overlapping public and voluntary service systems or federations (public social services, United Way agencies, community development, community mental health, Lutheran social services, Catholic welfare, Jewish family services, federation of Protestant Welfare, county human resources, etc.).

It is thus not easy to assemble a national quantitative picture. There are both public and voluntary suggested classifications and guidelines, but as yet no uniform definitions and comprehensive data collection systems.

If they are systematically reported at all, operational statistics usually refer to specific agencies and programs. They are often meant for promotional purposes, to impress budget makers (public) or contributors (voluntary). They certainly cannot be aggregated. Individual community surveys may remedy these defects but employ their own definitions or are narrower in focus. Occasional national surveys have been made, but none seeking user estimates for general social services specifically. If one had to make a very rough "best guess" on the basis of extrapolations and occasional one-community surveys, it would be that half of all "case" services — services to help, treat, or rehabilitate — are utilized by about 6–10 percent of the families in an urban population at a given time. The other half are more broadly distributed. No comparable estimate is possible with reference to developmental programs or access services — or for locations other than large cities — and the estimate given would hardly survive close scrutiny.

What follows is based on a national perspective. It is offered only for *orientation* purposes and to specify what some of the personal social service programs actually are. Agencies, programs, caseloads, and staffs are referred to — but all in a limited way.[3] The generalizations are, at most, somewhere near the facts, but they should not be deemed precise or appropriately qualified. In any *given* context, policy development or programming would require assembling considerable data about users.

Many of the concrete services referred to under expenditures cannot be here described in terms of users. Consumer statistics are few and vague. On the the other hand, social service planners report more detail on relationship and substitute care services. These categories of services tend to be better recorded, since they have long been the focus of social work agencies. Before turning to the materials that indicate the limited number of case service users, therefore, it may be useful to recall that in fiscal 1976 some 18.5 million people participated in food stamp programs, 23.9 million were Medicaid recipients, 1.2 million received housing assistance under means-tested programs, 125,000 received some supportive service under the work incentive (WIN) program, and 1.3 million were in Comprehensive Employment and Training (CETA) programs. (None of these programs are here defined as personal social services.) By 1977, about 11 million school children were participating in subsidized school lunch programs and 2 million were receiving subsidized breakfasts. In mid 1977 there were 11 million beneficiaries of Aid to Families with Dependent Children (AFDC) and 4.3 million beneficiaries of Supplementary Security Income (SSI) — the public assistance program for the aged, blind, and disabled. Social service planners would assess these as "high-risk" categories, people who might make heavy demands upon personal social services. It was estimated by federal authorities on the basis of reimbursement billings and statistical reports that 15 percent of all AFDC and 13 percent of all SSI recipients actually utilized Title XX and related services in mid-1976.

I here offer a limited national social services trend picture for late 1976, while stressing that the data are incomplete and in some ways inaccurate. It combines reports on Title XX (public assistance–related social services in our Table 3.1), Title IV-B (child welfare), and WIN-related social services. These are offered only to give some concreteness to the personal social service abstractions. The report system producing these data is currently in process of being developed. There are major inconsistencies in definitions and reporting among the states.[4]

These services were rendered to over 5 million people (counting mostly "primary" recipients) over a nine-month period — some 66 percent of them adults, the remainder children. The analysis for the most recent (and most adequately reported) quarter shows most recipients to be eligible for AFDC, SSI, Medicaid, child welfare service, and WIN benefits. However, some 3 percent of users were eligible for services for which means testing was not a bar (information and referral, family planning, protective services). The largest sums were spent for day care, foster care for children, and protective services for children. The largest numbers of users were recorded for health-related social services, counseling, and information–referral. The largest numbers of adult recipients were in California, Texas, and Pennsylvania; of child recipients, in New York, New Jersey, and Texas — in that order.

A review of the services most frequently offered yields the following data for the last reported quarter:[5]

SERVICES	AVERAGE NUMBER OF RECIPIENTS PER QUARTER (LATE 1976)*
Counseling services	509,843
Health-related services *(unclear category)*	490,658
Day care services — children	418,442
Protective services — children	338,745
Information and referral services	247,292
Family planning services	244,602
Education and training services	210,952
Case management services	191,115
Foster care services — children	174,423
Transportation services	166,514
Homemaker services	151,876
Employment services	150,256

*Subject to corrections.

State coverage was as follows for the thirteen most frequently reported services (but there are no data on intrastate coverage):[6]

SERVICES	NUMBER OF STATES IN WHICH OFFERED
Family planning services	51
Day care services — children	50
Protective services — children	48
Homemaker services	47
Counseling services	46
Transportation services	46
Health-related services	44
Education and training services	43
Protective services — adults	43
Adoption services	41
Employment services	41
Foster care services — children	40
Home management services	40

The delivery pattern through which these public services (only part of the total services covered by public expenditures) reach clients is only now being clarified as the reporting system is improved. Direct service provision by state or local government accounted for 51 percent of all costs in late 1976, purchase from other public units for 19 percent, and purchase from the voluntary sector (nonprofit or profit) for 30 percent. Since the pattern is a matter for state option there is great variation. States with high rates of direct provision by the responsible Title XX, child welfare, and WIN agencies are (numbers indicate percentage of all costs): Iowa (100), Idaho (99), North Dakota (96). If one adds direct public provision to purchase through other public agencies, the following states lead: North Carolina (100), Iowa (100), Connecticut (99), North Dakota (97), Kentucky and West Virginia (96). Five others are also over 90 percent. The states highest in "private purchase" percentages are: New Hampshire (69), Kansas (66), and both Vermont and Wyoming (65).

The following were the direct-operation services reaching the largest numbers of clients:[7]

SERVICES	NUMBER OF RECIPIENTS
Information and referral services	2,276,067
Counseling services	670,855
Health-related services	622,186
Protective services — children	305,842
Day care services — children	242,939

Home management services	214,897
Case management services	199,687
Protective services — other	190,525
Homemaker services	169,719
Education and training services	162,704

The following were the services purchased from the private sector reaching the largest numbers of clients in late 1976.[8]

SERVICES	NUMBER OF RECIPIENTS
Day care services — children	359,091
Counseling services	139,245
Transportation services	110,425
Family planning services	110,098
Diagnosis and evaluation services	91,645
Home delivered/congregate meals	90,559
Recreational services	89,386
Information and referral services	86,774
Homemaker services	64,385
Day care services — various	60,624

The overlapping is to be noted — as is the public agency's larger role in protective services and foster care. The services purchased from other public agencies are similar to those delivered in other states by social agencies or such specialized services as family planning, legal aid, or transportation. All categories and totals are only approximations.

The reader will have access to better data over the next several years. On the one hand, the statistical series on which the foregoing summary is based is being refined and will assemble more accurate annual data. On the other hand, the effort at federal realignment will create program units able to offer more accurate overviews of their domains.

For the present, the clarification of personal social service tasks and functions, and of the choices in their organization, requires some further illustration. For this purpose we offer brief overviews of several traditional domains. Because of administrative fragmentation and significant overlap, it is for the most part necessary to avoid quantification. Some of what follows is accounted for by the earlier service summary. The rest is earlier represented only in the expenditure totals.

Personal and Family Counseling

In theory, many millions of public assistance recipients have had access to counseling, help, referral, and various related concrete social services.

In actuality, most public assistance investigators (or "social workers," as they may be called) have had to concentrate on eligibility and employment issues. Few of them have been qualified for more than generalized "friendly visiting," even if accepted by their clients in, and able to find time for, a personal helping role. From the late 1960s to the mid-1970s, states were required by federal directive to separate the administration of cash assistance from service programs, to objectify eligibility and avoid coercion into service. Now the situation is in limbo as assistance is partly federalized (SSI) and partly the target of reform (AFDC and general aid). Whatever the outcome of the legislative debates, personal social service delivery will apparently not be reunited with the task of establishing eligibility in public assistance, even though there probably should and will be encouragement for case finding and social service referral by all income maintenance staffs.

Where, then, are the counselors in the personal social services? Who are the users? The data are fragmentary.

As we have noted, the report on Title XX, IV-B, and WIN indicates that counseling is important — but its depth and nature are unreported.

Within veteran programs, some 3,000 social workers and related personnel render individual and group counseling services. An unknown proportion of vocational rehabilitation funds and of medical costs is also devoted to counseling.

Relative to population size, the population at large has access to a small amount of private psychiatric and marriage counseling and to services by a number of voluntary family service agencies — some 282 agencies to which some 553,000 different families turned in 1975. In most cases, the contact is brief and the service limited, often a matter of a telephone call, a letter, one interview. However, some 232,260 families were seen two or more times. Although these family agencies are in geographic areas covering over half the U.S. population, a staffing pattern of 3.1 per 100,000 people means little capacity for extensive help to many individuals. Some 4,500 social caseworkers are employed by these family agencies. If one adds sectarian family agencies and small unaffiliated nonsectarian agencies, the agency total could reach 1,000; coverage, although untallied, is obviously still quite limited.

Counseling within the armed forces and by religious counselors, church-related social service programs, and many group programs is not here included. Nor can we estimate the extent to which school-based social workers, community mental health or hospital-based medical and psychiatric social workers, union and industry social workers, psychiatrists, or psychologists go beyond the helping situation that arises in the special setting to engage in a broader casework, counseling, or psychotherapeutic process. It is now expected that general hospitals, medical clinics, psychiatric hospitals, schools, community centers, and camps will offer special casework help to those whose situations call for assistance in utilizing the basic service and — perhaps — to those revealed to have personal problems impeding general adjustment.* Some of these facilities, especially hospitals, have facilitators or complaint adjusters, often erroneously called "ombudsmen." Many of the thousands of trained social workers in these agencies are engaged in casework services that may be described as intensive. Beyond this, in the general category of home or community care, or aftercare, many thousands of aged or mentally ill or defective or addicted or adjudicated or handicapped individuals are sustained through daily difficulties and given access to concrete services and resources by virtue of the activities of social workers (or counselors from related disciplines) affiliated with a diversity of institutional auspices. Protective services are becoming increasingly important for the aged living in the community, who may need outside intervention to avoid their being exploited or harmed.

Almost 900 antipoverty (community action) neighborhood centers are also the location of some social services. Counseling may be rendered by various categories of personnel, at levels of training ranging from the M.D. psychiatrist, the Ph.D. or M.A. psychologist, and the M.S. social worker, on the one hand, to the grade-school-educated area resident with the "instinct" and capacity for helping his neighbors. Caseload estimates do not exist. The service rendered ranges from sporadic "advice" or "information" to intensive personal help.

Child Welfare

Foster home care, adoption services, protective services, institutional care for children, and temporary shelter during familial emergency constitute basic social services. They have existed as long as social services have been known and have a history in the United States going back to the eighteenth century, even if we discount indenture and other precursors. They are bound to be important elements in any personal social service provision. The center of the delivery system for such services is a local public child welfare agency, usually in a working alliance with a group of voluntary child welfare programs, sometimes also connected

---

*It is not possible to go beyond numbers such as these: by late 1976 there were over 520 federally assisted community mental health centers and about 250 hospital clinics, most of them employing social workers and offering casework services, and providing about 1.6 million patients with various services, personal social services among them. Many psychologists and psychiatrists, as well as aides and nurses, also offered such services.

with a larger human services or personal service organization at the state or local level.* Most of the funding is public.

A relatively complete institutional census conducted in 1966 showed the following: 60,500 children in 955 institutions for the dependent and neglected (children without families or in danger from their families); 55,000 in 414 institutions for the adjudicated or adjudicable delinquent; 13,900 in 307 institutions for the emotionally disturbed; 8,000 in 145 psychiatric inpatient units; 6,000 in 201 maternity homes, 1,800 in 54 temporary shelters awaiting plans or facilities; and 10,900 in 242 more secure (detention) facilities awaiting court dispositions or facilities.

Left out of the census because of jurisdictional issues were 701 facilities for mentally retarded children and 373 for the physically handicapped. The child total was between 165,000 and 170,000 for the institutions included in the census and approximately 100,000 for the others. There is no detailed post-1966 census of children in institutions, but the 1970 general population census located some 300,000 children in all institutions (social service auspices, corrections, physical disabilities, mental illness and retardation). Demographic trends and deinstitutionalization have probably decreased this total, but the challenge of working with this group of children, whether in community or institution, remains substantial.

Whether through separately organized court services or in child welfare programs, several hundred thousand children also have exposure annually to social services of various degrees of intensity and competence rendered by probation officers and court intake departments and related services. Smaller numbers also are helped by trained juvenile police in special juvenile aid bureaus. Many children are held in jail detention with no service at all. Between 150,000 and 200,000 cases of dependent and neglected children may have some exposure to court social services annually as well. Social workers in child welfare agencies and courts deal, in addition, with perhaps 100,000–200,000 adoption cases, served by social agencies because nonrelatives are involved.

The core of child welfare work may well be the placement, replacement, supervision, and return home of children in long- and short-term foster home care (perhaps 395,000 at any one time) — and the efforts to head off trouble for the several hundred thousand referred to protective or preventive services as abused, neglected, endangered, or in need of supervision. In the third quarter of 1976, some 352,000 children received protective services under Titles XX and IV-B of the Social Security Act alone.

*Half of all U.S. children receiving child welfare services are served by one of the 376 public or voluntary (the majority) affiliate agencies of the Child Welfare League of America, a standard-setting organization.

Personal social services for children also include elements in the field of child care. Although part of day care and Head Start or nursery programs is categorized as being in the province of education, and much of the expenditure is tabulated as education under federal expenditure studies, a significant portion of all child care programs (center and family day care) and after-school day care may be seen as a developmental-socialization social service.* Most standard-setting groups see child care as a social service conducted jointly by educators, social workers, doctors, and related professionals. In addition to educational components, good programs are expected to include (or to ensure access to) social service, health, nutrition, and parent participation components.

In 1977, HEW reported 350,000 children and their families in Head Start programs administered by 1,350 grantees. There is a mandated social service component for such programs, as there is for the publicly funded center and family day care services to some 1 million children. To this one should add social service components present or needed in after-school day care programs, and in the private nursery and public prekindergarten programs, which in effect offer far more child care coverage than do the family day care and center day care programs. As labor force participation by mothers continues to grow, it is expected that the demands on personal social services will increase in these fields too.

This survey of child welfare services is rounded out with the mental health field. Children are psychiatric inpatients in general hospitals, state and county mental health hospitals, residential treatment centers, group psychiatric homes, community mental health centers, day treatment programs, and private hospitals. These overlapping service categories include programs with and without social service supports. Some are defined as part of a mental health or medical system, others as personal social services. Several hundred thousand children probably receive one form or another of psychiatric outpatient help in such facilities or in child guidance and outpatient clinics at any one time.

The Aged

Some of the counseling services we have described reach the aged. A significant subgroup of older people are served in community centers or settlement houses with recreation and other leisure-time group services. Others are in medically based nursing homes. Of those over sixty-five, about 5 percent, or more than 1 million, live in institutions of some kind. Larger numbers are housebound or have limited mobility. The aged in the

---

*There are debates as to which child care services are education and which personal social services.

community receive uncounted concrete as well as counseling services. Others, in hospitals, geriatric facilities, and psychiatric programs, are under medical care, also supplemented by general social services. Special apartments for the aged, as well as buildings, housing developments, or camps for them, often have supplementary general social services. However, the homemaker and home help programs and the major social service resources for the aged that exist in some other countries, often as rights under social insurance, are as yet little developed in the United States. Modest medically based home care equivalents, provided under Medicare, are expanding. Similarly, protective services for the aged, meals-on-wheels, and friendly visiting — regarded as basic social services in some places — are relatively rare in the United States. Given the size of the group and its population proportion, expansion in all of these realms is projected.

Adjunctive Social Services

Although there are debates about specific functions, social services — usually manned by professionally trained social workers — are located in or sought by schools, general hospitals, and psychiatric facilities in the United States. In a few foreign countries they are also to be found in industry, an infrequent occurrence in the United States. In some places they are sponsored by or located in labor unions — not the typical U.S. pattern despite considerable activity during World War II and some recent expansion.[9] These social workers focus on practical difficulties (illness of a spouse) or personal problems (extreme anxiety) or interpersonal conflicts (trouble with a former spouse) that interfere with a person's ability to meet responsibilities or use resources adequately.

It is generally agreed that in settings such as these the social services are adjunctive, that is, they are supportive of the primary mission of the host institution and of the individual's utilization of the core service (education, psychiatry, general medicine, and so on) or his functioning in his relevant role (worker, student, union member). However, social workers and aides in such social service programs also may conceive of themselves as carrying some responsibility to participate in defining the core policies of schools and hospitals as institutions and as contributing to organizational renewal. They also are in varying degrees preoccupied with the total well-being of the individual, even if it means not giving primacy to his role performance. Professional ethics at certain points dictate protection, even withdrawal, of a sick client in the face of unmanageable demands by a school, for example. Certain obvious problems in professional ethics follow.

General medical and psychiatric facilities that emphasize community care, as a substitute for or as a rapid follow-up to the time spent in the institution, place considerable emphasis on the role of social workers and others as adjunctive to the medical specialty. Day and night hospitals and various part-institutionalization programs, involving a segment of the day spent in a protected setting, also emphasize the general social service, as contrasted with the specific medical component.

Advocacy and Legal Services

Legal aid and neighborhood legal services have been recognized in recent years as having a major role in ensuring access to public housing, income maintenance programs, and similiar public programs. They of course also have central functions that are specifically legal, entering into cases relevant to a specific individual's interests, as well as into cases that "make" new law and policy affecting total classes of situations. There were in 1976 approximately 258 local legal aid programs with a total of 638 offices under the Legal Services Corporation and also a significant number of other legal aid units dealing with civil cases. Some of these programs include personal social service activities, others are more purely legal.

Vocational Rehabilitation

Although it is virtually impossible to separate completely programs that are basically medical from those in which general social services are a major component, it may be noted that professional practice in this field gives high priority to the role of the vocational counselor as a "coordinator" of the specialties as they are addressed to the particular case. He or she also carries responsibility for continuity of the care and for following outcomes. Social workers may play such roles, too, or may have some specialized tasks in rehabilitation. There are some 8,500 facilities and workshops that define themselves as rehabilitative in the United States, of which at least 2,000 are comprehensive centers. At least 15,000 counselors are identifiable. State programs may be serving over 1.2 million persons a year. In some ways the rehabilitation system is a comprehensive personal social services network for one category of cases.

Homemakers and Home Helps

It is estimated (1977) that there are 36,800 full-time and 44,000 part-time home health aides and homemakers in the United States, serving child welfare, the aged, and medical and family service programs. This total is a sharp increase over 1965, but it represents limited coverage compared to that provided by Britain, Holland, Sweden, and Denmark.

There are no comparable meals-on-wheels statistics. The program, which is highly developed in Britain and Scandinavia, is so small in the United States as to make ratios meaningless.

Community Centers, Settlements, and Group Programs

YMCAs, boys' clubs, sectarian and nonsectarian community centers (public and voluntary) for several or for all age groups, Aspira clubs for Puerto Rican children, settlement houses, scouting programs, Campfire Girls, local group programs under religious, nonsectarian, service, or charitable organizations, and other related groups serve millions of people. They combine character development, child development, talent encouragement, socialization, educational, camping, recreational and therapeutic components in various proportions.* The core professional skills involved are social work (group work), education, physical training, and recreation. Many volunteer leaders and college students serve these programs.

It is virtually impossible to include estimates of participation in or even of units offering programs of educational-cultural enrichment under diverse auspices. Nor would one expect to be able to do so. For example, the National Federation of Settlements reported in 1977 that it had 130 member agencies in thirty states operating 420 centers and "reaching" approximately 2 million people. One cannot judge how much of this is personal social service, nor its intensity and coverage.

Family Planning

Here, the core professional service is medical. However, large numbers of social workers are also needed because of the promotional/educational, family relationship, personal adjustment, and management aspects involved. Special services have developed for teen-agers, and these tend to have extensive personal social service components. Services are increasing so rapidly in hospitals, Planned Parenthood centers, neighborhood health centers, and related facilities as to outdate available statistics. Social services have also rapidly expanded in connection with abortion clinics and hospital abortion services, as state laws have been liberalized. And hundreds of thousands of young people are enrolled in family life courses in schools, churches, and community centers.

*There are some 450 Jewish Community Centers and Ys. Four youth-serving organizations (4-H, Boy Scouts, Girl Scouts, Campfire Girls) reported 11 million members in 1970.

Job Placement and Training

Auspices are provided by official state and city programs, several federal employment and training programs, local antipoverty units, educational facilities, veteran and rehabilitation programs, and medical facilities, among others. There has been an enormous new growth during the 1970s in response to high unemployment. Staffing of these programs is by job placement specialists, vocational and basic educators, psychologists and testers, group counselors, and a limited number of social workers and others who focus on problems of adjustment, participation, and personal counseling. In our sense, the latter are the general social service concerns. Recent emphasis on "workfare," the tying of public assistance eligibility to participation in public works, public employment, counseling, and training programs by those unemployed and deemed employable, is rapidly expanding the social service component in manpower programs. Boundaries between labor market placement programs and programs that may be considered to belong in the personal social service family remain permeable.[10]

Participation

There is no estimate of service "volume" in this vague category. Included are a diversity of programs under the successors to the antipoverty Community Action program, based in at least 800 centers; policy-advisory-planning committees or groups in programs sponsored by various community development efforts supported by HUD (Department of Housing and Urban Development); many state and regional planning enterprises under federal health-planning mandates; some local participation in advising or planning community mental health centers; various types of local participation in, or reaction to planning in, urban renewal, public housing, or highway programs; local multiservice centers under several programs; tenant organization; new forms of community "control" or participation in urban ghetto schools; local organization under settlement house auspices; a diversity of other programs related to self-help or the search for political power by deprived ethnic minorities; and — central to our concern — a mandated public participation opportunity that is part of the state planning process required if state Comprehensive Annual Service Plans are to be approved for federal funding under Title XX of the Social Security Act (social services). Some of these programs are professionally or subprofessionally staffed by community organization or community development personnel; some are truly locally controlled; some grow out of interest group initiatives; and some are neither staffed nor truly autonomous. Some see participation sociotherapeutically; others, politically. To some it is window dressing.[11]

Personnel

The broad definition of social services implies recognition that a variety of disciplines and professions may be involved in any given program. As we have narrowed the field, separating education, employment, health, and housing, we have eliminated programs in which educators, doctors, nurses, and architects are the primary movers, while noting that some general social service components may be related to their efforts.

The more restrictive definition of personal social services constitutes it as a field in which — with some exceptions — social workers are the core or "host" profession. The major exceptions occur in employment, in group–community center activities, and in family planning. Of course, as already indicated, even in fields like child welfare and family counseling there are major interdisciplinary aspects.

To estimate the non–social work component in each of the personal social service areas would be tedious, inaccurate, and relatively point-less. It is more productive to orient the discussion to basic policy questions and to issues of program strategy by an overview of the social work manpower situation, since this is the core on which one must build.

The 1970 Census reported 216,600 social workers, exclusive of those in recreation work. Using a similar definition, the Current Population Survey counted 300,000, both figures exclusive of managers. Various projections for 1980 range between 323,000 and 402,000, the latter figure rising to 440,000 if one adds managers, officials, and proprietors.[12]

Some two-thirds of all social workers are employed by governmental units; others, in voluntary nonprofit agencies, may actually be in receipt of salaries provided out of public funds. The last survey of social worker education level was conducted in 1970, but the ratios are expected to remain quite similar by 1980: 19 percent without college education, 13 percent with some college work, 38 percent with bachelor degrees, 30 percent with some graduate study. Of presently employed social workers, at least 60,000 have master's or doctoral degrees. There are currently some 17,000 graduate students enrolled in social work M.S. programs.

The public social work staffs concentrate in public assistance and child welfare. From the point of view of policy planners, the issues are the training levels essential for different functions, the organizational patterns for interrelating personnel with different types of credentials, the suitability of current training for new modalities of service, and the core professional discipline for the training of certain categories of personnel. There are many proposals and pronouncements about these matters but no general patterns or empirically validated standards. The discipline is in flux.

Social services have, traditionally, engaged large numbers of volunteers; in the United States, early social service programs were manned completely by volunteers until late in the nineteenth century,[13] when professionalization began. The American ethic has, from the beginning, valued voluntary good works, and millions of citizens are willing to serve their fellows who are under stress and have special needs. Hospital "gray ladies" and "candy stripers" are universal phenomena. Reading tutors, escorts who take aged citizens to clinics, and "friendly visitors" to institutions serve in many places. Peace Corps and Vista volunteers and members of the Teachers Corps have become widely known in recent decades. A federal agency known as Action, created in 1971, unifies them.

Volunteer efforts other than fund raising may be classified to distinguish among (a) assistance to others (case services), (b) mutual aid, and (c) social action and class advocacy. Because definitions are loose and comprehensive data nonexistent, it is impossible to say whether the use of paid social service staffs has been accompanied by a decline in voluntary service. Action is seeking to recruit even more volunteers and to broaden the range of concerns.[14]

Social service agencies everywhere, whether operated under public or private auspices, deal constantly with the question of which services are appropriately conducted by volunteers and which by paid staff — and how personnel in the two categories may interrelate. If the 1950s was an era of high professionalization and constriction of volunteer opportunity, and the 1960s a period of expansion of paraprofessionals and of offering the poor job opportunities in the social services, the 1970s was a time in which an effort was made to restore volunteering to a more central place in social services. It is not clear whether such efforts have succeeded in a context of large-scale organization — and with people tending to seek paid social service jobs. Nonetheless, extensive voluntarism seems likely to continue on the scene in the predictable future.* It has been estimated that as many as 30 to 50 million Americans volunteer now during a given year, although such totals include many people whose activity is quite limited.

Effects

It is traditional in "ideal" policy and programming discussions for the analysis to move directly from review of services rendered and of costs to an analysis of effects and differential effects. The questions are: what is offered? at what price? what is achieved? at what unit cost? and for whom? But, in the real world of social services, harsh realities intervene and generally defeat this logic.

*The issue of voluntary as contrasted with public *auspices* for programs is separately discussed later.

The problem of effects has historical roots. Traditional nineteenth- and early twentieth-century voluntarism was its own justification; providing an outlet for individual good works, its religious merit was an overriding consideration. No one asked whether the recipient was actually helped, since it was assumed that what was offered as charity was received as such, and that good motives automatically assured effectiveness.

Furthermore, traditionally, many social services have had manifest or latent social control goals, and effectiveness could be seen or assumed: criminals and delinquents were locked up or supervised in the community; mentally ill people were removed to institutions; poor people were fed enough, so that they did not riot or die of starvation; abusive parents were warned or jailed; unwed mothers were made to see that they had acted improperly and were guided toward personal reform. Along similar lines, if settlement houses, Ys, boys' clubs, and other character-building services reflected the controlling ethic and stressed acculturation, skill training, or socialization congruent with the dominant ethic, few questions were raised about effectiveness.

To some extent, then, the matter of proven effects has and will probably continue to have low priority for many citizens, when raised with reference to social services. If activities and outlook are in harmony with cultural trends and the programs are provided by a voluntary or public service system that — in context — is defined as charitable or humane, large elements of the public will raise few questions. Volunteer tutors, "gray ladies," "big brothers" are manifestly good — and not to be questioned. Public community centers and pools, community lunches, foster homes, marriage counseling, are obviously needed and "worthwhile."

Yet, as controversy arises about social strategies, the matter of effects cannot be ignored simply on the grounds that the programs involved are compatible with other things on the social scene and have gained acceptability with many citizens. If there is a debate about income, political power, and social service strategies as alternative pathways out of poverty, should the evidence for each not be assessed? Similarly, if there are controversies within a social service field about the validity of different programs or the relative effectiveness of given techniques, should one forgo evidence? For example, can it not be determined whether a Head Start program improves a child's chances of succeeding in elementary school, and whether the existence of such a program brings about changes in the basic elementary school programs — both identifiable goals of the effort? Can we not find out whether probation, at a relatively low per capita cost, is or is not as effective as the more expensive residential treatment? whether counseling with all family members as a group is or is not more effective than work with individual members one at a time? Is it not possible to know whether group "encounter" approaches to changing addicts of various kinds via the social-psychological pressures of a peer group are more or less lasting than medical strategies?

For the policy planner and programmer there is no way to evade the responsibility of such questions, lest services merely gravitate from fad to fad. Yet hard data about effects are scarce in policy debates. Specific assertions are difficult for a number of reasons.

1. Social services are usually initiated at a time and in a place where *many other things are going on* (e.g., the multiple innovations of the New Deal at a time of major political and value shifts in the society, or the services of the U.S. antipoverty war in the context of the civil rights movement and the Vietnam escalation). If the objective is large-scale effects, it is usually impossible to isolate the amount of change attributable to the specific social services innovation. William Gorham was reflecting a widely shared perspective when he reported, after a period of experimentation within the Department of Health, Education, and Welfare with a planning-programming-budgeting-system (PPBS):

Let me hasten to point out that we have not attempted any grandiose cost-benefit analyses designed to reveal whether the total benefits from an additional million dollars spent on health programs would be higher or lower than that from an additional million spent on education or welfare. If I was ever naive enough to think this sort of analysis possible, I no longer am.[15]

Major innovations in service will always be carried out in conjunction with other major innovations or significant political or social change. The society will often need to react to and evaluate such innovations without having solved the complex research problems of control, isolation of variables, and measurement.

2. *Value components cannot be avoided in evaluation,* and in a diverse country different population elements and regions emphasize their own value perspectives. Again, quoting Gorham:

The benefits of health, education, and welfare programs are diverse and often intangible. They affect different age groups and different regions of the population over different periods of time. No amount of analysis is going to tell us whether the Nation benefits more from sending a slum child to preschool, providing medical care for an old man or enabling a disabled housewife to resume her normal activities. The "grand decisions" — how much education, how much health, how much welfare, and which groups in the population shall benefit — are questions of value judgment and politics.[16]

Large social policy choices are made in terms of values and political perspective, not through weighing effectiveness. But even where it is seen as urgent and relevant the measurement of effectiveness does not escape controversial value choices: Is divorce "success" or "failure" as a family counseling outcome? Is placement of an old person in a nursing home "good" or "poor" service? What of the giving up of an out-of-wedlock child for adoption, the dropping out or continuance in school by an adolescent, the mastery of contraceptive technique by yet another unmarried adolescent, the organization of a protest group to combat or fight a public housing authority? Clearly, then, value components exist in the criteria that are posited by researchers and administrators in all efforts to measure and evaluate the results obtained. Only those studies of effectiveness are possible that can resolve the difficult value choices inherent in defining success. Furthermore, only those studies will be taken into account whose criteria of effectiveness coincide with the basic expectations of those to whom the studies are addressed.

3. *Many social services or service components are not sufficiently standardized* to permit generalization from a given evaluation effort. Thus, well-publicized studies may show that counseling is ineffective with "potential" delinquents or that casework is unable to resolve the problems of multiproblem families, yet they are readily dismissed on the grounds that service inputs were below standard in the experiments studied.*

To illustrate from other social service fields: Failures of foster care may be attributed to poor screening of foster parents, successes to unusual and atypical care in selection. The outcome of a homemaker program may be ascribed to the typicality or atypicality of the specific personnel. Congress may complain that its investment in social services yielded no noticeable effects in rehabilitating AFDC families (1962 Social Security Act amendments), whereas a research group may respond that no results were to be expected. (There was insufficient availability or utilization of social services in public assistance in the one state studied intensively.)[17]

In short, even where one would undertake modest studies of effects and effectiveness, as appropriate, there are complex research problems of control, outcome criteria, and standardized service ("inputs").[18] The interplay between these true obstacles, on the one hand, and the traditions that question whether one should probe too closely for effectiveness of services that reflect benign humanitarianism and charity, on the other,

---

*This type of critique, readily sustained, decreased the usefulness of three expensive, extensive, and promising efforts to evaluate casework and personal counseling. See Edwin Powers and Helen Witmer, *An Experiment in the Prevention of Delinquency* (New York: Columbia University Press, 1950); Henry Meyer, Edward F. Borgatta, and Wyatt C. Jones, *Girls at Vocational High* (New York: Russell Sage Foundation, 1965); and Gordon E. Brown, *The Multi-problem Dilemma* (Metuchen, N.J.: Scarecrow Press, 1968). Casework critics and planners will nonetheless continue to rely upon the results of these studies unless or until there appear equally careful and extensive efforts whose experimental services are deemed competent by professionals and that yield more impressive results.

creates overwhelming blockages to evaluation. A situation results in which too little can be said with a high degree of certainty even where it would be reasonable to ask for evidence. However trite and repetitive the call, students of social services must urge that, in any given field, policy planners and programmers exploit research and evaluation reports to the fullest degree possible and that selective and expert evaluation be given high priority as new programs and agencies are developed and old ones renewed and reformed.[19]

It would appear reasonable, in a total social service strategy for a given territorial unit, to expect the following components in an "effectiveness package":

1. *Social indicators* — ongoing social statistics and indexes based on them, compiled routinely and over time, to measure the state of social sector "health" and thus presumably reflecting the results of a diversity of measures. The conceptual and methodological problems are many, but interest in indicators has developed, and significant work has been done since the early 1960s.[20]
2. *Carefully designed and controlled evaluation studies* to determine the specific effects of new, experimental, significant, controversial, or otherwise important programs. Such studies are costly and difficult. They should be carefully selected and carefully carried out, and their results should then be considered seriously.
3. *Cost-benefit studies* to select from among competing methods of known or discoverable effectiveness those that deliver the most service of acceptable consequence, at lowest per-unit cost.
4. *Channels for consumer response and evaluation* to provide holistic judgments about services. While user evaluations may not tell or scientifically measure exactly what is right or wrong, they tell something that is central to the enterprise: how those for whom a service is designed experience and evaluate it and how they would improve it.

Some progress is being made in all of these categories and in relation to many social service fields.[21] Recently, cost-effectiveness studies have been developed in many new fields, and, where they ask modest questions and avoid efforts to quantify "human gains," they are useful. Movement toward client participation and community control has increased the sources of consumer feedback about programs, and follow-up and evaluation studies have been successfully carried out in some fields. The social indicator experiments are at a beginning phase but are promising.

Federal planning requirements under Title XX of the Social Security Act include provision for an evaluation process. This has been variously interpreted. Overviews of experience to date do not suggest that, in general, evaluations have significant impact on plans or that they thus far should provide major guidance to decision makers. Few observers dispute the need to change this situation over the long run, without denying that the record does not encourage optimism. On the one hand, evaluation is difficult; on the other, interest group and bureaucratic pressures may serve to offset or contain the results of assessments — whatever they may show.

For present purposes one must cite evidence of considerable service failure in many fields (state training school recidivism, foster home replacement, family agency case dropouts), of overlapping, wastage, and lack of service access. Many consumers indicate that agencies do not offer the help needed; many agencies proclaim clients to be "unmotivated" or unable to use help. There also is evidence that popular services exist on too small a scale to meet needs as users see them: the waiting lists for day care, homemakers, and public housing serve as illustration. Finally, there is evidence that agencies often become mired in their interventive procedures and organizational structures, to a point where innovators must begin anew, often in unorthodox settings and without a community's formal backing. To illustrate, we note that most of the attractive and innovative adolescent social services of the early 1970s seemed to develop outside of the traditional social agency network — as young people created self-help programs to cope with drug "emergencies" and related problems. Many of the most innovative family counseling, supportive, and educational programs of the late 1970s were based in self-help groups.

These impressionistic generalizations rely on reports and studies, but they rest on too little empirical evidence to permit quantification. Equally impressionistic and imprecise are a group of positive findings: Certain services remain popular with their constituencies and usually have waiting lists. Some programs routinely achieve results that all observers are willing to evaluate positively. When disadvantaged people are given a voice in the expenditure of funds, they often want to duplicate or expand traditional services. When public hearings are held to assess state or local social service or community mental health plans, many advocates of program expansion are present, few proponents of cutbacks.

As one balances positives against negatives, analyzes the uncertainties and the controversies, it is clear that there is cause for concern. In much of what is done there is little evidence of success, much evidence of dissatisfaction, and considerable evidence of failure. There is no escaping the need for innovation, more knowledge, better-ordered service priorities. While there is no case for abandoning the social service system in the interim — since some needs are being met, and needs exist that people want to have met — simultaneous efforts must be directed toward developing measurement tools and methods that will facilitate a more rational sorting out of the effective from the ineffective and provide a basis for informed choice. For, money and personnel will always be in short supply, and the visible needs considerable.

We shall note, in the ensuing discussion of policy approaches, that operations research and systems approaches often emphasize efficiency and related criteria as the major or sole basis for choice. But other approaches posit different values as particularly relevant to the social services. There is merit in both types of approach. While it is in the nature of social welfare to go beyond efficiency, there is no logic in closing our eyes to unit costs, effects, and effectiveness. On the other hand, the lofty rhetoric used to justify operational efficiency is no excuse for ignoring the questions of what is actually achieved and how consumers feel about it.

What of the considerable practice-oriented research into the social services? Does this not make a policy contribution?[22]

Much research into the social services is actually basic social science research employing social service materials. As such it is not specifically oriented to helping policymakers or to answering questions about effects and effectiveness. Nonetheless, appropriately employed, it may aid the analyst. Much of the research is oriented to what might be called practice issues: how to select foster parents, the grouping of children in institutions, the differential response to various interviewing or treatment techniques. As such, it may contribute to the work of the individual practitioner and to administrative decisions on the immediate level. The relevance to larger issues depends not only upon design but also upon the ability of a policy analyst to relate it to other studies that, in their totality, may shed light on significant questions.[23] Some of the research is directed to questions of need and of user response to service — this too may be applied by the analyst to policy questions. Finally, although only a limited amount of research has focused specifically on policy questions, interest has begun to develop, and expansion is anticipated.[24] New organizational structures in the form of policy centers and comprehensive programmatic research enterprises have been created to foster such development.

Needs?

In an interesting critique of a major British report on the social services, Peter Townsend emphasized the committee's failure to relate services to needs.[25] Our discussion of programs and personnel may be similarly faulted. More specifically, Townsend argued that while the formulation of goals may be influenced by the opinions of the consumers and suppliers of service, as well as by conventional views of need and standards of service, one should also attempt objective assessment of needs and standards: "Needs can be shown to exist independent of the feelings engendered within a particular society and independent of those recognized by society's institutions."[26] One would, in Townsend's strategy, seek several measures of inequality and of deprivation and relate these to objectively developed standards of service, as part of the social service planning process.

We have not attempted such analysis, since the present undertaking makes no pretense of social service planning for a field or locality. Our goal, rather, is to define the parameters of personal social services in the United States and to provide sufficient illustrative detail to introduce current policy issues. Such issues would be of concern to planners and programmers at all levels.

Clearly, Townsend's logic is right for those who would plan services at a given time and place. The complexities are enormous. To illustrate:

1. Basic physical requirements for clothing, shelter, and essential caloric intake aside, most "needs" are conditioned by societal context and the expectations engendered. Indeed, the form and level of need satisfaction is culturally set.
2. Service standards (number of teachers per 100 pupils, number of doctors per 100,000 population, and so on) are occasionally validated empirically as assuring a defined level of service. More often they incorporate some elements of folklore and faith. They always assume a specific pattern of operations, and the pattern may not be acceptable to innovators and reformers.
3. What is need satisfaction at one time and what is an acceptable service pattern at a given point become outmoded as aspirations change in response to greater affluence, improved communication, scientific progress, and so on. Indeed, policy decisions (about equity-equality, for example) affect levels of expectation.

Thus, while one might at a given time and place solve the "needs" problem in the sense of arriving at definitions and agreements that would empirically compare social deficits with resources assigned to cope with them,[27] it would not serve our purposes in the present volume to go beyond the illustrative and incomplete survey of some of the social services already presented.

It is of interest to note nonetheless that "needs assessment" has been the object of enormous attention and investment since the inauguration of Title XX social services planning in the United States in 1975. Many guides and manuals have been published. According to an overview from the Urban Institute, the major assessment techniques employed for 1977 have included reference to census or program data (twenty-seven states), attention to socioeconomic indicators (three states), provider questionnaires (eighteen states), client and citizen questionnaires (thirteen states), community needs surveys or studies (twenty-two states), and lists of inquiries from information and referral services (three states), as well as information from advocates and case data. This array provides little evidence of agreement as to exactly how one goes from alleged indicators of need to the setting of interprogram priorities or the invention of new programs. The Urban Institute survey uncovered evidence that the studies had had a major role in priority setting in only one-third of the states.

Considerations such as these also make it undesirable to attempt here an assessment of the *resource* picture presented in the earlier expenditures section. As needs are redefined and standards reformulated, a program's service deficit may be computed. This, then, becomes one of a series of competing claims upon the country's productivity. The decision as to the size of the allocation is of course affected by the nature of the other claims that arise, the values that are dominant, and the distribution of power among competing claimants.

One may ask whether assignment of more resources to social services would change or redefine the policy issues dealt with in the next section. The answer is yes, in the sense that fewer choices would have to be made if resources were plentiful; more diversity and acceptance of opposites might be tolerated (public-voluntary, integrated-separatist, cash–in-kind benefits, and so on). The reality is that resources are always scarce, never unlimited. Furthermore, some of the policy alternatives *are* mutually exclusive or at least do affect one another. Finally, availability of resources for a given field is also affected by policy choice, since — in turn — it influences the creation of a constituency and the costs of implementation. We doubt, therefore, that most analysts can solve the policy equation by starting out with an attempt to define its resource side.

For present purposes we have noted:

1. The relatively low current priority assigned what we call personal social services within the totality of social welfare (social service) expenditures
2. Illustrative evidence that personal social services may be considered quantitatively and qualitatively inadequate almost everywhere
3. An analysis of social change in modern society that suggests that social services will be essential in the predictable future and perhaps should be given a higher priority if certain amenities and protections are not to be ignored
4. The urgency of innovation and social invention, which would make

any long-term quantitative projections out of present service patterns quite insufficient

In sum, as long as society is responsive to need, social services are destined to continue — even to grow — and to change. Those who would guide this development cannot ignore issues of policy.

Notes

1. Ida C. Merriam and Alfred M. Skolnik, *Social Welfare Expenditures Under Public Programs in the United States, 1929–66,* Research Report no. 25, Office of Research and Statistics, Social Security Administration (Washington D.C.: Government Printing Office, 1968). Annual analyses to supplement this report appear in the *Social Security Bulletin.*

    Our exclusion of education, health, and housing in the discussion of personal social services, and the nature of available reporting systems, inevitably leaves out certain activities that many would list as personal social services in the narrower sense — but the omissions do not distort the basic relationships (social services to all social welfare) and this is currently the only practical approach.

2. These expenditure estimates were provided by HEW staff at House sub- committee hearings in September 1977. Subcommittee on Select Education, Committee on Education and Labor, House of Representatives, Hearings, "Reorganization of the Office of Human Development," September 8 and 12, 1977 (Washington, D.C.: U.S. Government Printing Office, 1977).

3. Good points of departure for seeing programs, usually from the perspective of the responsible administrative agencies, are the following: *Encyclopedia of Social Work, Seventeenth Issue,* 2 vols. (New York: National Association of Social Workers, 1977); *Statistical Abstract of the United States,* U.S. Department of Commerce, Bureau of the Census (Washington, D.C.: Government Printing Office, 1978); *Social Security Bulletin, Aging, Children Today, Social Services U.S.A.* — all published by the U.S. Department of Health, Education, and Welfare. Also, see reports from the Family Service Association of America, Child Welfare League of America, United Way, and other national voluntary planning and coordination agencies cited in the text. For contrast, see *Social Trends* for recent years, Central Statistical Office (London: Her Majesty's Stationery Office); or the latest edition of *Social Welfare of the Northern Countries* (Stockholm, published annually).

4. *Social Services U.S.A.* and HEW advance tables.

5. Ibid.

6. Ibid.

7. Ibid.

8. Ibid.

9. See topical articles in *Encyclopedia of Social Work.* Also, Sheila B. Kamerman and Alfred J. Kahn, *Social Services in the United States,* (Philadelphia: Temple University Press, 1976); and Alfred J. Kahn and Sheila B. Kamerman, *Social Services in International Perspective* (Washington, D.C.: Government Printing Office, 1977).

10. See the most recent issue of *Setting National Priorities* (Washington, D.C.: The Brookings Institution). Also, Sar A. Levitan and Robert Taggart III, *Jobs for the Disabled* (Baltimore: Johns Hopkins Press, 1977); or Sar A. Levitan, *Programs in Aid of the Poor,* rev. ed. (Baltimore: Johns Hopkins Press, 1977), or *The Great Society's Poor Law* (Baltimore: Johns Hopkins University Press, 1969).

11. See Charles Grosser, *Community Organization: From Enabling to Advocacy* (New York: Praeger, 1972).

12. Sheldon Siegel, *Social Service Manpower Needs: An Overview to 1980* (New York: Council on Social Work Education, 1975).

13. Roy Lubove, *The Professional Altruist* (Cambridge, Mass.: Harvard University Press, 1965).

14. See *Voluntary Action News* published regularly by the National Center for Voluntary Action, Washington, D.C.

15. See William Gorham, "Notes of a Practitioner," *The Public Interest,* No. 8 (Summer 1967). The quotation is from his testimony before the Joint Economic Committee, *The Planning-Programming-Budgeting System: Progress and Potentials,* 2 vols. (Washington, D.C.: Government Printing Office, 1967), Vol. I, p. 5.

16. Ibid.

17. Joel Handler found, in his Wisconsin study, very little direct service in public welfare, despite the intensive efforts to free public assistance workers for a casework role in the 1950s and early 1960s. See Joel Handler and Ellen Jane Hollingsworth, "The Administration of Social Services and the Structure of Dependency: The Views of AFDC Recipients," *Social Service Review,* 43, 4 (December 1969), 406–420. Or, the same authors, *The "Deserving Poor": A Study of Welfare Administration* (Chicago: Markham Publishing Co., 1971).

18. Herbert H. Hyman, Charles R. Wright, and Terence K. Hopkins, *Applications of Methods of Evaluation* (Berkeley and Los Angeles: University of California Press, 1962). Also, Edward Suchman, *Evaluative Research* (New York: Russell Sage Foundation, 1967); Frank Caro, *Readings in Evaluation Research,* rev. ed. (New York: Russell Sage Foundation, 1976); and Carol H. Weiss, *Evaluation Research* (Englewood Cliffs, N.J.: Prentice-Hall, 1972); and *Evaluating Action Programs* (London: Allyn and Bacon, 1972).

19. For a useful review of the state of the art, see Henry Maas (ed.), *Research in the Social Services: A Five-Year Review* (New York: National Association of Social Workers, 1971). The manpower field has been subject to as much or more measurement and evaluation as any in the past decade. For an informed and wise appraisal of experience, and an assessment of possibilities, see Sar A. Levitan and Robert Taggart III, *Social Experimentation and Manpower Policy: The Rhetoric and the Reality* (Baltimore: Johns Hopkins Press, 1971).

20. The topic is large and complex. How, when there is no conceptualization of "social system" that can be operationalized, does one develop indicators of the social health and characteristics of a society? How does one choose dimensions to monitor that have long-term normative significance? Given present sources and methods of collecting good statistics and current thinking about social factors, is there any way to aggregate statistics into major index items? For an introduction, see Raymond A. Bauer (ed.), *Social Indicators* (Cambridge, Mass.: MIT Press, 1966); Bertram M. Gross, *Social Intelligence for America's Future* (Boston: Allyn and Bacon, 1969); *Toward a Social Report,* U.S. Department of Health, Education, and Welfare (Washington, D.C.: Government Printing Office, 1969); Eleanor B. Sheldon and Wilbert E. Moore (eds.), *Indicators of Social Change* (New York: Russell Sage Foundation, 1969); and *Statistical Abstract of the United States, 1978,* U.S. Department of Commerce (Washington, D.C.: Government Printing Office, 1978). A sophisticated review of conceptual issues appears in Eleanor B. Sheldon and Howard E. Freeman, "Notes on Social Indicators: Promises and Potentials," *Policy Science,* 1, 1 (Spring 1970), 97–112. For a British illustration, see *Social Trends,* Central Statistical Office (London: Her Majesty's Stationery Office). On the city level, an approach is offered in Martin V. Jones and Michael J. Flax, *The Quality of Life in Metropolitan Washington, D.C.: Some Statistical Benchmarks* (Washington, D.C.: The Urban Institute, 1971). Also, *State of the Child Report* (New York: Foundation for Child Development, 1976).

21. Maas, *Research in the Social Services.*

22. For example, see Henry S. Maas (ed.), *Five Fields of Social Service: Reviews of Research* (New York: National Association of Social Workers, 1966); and Maas, *Research in the Social Services.*

23. As exemplified in the contribution of Alfred Kadushin in Maas, *Research in the Social Services,* in his summary of foster care and adoption research.

24. See Jack Rothman, "Community Organization Practice," pp. 70–107, and Genevieve W. Carter, "Public Welfare," pp. 192–230, in Maas, ibid.

25. Peter Townsend, "The Objectives of the New Local Social Service," in *The Fifth Social Service: A Critical Analysis of the Seebohm Proposals* (London: Fabian Society, 1970).

26. Ibid., p. 9.

27. For illustration of several approaches, see Eileen Younghusband, et al., *Living With Handicap* (London: National Bureau for Co-operation in Child Care, 1970); Jean Packman, *Child Care: Needs and Numbers* (London: Allen and Unwin, 1968); Florence Ruderman, *Child Care and Working Mothers* (New York: Child Welfare League of America, 1968); Alfred J. Kahn, et al., *Neighborhood Information Centers* (New York: Columbia University School of Social Work, 1966); and Alvin Schorr, *Poor Kids* (New York: Basic Books, 1966).

II

▶▶▶▶▶▶▶ POLICY ISSUES

The Framework of Social Service Policy ◄◄◄◄ 4

In deciding to develop or to expand social services, a group, organization, or government adopts a policy — as it does in electing one category of services rather than another for emphasis. Similarly, the designation of organizational forms for the services and the selection of a delivery system for any specific service represent significant policy choices. Such choices have consequences, whether or not immediately visible during the choice process and whether or not the choosing is deliberate, or even conscious.

What do we here mean by policy?[1] To the planner, a policy is a "standing plan," a "guide to future decision making," or a "continuing line of decisions or set of constraints upon individual decisions." It is the implicit or explicit core of principle that underlies specific programs, legislation, priorities. "Social policy" may be described as the common denominator of decisions and constraints with reference to social welfare or social service programs. Or one may specify policy with reference to a given service system (family welfare, social insurance, and so on) or a given type of social issue (degree of localism, use of market-type instruments).

Policy questions raised about social services in the more distant past were quite different from the ones we are facing here. Before the personal social services began to serve people other than the poor and the unacceptably deviant (that is, before the late nineteenth century for the most part), there was little concern with the stigma associated with service. To those who rendered charity, for that is what the services were, there was no doubt that "it is better to give than to receive." To the general public it was acceptable or even desirable that charity in some way constrain the recipient or perhaps even punish him because of his need to accept aid. The notions of professional skill and specialization were generally not yet developed. If a distinction was made among the categories of people making use of services, it was so as to permit a somewhat different moral assessment of various "clients." Thus, it might be held that children should not be kept with adults, dangerous criminals with the "impotent poor," or the extremely disturbed mentally ill with "innocent" women and children. Since the giving of help, the offer of aid, was its own justification and reward, there was little accountability for results from a user perspective (an arena in which change has been very slow). Therefore, questions of coordination, case integration, and service accountability did not often arise. And, given a view of the poor or the deviant that accentuated moral failure and inferiority, there was readiness to concentrate on in-kind benefits and indoor (institutional) relief — approaches that appear to facilitate control of recipients — rather than upon cash, vouchers, and market-type devices.

What is the occasion today for the considerable attention to social service policy? Why do some — but by no means all — of the concerns reach the mass media, public debates, legislative bodies, and other political forums? The order of the listing of relevant factors varies with individual perspective.

First, more people from all social classes are affected by social services. The problems of the "invisible poor" may generate little interest and debate, but women of all classes care about day care. Citizens of many backgrounds are interested in treatment resources for drug addicts, in service for unwed mothers, in abortion counseling services, in facilities for senior citizens, and so on. Many citizens are concerned with communal solidarity and consider social services as a possible vehicle for its achievement.

Second, the poor and disadvantaged have become quite visible. Certainly among the major factors in making the policy debate more general was the rights revolution. In the early and mid-1960s black leaders and their allies began to ask whether the scarcity of ghetto social services and the control of social services by public and voluntary groups outside of the ghetto community did not represent a kind of "welfare colonialism." In this connection they raised two kinds of questions. First, in the early 1960s they asked why ghetto residents had to go to central offices, why services were not in the neighborhoods of people to be served, why the controlling boards were always "downtown" white people. Later on they asked: Were the services appropriate? Were the priorities right? Did the existing balance among services not confuse the fundamental issues as ghetto citizens perceived them? In the latter connection, they increasingly cited the prevailing emphasis on therapeutic and adjustment services, when in their view the priority need was for education, jobs and job training, housing, and urban amenity.

From the mid- to late 1960s, the critics of the system took another step. The antipoverty war had stressed work and work training, while playing down personal treatment. But, graduates of training programs for the deprived often could not find — or could not hold — jobs. The available jobs were frequently considered to be "dead ends." The local milieu did not change as much as people hoped through the community action programs that generated health, child care, and other social services, plus "participation." Now the charge was made that these were the wrong priorities. Some reformers turned their emphasis toward public assistance reform or the achievement of a minimum guaranteed income. Why not end poverty with money rather than with service? Others stressed "local power" as the target, seeing this as the dynamic for "basic" institutional change. General social service was either diversion or target, not a major instrument.

These were not the only factors that created awareness of the policy issues in social services. Both the commitment to end poverty and the increased alertness to economic growth and its relationship to an accelerated inflation have highlighted certain staffing issues. There is recognition of the increased proportion of the labor force available for both commercial and nonprofit services, of the reservoir of noncredentialed and unskilled people in search of work. The question arose, and became urgent in social policy, as to whether what had previously been defined as professional tasks in education, social work, and health could be restructured and subdivided to create nonprofessional roles. Initially the idea was attractive as a way of coping with staffing needs, but by the late 1960s, as some personnel shortages began to ease, the question arose as to whether the new trend was not in itself desirable: Were some jobs not made artificially inaccessible? Were the "noncredentialed" better qualified than degree holders or college graduates for certain jobs in the sense of knowing consumers and their needs, as well as localities and their resources?

Similarly, the need to assure responsiveness of services to ethnic and cultural diversity, particularly to the unique problem of urban ghettos, spurred a movement toward decentralization in social services by the mid-1960s (or, alternatively, the creation of locally based but centrally controlled service outlets). This trend, too, had wider ramifications. Society's response to increasing bureaucratization and the creation of large-scale organization has taken a number of forms. Increased localization of outlets has become popular and indeed urgent. Even governmental authorities, long ready to increase centralization of power and resources in Washington, have sought to define a "new federalism," involving redistribution of funds (revenue sharing) and power to lower levels. The policy debate about degree and modes of decentralization in social services is to be viewed in this context.

Concern with service effectiveness or cost effectiveness has also contributed to social policy alertness within social services. The search for increased domestic expenditure to deal with urban blight, poverty, and racial injustice has taken place in a time of fiscal stringency; inflation has been a major problem, as has unemployment. Within government, increased adoption of cost effectiveness and program budgeting techniques, a trend that began with the defense establishment in the 1960s and spread to all federal departments, and to many state and local units as well, has tended to highlight issues of priority and policy.

While operations research, systems analysis, and various efficiency or economizing approaches were gradually applied in the period after World War II to plans for the development of natural resources and to defense policy and programs, they began to receive serious attention with reference to many aspects of the domestic scene during the late 1960s and 1970s. Economists and political scientists, in particular, responded to the increased emphasis on the domestic sector by adapting, or attempting to adapt, their policy-analytic approaches to new kinds of issues. This in turn has raised questions about traditional value perspectives in American social service policy and has introduced alternative options into the debate. It has also highlighted the need to reconcile the efficiency and the other-value orientations to social service policy, just as all American institutions, including the corporation, have begun to face the need to reconcile the "economizing" mode (rationality as profit optimization) with the "sociologizing" mode (an attempt to use a variety of values in judging the public interest).[2]

Consumerism has become a large and respected movement in American society. Ralph Nader's leads are being followed in many fields. Within the social services, concern with the indictment by the minority community, organized poor people, and youth has created a readiness to review effectiveness in relation to expenditure — as an aspect of accountability. At the same time there are social service proponents who have cautioned against pragmatic and utilitarian approaches that would justify efficiency criteria while ignoring important societal processes, particularly the end of social solidarity — which is seen as a higher value.

For board members, administrators, budget authorities, and planners, the proliferation of social services in the last two decades has generated yet another category of policy concern. By the 1970s, a middle-sized or large American city had three overlapping systems of social services:

1. Those traditionally associated with *public welfare,* now often called public social services, including the public psychiatric hospital and aftercare programs (concentrating on recipients of public assistance and Medicaid and on other poor people but — as in the case of child welfare — some others as well)
2. The *voluntary* family, child welfare, and child guidance agencies, which often — but not exclusively — served users from the working and lower-middle classes, but whose caseloads increasingly included more of the very poor, as public reimbursement contracts became available under Title XX in the late 1970s
3. *Community action* programs, created during the antipoverty effort, originally an attempt at a "new look" service for the poor, now with a mission overlapping with public social service programs, but more likely to have consumer participation as well as indigenous personnel.

For close observers of these overlapping, competing, and generally unsatisfactory systems, the issue had become — given the several initiatives to create new income maintenance programs separating the administration of cash assistance from nonmonetary social services, given the pressure to relate antipoverty programs to long-existing services, and given the evidence that fragmented services were costly, ineffective, and irresponsible — what should be done? This question led directly to many basic policy issues, particularly to the matter of universalism versus selectivity (see pp. 76 ff.) and to the public-voluntary pattern (see pp. 86 ff.).

Solutions were not readily discovered. By the late 1970s, the programming confusion and policy sprawl had only increased: many social services were being offered under community mental health, Law Enforcement Assistance Administration, and proprietary auspices, and there were new categorical efforts for abused children, runaways, teen-age mothers, and the aged. Social services for many types of handicapped children and adults continued to expand under still other administrative arrangements. And, in the marketplace, there were personal social services on a fee basis, seeking access as well to "third-party" insurance and related payments.

The most basic among all the factors encouraging attention to policy follows from all that has been said. It has become clear that, in seeking to meet the basic human needs of families and individuals, to solve its social problems, and to achieve urban amenity, racial equality, communal integration, social justice, and an end to poverty, the United States will rely heavily upon personal social services as a prime instrument. Social mobility, greater individual opportunity, geographic mix, and distribution of specific goods can be implemented through social service programs. Furthermore, as suggested in Chapter 1, social services become increasingly important to all segments of society and all social classes in facilitating response to social change. Social services now are matters of great urgency to an urban-industrial society. But this projection does not answer questions of what and how; it does not resolve issues of social policy and programming strategy. Because the questions and issues are complex and have many political and economic ramifications, the social services debate arouses interest and feeling.

Human Services Within an Existing Societal Context

Mention has already been made of the position that holds that social services are and have always been a means of diverting attention from the need for more basic institutional change. (Sometimes the term social services is meant narrowly, sometimes broadly.) The allegation is true, we have noted, in the sense that unmet human need sometimes generates irresistible pressure for major social innovation and shifts in power relationships. Such shifts set off chains of circumstances with unpredictable outcomes. No one seriously contends, however, except perhaps the more diabolical among political revolutionaries or the naïve who assume that apocalypse leads inexorably to Utopia, that a serious case can be made for opposing all social services in the hope that significant changes will follow and that such changes inevitably will be benign. A more valid argument may occasionally be offered against specific services proposed, where it is shown that such services are likely, whether or not so intended, to defer or interfere with more basic or more favored measures: a self-help project where participation in an election contest is an alternative; services to develop personal insight where one might launch an economic program; services to care for children so that mothers may be required to work whatever their overall situation or preferences, where what they may need is income to enable them to remain home to care for their children if they wish to do so.

These illustrations suggest that the promotion of constructive institutional change may take the form of advocating and implementing social services — using the term broadly here to include education, employment programs, health, and income maintenance. The pace and type of institutional change may be as much a matter of the *type* of social service created as of the presence or absence of any service at all. This is so because desired institutional change, as sought by reformers, must be understood as an evaluative category, describing a point on a continuum in which shifts in power relations, resource distribution, institutional procedures, overall policies, and program balance bring about qualitative, sought differences in distribution of resources, primary and secondary social relations, social structure, and culture. Social service policy and programming decisions may be important factors here, even though no one would argue that they represent the sole approach.

In this sense, then, for those concerned with personal social services in the narrower sense of the present volume, the policy questions at a given moment may be formulated as follows:

1. Is this the time for investment of energy, attention, and resources in social services (as contrasted with economic or political measures), and if so what should be the mix among these several components?*
2. What mix is desirable of different types of social services — broadly conceived to include education, health, employment, and housing, as well as the personal social services?
3. What is the appropriate balance among cash and in-kind transfers, public social utilities (which we shall define as services available at user option or status), and case services (services with a "diagnostic" doorway)?†
4. Among the personal social services, particularly case services, what is to be the mix of concrete services (nutrition programs, escort services, chore services) and relationship services (counseling, casework, guidance, and so on)?

Social utilities and case services, two major concepts, are yet to be introduced. The expansion of public social utilities would indeed represent significant institutional change. These notions require some background discussion.

Social welfare history began with the assumption that most "normal" people managed satisfactorily on their own, through their own energies and resources and with the assistance of primary group members and such traditional institutions as work and church. Temporary catastrophe and personal misfortune (flood, drought, war, accident, depression) might require public intervention, but this was temporary. Social welfare was a sometime thing; it "withered away" if times were good. Of course, some

*Political and economic judgments are here called for — as well as data about program complementarities. The "art" is in a primitive state. On the notion of "mix," as an alternative to the more traditional "priorities" approach, see Kahn, *Theory and Practice of Social Planning,* pp. 223, 229, 242, 243.
†The cash or benefits-in-kind debate is reviewed in Chapter 6.

people were incapable of managing on their own or they were morally defective and "exploited" others, expecting help when they should have been able to manage — these were the unworthy poor, the malingerers. Whatever programs proved necessary for them should have deterrent and control features and should avoid encouraging continued dependency.

This view of social welfare, now generally named the residual perspective ("the need is temporary"), goes back to the seventeenth century, when the beginnings of organized provision in the modern sense were visible in the West. It is a view that expanded with industrialization. In the United States, at least, it had no serious challenge until the latter part of the nineteenth century and, again, during the Great Depression of the 1930s. It is a widely held view today, particularly where personal mobility is visible and elements of frontier tradition are strong.

A residual view of welfare tends to give almost sole emphasis to what may be called case services, or what Willard Richan has named "social intervention." Case services are available by individual diagnosis or evaluation. They are intended to restore or enhance functioning in an individualized manner. The assumption is that an outside environmental force or a personal illness or problem is in the way of adequate functioning. Treatment or help will bring improvement or cure; the recipient is considered to be a patient.

But the residual view hardly describes the total social reality of an industrialized or a postindustrial society, and case services do not encompass all the necessary societal responses. It is now understood that a successful industrialized society generates new problems and new needs by virtue of its success. Technological advances in production, increasing worker productivity, may create unemployment because some workers are not required or because members of the existing labor force lack the required skills. Scientific and public health advances increase substantially the number of the aged who are alive for significant periods after retirement from the labor force, thereby generating new needs in the fields of health, housing, income security, leisure, protective services, and so on. This alternative, or institutional, view of social welfare holds that out of its normal functioning the society constantly develops pressure for new provision for meeting newly emerging needs. This is as legitimate and appropriate a process as was the process that created the basic institutions serving an agricultural or early industrial society — family, church, local government, guild, and so on. New institutions must be invented to meet new societal requirements, and the process should be understood and welcomed. Social welfare, if the term is employed to mean the societal provision or action to meet such needs, is thus a continuing and expanding aspect of the modern world.

The institutional view of social welfare gives support to the concept that some social services might be regarded as public social utilities, rather than as case services. Even extreme laissez-faire-ists do not question the need for such communal services as a water supply, postal system, sewage system, public transportation, or highway network. These are the infrastructure of the industrial society, and their use does not bring any stigma. There may be user charges, and the system is constantly updated to reflect changed need as well. Similarly, some social services are generally accepted as representing social infrastructure, although the listing varies by place. Generally included are elementary and secondary schools, parks, libraries, museums, and some aspects of public health. Included in some places are general health services, junior or community colleges, family planning, housing, employment services, credit unions, and information and access services. Often proposed and sometimes provided are nursery (prekindergarten) programs and day care centers for children below elementary school age, family or youth centers, and centers for the aging.

Where a system is widely accepted as a public social utility, it may take on its own institutional autonomy outside of the general social services field. This is true, as already noted, of education, medical care, public housing, and — to an extent — employment services.

Public social utilities may be divided into those available at user option (library, museum, general community center) and those available by user age category or status (day care, center for the aged). The user is citizen, not patient. He does not need to prove poverty, illness, or problem. He enters at will, not after a diagnosis or a means test.

The social planner and policymaker thus faces the issue, in contemplating new or improved personal social service, of clarifying the balance among case services, to be reached through diagnostic or evaluative channels, and public social utilities, including those to be available by user option and those to be open to individuals of defined statuses. A full social service system would apparently require a mix. An institutional view of social services includes the notion that case services and utilities are normal, permanent, inevitable, and enriching — not regrettable — components of modern societies. Public attitudes and preference — and particularly the determination of whether user wish is to be regarded as the criterion of need for service — will determine the readiness to create a utility and will clarify whether the utility is to be completely free or, as in the instance of water or transportation, to be associated with some pattern of user charges.

Students of American social welfare will recognize that, just as modern cities currently suffer because of inadequate public physical utilities — note the new concern with transportation, water, antipollution devices, and housing — so do cities also suffer because of public social utility lags. There has been a poverty of social invention and a deficiency in public investment in the social sector. Cities now need to find new primary group supports, new facilities for the very young and for youth, new provision for the aged, new enrichments for family life. Some of the services will be concrete; others, relationship. The topic should be at the heart of public policy in coming decades, and estimating whether a service is or is not to be organized as a utility will occupy planners increasingly.

Universalism versus Selectivity

Closely related to the case service–public social utility dichotomy, and growing out of the distinction between the residual and institutional approaches to social welfare, is the differentiation between the universal and selective approaches to social welfare.

Universalism is associated in Great Britain with the names of Beatrice and Sydney Webb and Sir William Beveridge. Particularly in the egalitarian atmosphere of World War II, it was decided to develop social welfare measures, especially social insurance, on a flat-grant basis. All would pay at the same rate and benefit at the same rate, a social minimum. All social services, envisaged as reflecting a social minimum conceived in social justice and nurturing equality of opportunity, were by their nature to be universal.

Family allowances are universal income maintenance programs in most industrial countries. The assumption is that society thus equalizes the cost burden of rearing children for those with no or few children and those with several. The payment is automatic. The tax system may be designed to recoup family allowances from the prosperous, as it may to ensure that the affluent pay their fair share for all universal services.

Universalism (service eligibility regardless of economic status) as an idea is appealing to people with democratic convictions. It breaks away from poor law notions that only the inadequate, the failures, need the resources of the social welfare system. Indeed, to the Webbs, it destroys poor law completely. Universalism also departs from the residual notion that social services are temporary and needed only in time of special stress or catastrophe. It encourages constant updating of social services in the light of social change. It recognizes the large part that social services play in the economy and manpower strategy of any society. It offers leverage to ensure that social services are quality services: where services are only for the poor or for the "unworthy," one cares little for making them attractive. Where they may serve anyone, they must meet the standards expected of any general communal provision.

Why, then, would there be any doubt at all about a policy of universal social services? Why, in the late 1960s, when the issue was publicly debated in Great Britain and much of Northern and Western Europe, should there have been considerable public support for the alternative of selectivity, a system whereby people become eligible for services only if they are below a specified income — that is, meet a means test?*

Modern proponents of selectivity (a means-test screen for eligibility) often agree that there should be some universal provision, some public social utilities; but they would limit this provision to a few high-priority fields such as public elementary education, where the communal stake is obvious and high. They hold that universal provision in many fields sets a norm for a greater volume of use than a country can afford. It takes out of the market, and relieves individuals of the cost of, many items that they should seek out for themselves and pay for out of earnings. If they are poor or have no income, it is held, let people apply on a means-test basis for public services. Then their service costs can be publicly met or free service provided.

After all, this position holds, any universal service must be paid for somehow. A service's universality could generate demand and encourage use where the individual would not accord it a priority were he to pay costs out of his own income. Where this occurs, services ranking low in consumer preference gain support through the tax mechanism.

There are, moreover, two very practical obstacles cited against universalism. First, whatever the views of public policy advocates, there are sizable elements in the population in significant numbers of places that do not conceive of some social services as generally needed. They regard such services as "all right" for people with special problems or needs (and they think this always means only poor people) but simply do not believe that programs should be designed and organized with the total population in mind. Second, services are expensive. Whatever the ideological stance, there are those who hold that universalism as a social service philosophy is simply unrealistic. Indeed, during the several European crises of public finance in the 1970s, a number of countries holding to strong democratic ideologies either added user charges or departed from universalistic approaches by introducing means tests.†

*Ryan poses the distinction as between "universalistic" and "exceptionalistic" approaches. Given the considerable background of the issue and the available literature, there would appear to be no valid reason to introduce a new vocabulary. See William Ryan, *Blaming the Victim* (New York: Pantheon, 1971).

Steiner differentiates "subtle" from "crude" techniques in coping with poverty, with the former corresponding roughly with universalism, perhaps tinged by economic aggregate demand concepts. Gilbert Y. Steiner, *The State of Welfare* (Washington, D.C.: The Brookings Institution, 1971).

†It is in fact uncertain that careful analysis would show universal services to be more expensive, once all societal accounts are tallied. Nicole Questiaux, Paris, personal communication.

It was yet another consideration that led to the strongest attack on universalism in theory and practice in the U.S. antipoverty war of the mid-1960s. The argument recurs wherever the debate is joined. A number of students of social policy, and some local and national leaders, believe that, when programs are universal, the very poor do not get their fair share. It is held that the educated and informed, or those with some resources to employ, are guilty of "creaming" what is intended as general public provision. The more advantaged permit services to reach the poorest only after skimming off the best for themselves. As evidence, one may cite how, historically, the very poor do not get a fair share of the best public secondary schools and colleges; how publicly supported libraries, museums, and concerts often are operated largely for the benefit of the middle class; how expensive, tax-supported beaches can be reached only by private car owners; how the very poor mentally ill may be incarcerated in state congregate-care facilities while the more advantaged receive ambulatory care and outpatient clincial service — and so on.

The strategy in response to these problems inherent in universalism was, of course, the U.S. antipoverty war. A national agency, the Office of Economic Opportunity, was set up in the Executive Office of the President in the mid-1960s as advocate on behalf of, planner and implementer of services for, and instrument of the poorest. Local counterpart agencies were funded and placed in the hands of boards more or less representative of, responsive to, or consisting of the most disadvantaged. Many new social services were designed on the premise of income-group separatism and provided with service delivery structures growing out of such policy. Unique staffing patterns followed. It was several years before many voices were heard claiming that, once again, selectivity had been self-defeating: these special services for the poor were often stigmatizing and of poor quality.

By the late 1970s, many observers had changed sides: they did not want the poor closed out, but they had come to consider universalism realistic, since many nonpoor people needed services, and selectivity generated the inefficiency of dual systems as well as stigma. They also had come to believe that universalism was a better path to stability and quality of programs.

In short, on the one hand, selectivity is a response to creaming. Also (although the argument has a constituency that may not care about creaming), selectivity is an approach that protects the public purse and ensures that limited resources go where they are most needed. In the economics vocabulary this latter point is summed up as "efficiency." Universalism, on the other hand, reflects egalitarian and social justice ideologies. It faces modern realities about the need for social services and is a response to the allegation that, because of considerable historical baggage, services designed for poor people tend to be poor services and to attract poor-quality staff. Selectivity by means tests creates stigma and limits "take-up" — the degree to which services are called upon by those who need them.[3] Administration of means-test eligibility for social services has proven very expensive too.

There is also a subtle, but increasingly influential, point yet to be noted. If many rights and benefits are means-tested, a welfare-eligible individual suffers a huge loss in standard of living (food stamps, medical care, housing benefits) if his/her income rises just above the eligibility line. Where benefits are universal, the disincentive is far smaller: universal benefits are not income-conditioned.

Social service policy clearly will continue to deal with such matters. In the sense that an income tax form is a type of means test, it has been shown that stigma and status inferiority need not follow an effort to classify people by means. Affluent as well as poor parents in the United States quite readily submit income statements used routinely to determine the levels of college scholarships. The issue would, then, appear to be the generality and form of the means test, and how it is socially defined, not its mere existence.*

The analysis would tend to confirm Mike Reddin's view[4] to the effect that one cannot choose universalism or selectivity as a sole principle. The issue is one of emphasis, context, and nature of a composite policy. A democratic and relatively industrialized society might debate a solution along the following lines: First, there might be implemented quite generally the distinction we have proposed between public social utilities and case services. Utilities by their nature are universal. They would be employed at user initiative, since eligibility would be a matter of status (age, handicap, and so on) or one's wish or option. Case services would become available through intermediaries, expert "doorkeepers," who assess personal need. In neither instance would income affect access.

There would remain much room for maneuver in determining which utilities are to be paid for out of general revenue (that is, preferably progressive income taxes) and which are more efficiently used and appropriately funded by user charges. The community's stake in assuring access should certainly be the major determinant: Are users who cannot

---

*In "On the Stigma Effect and the Demand for Welfare Programs: A Theoretical Note," unpublished discussion paper from the Institute for Research on Poverty, University of Wisconsin (1971), Burton A. Weisbrod suggests, from an economics perspective, that it may be useful to think of "marginal stigma cost." The importance of stigma depends upon benefit levels, he believes: "with an increase in benefits it pays to incur greater stigma costs." The matter requires research. For some findings that ran contrary to expectations about AFDC, see Joel F. Handler and Ellen Jane Hollingsworth, *The "Deserving Poor": A Study of Welfare Administration* (Chicago: Markham Publishing Co., 1971).

or will not pay to be encouraged? Would fees close the doors to those the community wishes to attract? Is the priority high enough to merit public funds?

Since case services always reflect personal or familial need and signify the presence of a problem in adjustment or functioning, readiness to pay charges should never be an access factor. Nor should mode of payment determine the quality of service. The doorway of a case service should diagnose, evaluate, categorize — but only with reference to problem or need for the particular service. The question of payment should be raised after the service plan is made, the required help ensured. Payment for case services is possible in a variety of modes, none of which compromise universalism. First, the service might be a free, statutory one, financed out of general revenues, preferably through a graduated income tax. Second, it might be paid for on an insurance basis, with government meeting all or some of the premium payments for the poor (again, financing by means of a graduated income tax). Or, whether through a public or a voluntary service agency, a service might be delivered on a universalistic basis, with payment determined and specified only after case acceptance — and varying with individual means. There might be free service for the poor and near-poor, low fees for the middle group, economic fees that meet the actual costs of the service for those who are better off. In fact, voluntary agency and United Way fund raising could be used to subsidize fees for those in the middle group.

Societies that accept such an approach to the universalism-selectivity issue will need to adapt it in light of the degree of their wealth, service development, and manpower resources. Less-developed societies will have little choice but to begin with more selectivity in the earlier stages of their development, employing individual means tests or giving priority to specified groups.[5] Day care for workers in favored industries or workmen's compensation for the labor force in a pioneer industry illustrate this approach. All societies may assign special priorities to underprivileged groups or regions.

A final comment: Completeness would suggest listing a third category, so that the policy options referred to here would be labeled as "universalism," "selectivity," and "exceptionalism."* Studying programs of aid for poor veterans, Steiner has shown how superior or special programs are developed in response to strong political pressure by veterans' lobbies, even though there is no rational justification for such positive discrimination or preference ("separate and unequal"). A special rhetoric and administrative machinery is invented for veteran relief to avoid

---

*Here, exceptionalism means a favored category, unlike Ryan's sense of the term, which makes it synonymous with selectivity. See footnote on page 77.

stigma. Veterans receive aid for non–service-connected disabilities and face rules about assets, earnings, dependents, and so on quite different from those that apply to nonveterans and unrelated to service disability, compensation for time in service, or the easing of return to civilian life.

Exceptionalism is a policy that could be defended if it paved the way for others, as did the successive separation of several disadvantaged categories from the "poor law" mass in the nineteenth and early twentieth centuries. The Steiner studies appear to demonstrate that, in the case of veterans, the possibility of exceptionalism allows society to ignore the plight of others served by inadequate programs.[6] There is also in the United States a history of sectarian and ethnic exceptionalism in the voluntary social service sector. One would regard such policy differently where it is self-financed than when it is publicly financed through subsidy or fees for service.

Social Service Rights and the New Property

Students of social policy have talked increasingly of "the new income," "the new property," or "the social wage," seeking to call attention to the fact that one's standard of living depends in the modern world not only upon monetary income but also upon access to guaranteed assets, services, and resources.[7] Particularly relevant to social policy are pension and social insurance entitlements, housing, and broadly conceived social services such as education, health, and neighborhood amenities for recreation and leisure. Charles Reich and Harry Jones have elaborated a legal doctrine that argues, in effect, that this new property is as critical as is one's wage income and that the enactment of income security and social service legislation represents the conferring of property rights that can subsequently be protected in the courts.

It will be recognized, immediately, that such doctrine would tend to develop and flourish in the atmosphere of universalist social policy. While even Elizabethan poor law placed certain obligations upon the local parish for relief of some categories of the needy, thereby by implication assuring the latter of certain benefits, perhaps as a matter of right, the essential attitude to pre–poor law and poor law social provision is that it represented charity and individual beneficence, not the meeting of statutory obligation. In the United States, for example, President Pierce in 1854 vetoed a congressional grant of considerable acreage in support of mental hospitals on the grounds that the Constitution did not permit the federal government to enter into welfare activities. It was argued routinely that no precedent should be set that would seem to imply that welfare services or financial assistance may be regarded as a commitment of government and a right of recipients.

The changes in philosophy occurred initially in services that were to be universal. Elementary education was first privilege, then right, then requirement; a rights conception was essential if attendance for the young was to be made compulsory, an inevitable development in a society demanding literacy for labor force and political reasons. A variety of types of social insurance were enacted, beginning with the twentieth century, mandating in very specific terms participation in financing by employers, employees, and government, and specifying the risks covered and the conditions for the award of benefits. The social insurance provisions of the 1935 Social Security Act were quite specific in this regard: payroll deductions and employer taxes were precisely defined, as was the pattern of benefits. Thus, government could enforce the law as it related either to responsibilities for insuring oneself or one's employees, or to the setting up of state employment services. Authorities could demand precise implementation of the law as it specified the exact financial benefits for a person of a given salary level; years of work; age of retirement, disability, or death; and number of dependents. A true legal right, in the social insurance sense, is a justiciable right; if benefits are not paid under the specified conditions and in the specified amounts, the claimant may call upon the power of the courts. Such right is the reciprocal of concomitantly specified obligations.

The concept is confused because the word "right" is also employed in the moral sense, as in the U.N.'s International Declaration of the Rights of Children or in similar affirmations made by many bodies over the years in many fields. It is further confused because some so-called rights are actually partial, justiciable in only a limited sense. As interpreted by the courts for many years, for example, public assistance in the United States was such a partial right. An applicant could demand court action if he could show that policies and grant levels were not uniform as among jurisdictions within a state or as among groups. However, he could do nothing in the courts if the state legislature had appropriated so little money that welfare departments could meet only a portion of need as computed under their own budget standards. On the other hand, federalization of adult assistance categories into Supplementary Security Income since 1974 has, in effect, created a right to a modest income guarantee for the aged, blind, and disabled — under specified conditions.

If a state or city develops a public housing program, there might be limited legal recourse in instances of discrimination, personal abuse, or the imposition of restrictions on tenants that infringe on fundamental constitutional rights. However, there is no justiciable right to housing, no matter how frequent the moral affirmations in this realm (usually in the preambles of housing acts), that could compel public authority to offer adequate provision and on a scale to meet all need. A dynamic does seem operative, converting some moral rights to partial and then complete legal rights. Yet the total amount of achievement with regard to social services remains limited.

For the fact is that a true rights concept has reached social services only gradually and in a modest sense: elementary and secondary education in most places in the United States, community college and four-year college in a few; limited medical and hospital service, on an insurance basis for some and on means-test basis for others; social insurance; a scattering of other areas, with little uniformity throughout the country; and some aspects of veteran programs.

The latter part of the 1960s saw the development of neighborhood legal services as part of the antipoverty program; and a series of "class action" court challenges of administrative practice in public assistance and housing began to increase the rights component, in the sense that certain administrative rules were defined as infringing on constitutional rights — for example, residence laws, "man in the house" rules, unannounced home visits. By the 1970s, certain sex-linked discrimination in social insurance had been outlawed by the courts.

In such an atmosphere, it was also inevitable that some attention would be directed to the right to such personal social services as day care, family counseling, child welfare, services for the mentally retarded, family planning, institutional care, rehabilitation, and so on. In a few instances, higher courts sustained the claim that a child had to be returned to his home if an institution to which he had been committed as a delinquent could be shown as unable to provide the help he was deemed by the committing judge to need. In at least one state, a mental hospital patient was awarded substantial damages because inadequate treatment was considered the cause of long confinement and consequent loss of earnings.[8] A court instructed one state exactly how institutional care for the mentally retarded was to be improved (Alabama, 1972). Another court (New York, 1972) specified a detailed service improvement and deinstitutionalization plan for a very large institution for the retarded. The concept has increasingly been advanced that if the state takes corrective or protective action, if it mandates placement or confinement, it simultaneously assumes the obligation to provide adequate services and thus establishes rights for those taken into care. Less definitively, in some cases of handicap, judges have mandated that agencies offer certain specified help, thus creating a right.

The initiative for service rights has not been confined to the courts. The Advisory Council on Public Welfare recommended to the Secretary of Health, Education, and Welfare that steps be taken to develop within the public welfare system comprehensive social services "readily accessible as a matter of right at all times to all who need them."[9] While, with reference both to income assistance and to social services, the report refers to application process, appeals machinery, legal aid, and publication of rights, it does not confront the issue (with reference to nonmonetary services) of how a service level and range can be statutorily specified, protected, and financed.

The efforts of recent years suggest that the subject is complex. Agencies announce appeal and hearing procedures and specify entitlements, but courts are expected to offer ultimate protection. However, while courts may mandate "treatment," order "community care" (as opposed to institutional confinement), and specify "state of the art" provision, courts cannot be expert in everything and control the public purse everywhere. They must turn to administrative agencies and experts for advice in writing compliance orders. Furthermore, since social service resources remain scarce and the state of the art quite limited, court efforts to enforce rights are inevitably constrained. The process is successful for a few cases, even a few small programs, but bogs down when it demands enormous new resources for one entire service system (retardation) as contrasted with others (education, roads, health, etc.). Nor is it always obvious that the chance priorities of courts, based on the cases that happen to come to them, should necessarily supersede those of elected legislators and executives with more current information, overviews, and public mandates. Ultimately, real progress in guaranteeing good services will have to be dependent upon conceptual and organizational initiatives by those who work in the service fields and by government leadership. When legislatures and executives meet these commitments energetically, within their constraints, courts should be prepared to withdraw.

In short, the topic remains open for exploration and debate. When and how should courts take over legislative and executive branch budgeting and service implementation prerogatives for any level of government? What is possible? How can service personnel assist the courts? How should they respond to court orders? How are courts to avoid creating problems in one place as they address them in another?

For the present, then, we face the reality that many personal social services in the voluntary and public sectors are privileges or partial rights, not full rights. Some services should probably become rights, but — like the citizens of the Federal Republic of Germany, who are dealing with the same questions — we are not exactly sure what this means. At the very least we now should have administrative accountability machinery to ensure that protective and corrective services are available to endangered people, victims, and those deprived of liberty by the society. The state's right to intervene, and obligation to protect and treat, in the instance of contagious diseases may here be at least partially analogous. With reference to such case services, perhaps the rights notion might at this time translate itself into adequate machinery for case finding, evaluation, referral, case integration, accountability, and ensuring that a case so located and processed will not be dropped except in relation to well-defined community policy and by the actions of clearly designated community instruments. The policy becomes more uncertain as one turns to case services that do not respond to a "clear and present danger" to self or to community. Here we may note, to initiate the exploration, that at the very least if a service is to be defined as a right it must in some sense be standardized.

As the new income and new property philosophies of the welfare state develop (and this would appear almost inevitable in a highly urbanized industrial society), the rights question cannot be avoided. To the extent that personal social services are seen as universal public social utilities, whether available by user option or by user status, part of the answer appears to be clear: If a service is meant for all citizens or for all children or all old people, infringements on access are an interference with statutory rights and may be dealt with as such by the courts. This does not, however, eliminate the problem of ensuring legislative and administrative action to guarantee the quantitative sufficiency and qualitative adequacy of services. Do social services lend themselves to sufficient specification for such purposes? Elementary and secondary education offer an encouraging precedent, but many social services are far less easily specified. Moreover, in many of the areas of concern, the mere provision of service, even of social utilities, will not of itself completely accomplish the objective. It will require the considerable development of doctrine and the spelling out of clear provisions to ensure user access to service before full service rights may be said to exist.

Guarding Values as a Policy

No observer of modern society could expect social services to disappear in "normal" times and to become necessary again only in emergencies. The social services, in a basic sense, are a modern societal invention, responsive to new circumstances and needs. Clearly, however, services are both cause and effect, response and motive. A day care center answers to the needs of one group of mothers, but it also changes the environment in which other mothers live and arrive at decisions. A cash grant that enlists an adult daughter to offer daily service to her retired parent makes possible what would otherwise have been financially impossible for her, but it may monetize other relationships that would have been only affectional. Thus the dilemma about social service policymaking in an era of social change: there are core family, community, and other societal values, as there are life patterns and mutual commitments, that we wish to nurture and to preserve. The pace and specific character of our policymaking, the details of programs and their implementation, may determine on balance whether and how societies gain from the growth of personal social services. While large-scale efforts are needed, one cannot forgo subtlety and continuous vigilance. We need careful scientific work that is meshed with provision for tapping citizen values and preferences and for building upon "natural" community and social network mutual aid and social support systems. The decision as to what to do and how much to risk does belong ultimately to the consumer.

How shall services be delivered? The several earlier topics converge in this issue. An institutional perspective on social services, consideration of universalism, introduction of the notion of citizen rights to services — all these elements point to the question of auspices. Shall service delivery be assigned to the market? What are the most strategic roles for statutory and nonstatutory bodies? Should social agencies serve particular religious, cultural, or social groups?

Auspices: Public, Voluntary, and Proprietary

In today's terms, policy issues relating to the roles of public, voluntary, and proprietary social services tend to be posed in one of the following forms:

1. Should voluntary (that is, nonstatutory) services be publicly funded? If so, is there a limit to what part of the voluntary agency budget should be met out of the public treasury?
2. Are there some categories of service that public agencies should not undertake, or that are inappropriate for private agencies?
3. How may or should public and voluntary agency services be interrelated at the operational level?
4. Should profit-making organizations be employed to deliver social services that, presumably, should be accessible to consumers whether or not they are able to command such services in the marketplace through their own resources?

These issues derive from historical context and are consequently different in the United States from what they are in the Mediterranean or South American countries, for example. Basic to the Protestant ethic (and thus the United States) is the idea that goodness cannot be legislated, cannot be compulsory. Laws may forbid or deter evil ("blue laws"), but good works are voluntary moral acts — thus, church-state separation, the emphasis on personal volunteering, the long hesitancy to allow government to involve itself in social welfare activity and the preference for nonpublic (voluntary, private, nonstatutory) social agencies.

When such agencies could not assemble needed resources, a tradition grew in some fields and in some places (child welfare) permitting public subsidy. Public tax policy allowed a degree of credit for contributions to voluntary charities. Later, consumers-users of social services were given public vouchers that could be expended for voluntary agency services, even in profit-making organizations (rehabilitation and, then, nursing homes). Finally, following a pattern that had evolved in the industrial sector, particularly in connection with war industries, public funds might even be used to establish and capitalize a nonpublic agency (antipoverty corporations, hospital corporations). Should public money capitalize a profit-making social service? Inevitably, this was the next question.

A survey of the present pattern reveals historical residues devoid of logic or policy guidance. Most institutions for the mentally ill are publicly operated, institutions for the dependent or neglected child are heavily voluntary, but foster home facilities are as likely to be public. Settlement houses and family service agencies are private, but neighborhood service centers are public. Sometimes the auspices vary with the section of the country, the historical period when the service began, extent of sectarianism, or potential profitability of the undertaking (nursing homes).

From a practical point of view, the welfare or service society — which is an urban and industrial society — undertakes and requires so large a volume of social services and develops so considerable a rights component in its definition of entitlements (the new property) that voluntary agencies cannot be conceived of as meeting all needs by themselves. We have noted that voluntary expenditures for personal social services are only 15 percent of the total, if that. The issue then becomes one of whether the public agency should itself expend all public funds for social services or seek to use voluntary nonprofit (more accurately, nonpublic or nonstatutory) or even profit-making agencies as public instruments.

In the United States, at least, it would probably be easier to ensure coverage, access, uniformity, accountability, and universality with relation to public social utilities and basic case services if the access points themselves (see page 161 ff.) and some basic services were publicly, that is, statutorily, operated — or at least guaranteed. Planning, standard setting, licensing, and inspection require a public base. There is certainly a place in each county for a basic social service operation under government, with clear recognition that this is a national pattern and that expectations are definable. Elsewhere, I propose specifically that the local service should be staffed to offer access services, case integration, and basic counseling and to assume responsibility for case accountability.[10] There are other alternatives, of course, but the local public outlet with core functions is absolutely essential.

Succinctly stated, this may seem like very little, but the preceding paragraph contains important implications. It affirms that only public authority and sanction ensure the possibility of developing and enforcing standards over a large area. It accepts the premise that service rights can be defined and guaranteed either through public planning and operations or through careful contracting and policing by the public authority. It recognizes that social services are costly and that coverage can come only by means of support from the public treasury. It notes that, if public funds pay for the bulk of a service, there is public obligation to spend money carefully — that is, to plan and monitor the service or to deliver service directly. It acknowledges that, unless each governmental unit has an active public service outlet, probably at least at the county level in the United States, it cannot monitor services the public contracts for through the voluntary sector.

Beyond this, states, regions, and localities may face many options, with the parameters often definable on the federal level. That is, where federal funds are involved, as they are or will be in most major social services, the legislation will indicate whether the operation is to be public or whether local or state government (or, in some instances, Washington) may contract with nonprofit voluntary agencies or with profit-making groups to deliver service. Or, clients may be given cash or vouchers (food stamps, service "rights") to use in one or more types of outlets. Of late, federal legislation has been increasingly permissive, opening more options to the local level. The largest federal personal social services funding stream, Title XX of the Social Security Act, has permitted or encouraged contracting for services with voluntary sector agencies. States vary in their practices: some thirty-six states prefer public operation for services involving more than half of their expenditures;* fourteen states spend over half their services funds for voluntary services; this includes several states that lack the capacity for any delivery at all, preferring merely to pass the federal dollars through to private organizations. It is far from clear that this latter approach is effective in ensuring rational resource development, geographical coverage, or accountability. Policymakers at the federal level are therefore continuously alert to this policy sphere; and planners, legislators, and executives at the local level are engaged in major exploration of the subject.

Direct-service volunteering, of course, is possible in either publicly operated services (volunteer tutors in local schools) or voluntary agencies

---

*Mid-1976, preliminary report, and covering only Title XX, Title IV-B, and WIN services. *Social Services U.S.A.*, as of June 1976, subject to correction.

(child guidance escort volunteers or local committees that "adopt" institution cottages). The issue does not reside here. Pioneering and policy advocacy is found in either sector, too; the voluntary agencies have no monopoly on innovation or on pressing for client rights, despite the conventional wisdom, as any review of the last two decades of social service history will disclose. Nor is the voluntary agency truly autonomous, depending as it does on charters, referrals, subsidies, and tax-deductible contributions. Its role is susceptible to public policy making. Finally, consumer influence at the local level should be felt in both the voluntary and the public sectors.

By virtue of their nonstatutory status, voluntary services appear to have several unique possibilities. They might serve exceptional circumstances, for example, where there is societal interest in doing things for individuals and groups that cannot be formulated as legal rights and made uniformly available (the family service agency that offers a major investment to put a family on its feet, the economic development agency that invests in one city neighborhood). Voluntary agencies are excellent vehicles, too, where what is needed is so venturesome and risky as to be unlikely for a politically responsible and sensitive group (the foundation that funds an unusual consumer interest enterprise, the agency that backs a controversial drug or family planning service).*

Most important, the voluntary service may assure *diversity* even where there is public coverage — if diversity is valued. To serve a complex country, or a heterogeneous local community, a social policy may seek diversity in locus, staffing, philosophy, and/or techniques. Commercial products on the market appeal to a variety of tastes, and, while public services reflect some understanding of the needs of several types of consumers, the experience is that politically guided public services commonly must forgo some of the needed range for reasons of economy or caution. The voluntary sector here offers important flexibility.

Perhaps even more important is the fact that public services, while they

---

*Given political diversity and dispersion of authority among levels of government, there have been occasions when public agencies took on the venturesome and the risky. Sometimes, as in the case of the antipoverty war of the mid-1960s, this was even encouraged by Washington. It is in the nature of our political system, however, that governmental programs may often be stalemated and officials cannot take on high risks. It is at least helpful to have other sources of support.

To some extent, the ability of public agencies to take risks is determined by such things as whether different, but interacting, levels of government are under the control of the same political party; whether officials on different levels, whatever their party, are in rivalry; whether the program in question is a public "whipping boy," and so on. Voluntary agencies, too, are subject to many idiosyncratic factors: board composition, source of voluntary funds (foundations, United Way, endowment, investment, and so on), and nature of staffing.

may offer religious outlets to individuals (as in the instance of the prison chaplain, or the placement of a foster child with a foster parent of a similar religion "if practicable"), cannot have strong religious character. Otherwise, there would be the claim that government is allowing itself to be used to "establish" a religion. Yet there are people to whom religion is so critical a component of daily life that, precisely under circumstances during which they require social services, *they wish* sectarian services. Family counseling, child guidance, adoption, maternity homes, residential treatment programs, and senior citizen centers often fit into this category. This special kind of diversity, the agency offering the user a sectarian religious context reflecting cherished values and cultural identity, is something that under our Constitution can be offered only by the voluntary agency, not by the public.

Beyond these well-defined roles, for which there is much historical experience, there is the fact that in the current antibureaucratic climate, in which many Americans strongly favor dispersion of power and fear increasing centralization and the proliferation of important service under governmental authority, the voluntary agency is also suggested and employed as a contractor to deliver a service that is a public responsibility. Whether as a semipublic corporation (antipoverty community corporation, New York City Hospitals Corporation) or as an autonomous agency, this entity undertakes a public role on a nonprofit or a cost-plus basis. It thus parallels the defense contractors, research and development corporations, or private professionals who have similar relationships to government in other fields. Here, economy-efficiency criteria should obtain. When a new social service is to be launched, the planning agency might, if there is no existing public instrument, open the field for bids while public programmers develop their own costs, too, on the basis of circulated specifications. If all other things are "equal," that is, if no conditions obtain that make nonpublic operation highly desirable, then that agency should be selected — public, nonprofit, voluntary, or proprietary — that offers the community the best buy.

Clearly, then, one can and should project a continuing contribution by the voluntary sector in the social service field in the United States.[11] But many of the critical characteristics of such agencies would be lacking if they were completely publicly funded and could not recruit an active corps of volunteers. And public purposes would be defeated if the use of voluntary service was not guided and integrated by the responsible public body.

In addition, as will be seen in the discussion of vouchers and performance contracting, one can also envisage the entry of additional profit-making suppliers of service, so that some of the advantages of the marketplace, insofar as they affect delivery efficiency and service effectiveness, may be tested in their application to this field. Scale and scope, constraints and limitations, nonetheless require definition for those who would plan ahead. For some, the overriding considerations are pragmatic: what pattern will assure diversity, responsiveness, economy? Here, experimentation and research are needed. For others, the issue of accountability is so central that they would permit voluntary development largely in the interstices of a basic public network. Still others see state-church issues and constitutional challenges as paramount: let the voluntary services, particularly sectarian services, develop insofar as citizens support and pay for them, but do not subsidize such services with tax funds and do not establish administrative patterns that allow users no real options and, in effect, coerce them into using voluntary outlets. There are, too, those who believe that profit making negates key social service values; they cannot accept the notion that proprietary agencies belong on the team. Others prefer to look at the experience.

Wherever the dividing line is placed in the light of such considerations — and there is reason to expect a range of answers — the realization of the full benefits of the potential voluntary contribution will be dependent upon provision for coordination with the public sector. Social service guarantees need public affirmation; their translation into rights and benefits will depend on public implementation of planning responsibility.

General versus Separatist Services*

In an earlier period, this policy issue might have been formulated as "sectarian or nonsectarian programs," but the explosion of ethnic and racial separatisms requires a broader statement. Briefly, the issue is this: Granted that religious, ethnic, and racial groups have the right to establish and conduct social services for members of their own groups, and recognizing that these must be nonstatutory (voluntary) services, is it permissible or desirable that public funds or public tax policy be employed to permit or even encourage such separatism?

In this presentation we do not do full justice to the legal issues, which are yet to be fully clarified in the courts with reference to their constitutionality. There has been some erosion of the principle of church-state separation as it relates to the issue of public subsidy of sectarian education. The vehicle for departure from traditional restrictions has been a

---

*In some of the literature, the issue is phrased as "universal versus particularistic services," but this creates confusion with universalism-selectivity, the distinction described earlier, referring to presence or absence of a means test.

strategy of aiding individuals rather than institutions, or of paying for facilities and equipment, not for personnel. Yet to be settled to the satisfaction of some members of the legal profession is the question of whether the long-time distinction between child welfare (substitute parenting) and education can be constitutionally sustained. For approximately a century there has been direct and indirect public support of, and even preference for, sectarian child welfare services in some states, on the premise that this was not "establishment" of a religion.

The courts have held that the public may not finance a social service that discriminates against blacks, Mexican Americans, and other minority groups, even if government simultaneously funds a separate and similar program for such minorities. The "separate but equal" doctrine was discarded in the 1954 *Brown v. Board of Education* ruling of the U.S. Supreme Court. Not yet clear is how the courts will regard minority "discrimination" against majority group members or other minority groups in publicly funded programs. Can black or Hispanic or Indian separatist programs be legally sustained, or is the assumption that de facto separatism will simply develop and be tolerated because majority group members will not wish to utilize minority-run programs — even in areas in which so-called racial or ethnic majorities constitute a local minority? And will the courts perhaps hold that de facto discrimination of this sort is illegal for the minority, as it is for the majority?

These may appear to some as frivolous issues, but they are likely to be faced legally as the several racial-ethnic separatisms expand and as they dominate the scene in border areas and ghettos, where, in fact, some population elements will be deprived of service because of separatism. Even more often, one racial or ethnic minority group could, by either deliberate or de facto discrimination based on separatist impulses, be seriously depriving members of another — but locally weaker — minority.

Legal issues aside, the matter may be explored in a policy context focusing on value and factual components of the decision process. Historically, religious and ethnic minorities have developed their own social services in a spirit of mutual aid and also of self-protection because it was at times demanded of them if they wished to settle in specific colonies or cities. Social services have assisted acculturation and have introduced social control, often thus advancing the interests of an ethnic group. Such services have perpetuated or protected cultural values and distinctive folkways; they have provided supports and continuity for individuals and families moving from the old to the new. Sometimes members of previously integrated groups have aided the newly arrived out of sympathy for their needs or to hasten their acculturation.

The program forms have varied with the basic objectives: centers and settlements for acculturation simultaneous with preservation of old values; child care services to protect group continuity; family services also as representing social continuity but facilitating the taking of aid because of shared experiences of the helper and the helped; boys' clubs as vehicles for value continuity and for supporting ethnic identification; and so on.

The very goals suggest the negative arguments. Separatism, if it stresses the preservation and accentuation of differences rather than ensuring a vantage point for integration in which valued differences are not considered as requiring separation, may be continually divisive and may even complicate social adjustment. In some instances it may deliberately encourage intergroup conflict. Moreover, the more advantaged ethnic groups do well by their "own," whereas those who are poor are frustrated even further. Redistributional goals may be thwarted by ethnically separated services, unless funded out of general revenues. Help is needed across ethnic lines and should not await individual magnanimity. Social service has redistributional possibilities and obligations that should not be ignored.

Resolution of the policy issues in this field remains difficult, since various participants in the debate apply different criteria. There is evidence, for example, of some consumer preference for racial identity of social service professional and client — but the degree of preference may be affected by the type of task and is modified when competence is introduced as a variable.[12] In sectarian services the specific nature of the service (marriage counseling, child welfare, group activity, education) may be of considerable importance to this issue.

Some people feel that consumer preference should not be the determining factor. What of broad public policy, such as integration? To those for whom separatism, integration, and pluralism are the overriding legal or policy principles, questions of preference and effectiveness become secondary matters. Others, quite pragmatically, refuse to espouse a doctrine; they ask about the circumstances under which people in need are best reached and helped.

The issue is at the heart of current urban social policy debates and not readily resolved by social service planners alone. Those to whom black or Puerto Rican or Chinese or Japanese or Chicano separatism has become a major, new social goal may abandon many of the traditional liberal social policy guidelines. They will encourage separate services, segregated staffing, and public subsidy of it all, without needing to know if more people are actually better or less satisfactorily served as a result. For those espousing a liberal pluralism, the emphasis will be on allowing the consumer-user maximum options and choices: public or voluntary service, sectarian or nonsectarian, unified or separated. They will probably back a basic public "coverage" service for most users, seeing such service as the vehicle for a public service guarantee and a prerequisite for planning, accountability, and case integration. At the same time, individuals preferring voluntary services, whether sectarian or racially or ethnically separatist, would be permitted to elect such service. This need not be difficult to arrange where services are financed out of insurance awards or by vouchers available to consumers by status or need. The issue encounters controversy as proposals are made for public purchase of care (less difficult) and subsidy (the most difficult issue). Here there is need not only for legal clarification, as proposed at the beginning of this section, but also some way to ensure that the public purse is being employed to do what people want (diversity, choice, pluralism) and not to impose or induce preferences that are not prevalent (that is, giving a publicly supported monopoly to a separatist service whose main goals are political or religious-sectarian).

Finally, those to whom social solidarity is the cardinal principle will reject these rather pragmatic strategies and utilitarian rationales. While respecting individual freedom and difference they would not permit policies that undermine a society's integration. Thus,

there must be no allocation of resources which could create a sense of separateness between people. It is the explicit or implicit institutionalization of separateness, whether categorized in terms of income, class, race, color or religion, rather than the recognition of similarities between people and their needs, which causes much of the world's suffering.[13]

Notes

1. See Alfred J. Kahn, *Theory and Practice of Social Planning* (New York: Russell Sage Foundation, 1969), Chapters 5, 6, 7, and *Studies in Social Policy and Planning* (New York: Russell Sage Foundation, 1969); Martin Rein, *Social Policy: Issues of Choice and Change* (New York: Random House, 1970), especially Part 2; and Richard Titmuss, *Commitment to Welfare* (New York: Pantheon, 1968), Chapter 1.

2. On the latter distinction, see Daniel Bell, "The Corporation and Society in the 1970's," *The Public Interest,* No. 24 (Summer 1971). For a review of the various policy approaches in the "optimization" tradition, see Richard Zeckhauser and Elmer Shaefer, "Public Policy and Normative Economic Theory," in Raymond A. Bauer and Kenneth J. Gergen (eds.), *The Study of Policy Formation* (New York: Free Press, 1968), pp. 27–102.

3. Universalism is defined as "services good enough for any American," in *Services for People,* Report of the Task Force on Social Services (Washington, D.C.: U.S. Department of Health, Education, and Welfare,

1968), pp. 37–38. The British discussion is reflected in Mike Reddin, "Universality Versus Selectivity," in William A. Robson and Bernard Crick (eds.), *The Future of the Social Services* (Baltimore: Penguin, 1970), pp. 23–35. The universalism case was also made in Kenneth Keniston and the Carnegie Council on Children, *All Our Children* (New York: Harcourt Brace Jovanovich, 1977).

4. Reddin, "Universality Versus Selectivity."

5. A British analysis is offered in Richard M. Titmuss, "Choice and 'The Welfare State' " and "Universal and Selective Social Services" in his *Commitment to Welfare* (New York: Pantheon, 1968), pp. 113–123, 138–152. Recent U.N. literature has reflected stronger support for universalism, even in poorer countries.

6. Gilbert Y. Steiner, *The State of Welfare* (Washington, D.C.: The Brookings Institution, 1971), Chapter 7.

7. In this connection, see S. M. Miller and Frank Reissman, *Social Class and Social Policy* (New York: Basic Books, 1968); Charles Reich, "The New Property," *Yale Law Journal*, 73, 5 (April 1964), 773–787; and Harry Jones, "The Rule of Law and the Welfare State," *Columbia Law Review*, 58, 2 (February 1958). Also, see Harold L. Wilensky, *The "New Corporatism," Centralization, and the Welfare State,* Sage Professional Paper Series #06-020, Vol. 2 (Beverly Hills, Calif.: Sage Publications, 1976). The social wage discussion is illustrated in Chris Trinder, "Inflation and the Social Wage," in Peter Willmott (ed.), *Sharing Inflation: Poverty Report 1976* (London: Temple Smith, 1976), pp. 57–84.

8. William J. Curran, "The Right to Psychiatric Treatment," *American Journal of Public Health*, 58, 11 (November 1968), 2156–2157.

9. *"Having the Power, We Have the Duty . . .,"* Advisory Council on Public Welfare (Washington, D.C.: Government Printing Office, 1966).

10. See Chapter 7. Also, Sheila B. Kamerman and Alfred J. Kahn, *Social Services in the United States* (Philadelphia: Temple University Press, 1976), Chapter 8, and Alfred J. Kahn and Sheila B. Kamerman, "The Course of Personal Social Services," *Public Welfare*, 36, 3 (Summer 1978), 29–49.

11. A good current statement advocating the voluntary sector position is Gordon Mauser and Rosemary Higgins Cass, *Voluntarism at the Crossroads* (New York: Family Service Association of America, 1976).

12. Donald Breiland, "Black Identity and the Helping Person," *Children*, September–October 1969, 170–176.

13. Richard M. Titmuss, *The Gift Relationship* (New York: Pantheon, 1971), p. 238.

Goals
Meet Technique ◀◀◀◀ 5

Redistribution as a Social Service Objective

One of the major tensions in social welfare policy arises from the differences in viewpoint between (a) those who assume that the purpose of programs is to aid the unfortunate and handicapped in the context of the economic and social status quo and (b) those who conceive of social welfare programs as an instrument of equalization. Indeed, it is the perception of this issue and the recognition that extensive social welfare programs may very well have some redistributional effects that lead some people to oppose the "welfare state" as socialist. On the other side, it is the potential for redistribution through both cash and in-kind programs, on the one hand, and service programs, on the other, that leads other people to conceive of redistribution as the central justification for, and beacon light of, social policy.

What, then, are the facts? Serious study of some aspects of the subject is only recent, and there are many uncertain areas;[1] yet several generalizations seem to be sustained. If by redistribution we mean a system of transfers of money and nonmonetary benefits and services, so arranged that members of a given group end with a balance different from that which is created by market transactions, then we may hypothesize:

1. Governmental taxation, grants and service programs, and various government-sanctioned and -aided insurance and fringe benefit schemes are sometimes redistributional, but by no means always in favor of the very poor or even of the working class.
2. Means-tested income maintenance programs, cash and in-kind, are the most clearly redistributional in favor of the severely disadvantaged; other types of income maintenance may be less so or not at all.
3. Some service programs are redistributional in favor of the most disadvantaged, some in favor of other population elements.

These, at least, appear to be reasonable hypotheses.

Systematic analysis by the Congressional Budget Office showed that, for fiscal year 1976, using the standard definitions of poverty, social insurance grants cut the percentage of U.S. families in poverty from 25.5 to 14.1 percent (before taxes). Other cash transfers reduced the total to 11.4 percent. The in-kind transfers, especially food stamps, medical care, and housing subsidies further reduced the poverty percentage, after taxes, to 6.9 percent. This calculation does not consider personal social services, which are not readily assigned cash values.[2]

An earlier analysis at the Institute for Research on Poverty states that over 85 percent of the costs of social services tied to public assistance and community action programs are expended on the pretransfer poor. This is to be expected for programs that conduct means tests at the doorway or are assigned to the poorest of neighborhoods. Other services spend far smaller proportions of their budgets on the pretransfer poor.[3]

Many governmental efforts and activities are not specifically oriented toward redistribution on behalf of the poor. In 1972, for example, only 5 percent of payments to farmers were spent on the pretransfer poor, as was 21 percent of unemployment insurance, 42 percent of Model Cities housing expenditure, 48 percent of Medicare costs, 33 percent of veteran education expenditure, and 48 percent of expenditures under the Elementary and Secondary Education Act.[4]

Other analysis notes that increases in redistribution through transfer payments and in-kind benefits may be offset by growing tendencies to rely for program financing on regressive sales and payroll taxes.

The nature of existing payment and service arrangements makes these results almost inevitable. Income taxes are graduated, but there are many loopholes available to the more prosperous and to people in upper-income brackets. Because the sales tax and social security tax are regressive and proportionately more important to low-income people, their total tax "bite," as of this writing, is of the same dimension (as a proportion of pretax income) as that of upper-income people, although some remedies are now beginning to change the picture. The U.S. Congress was unwilling until 1970 to eliminate income taxes of $2 billion on those below a governmental poverty line. Benefits to agriculture and corporate industry benefit the more affluent, and the pattern of mortgage insurance and tax deductions for mortgage interest and for real estate taxes may bias the governmental housing subsidy in favor of purchasers of detached suburban dwellings. Income maintenance programs that use the means test — largely public assistance — are redistributive but at a low level. Social security income testing for the aged is very limited, but there is transfer from middle- and high- to low-wage earners in the pattern of benefits. Distinctions between capital gains and income aid the wealthy. Minimum wage laws could be redistributive for the poor, but many low-wage jobs are held by second or third earners in a family in which there are already well-paid earners.

Education, health, and housing — social services in the broadest sense — seem to be redistributive in favor of the very poor only as they emphasize a basic minimum (elementary school, which is compulsory, universal health checkup and inoculations). To the extent that they offer higher levels of education, more sophisticated or intensive health services, or housing that goes beyond the minimum, such programs may actually favor the more stable elements of the working class, the lower-middle class and even the upper-middle class. The sophisticated and informed, the people who know how to take advantage of possibilities, families motivated to get more for their children, do seek out and employ services that go beyond the compulsory minimum. Families with resources more often know about and have access to more programs. To illustrate, in some places secondary education and junior college, publicly paid, is of help only to the middle class because others cannot afford to have their children out of the labor market or cannot meet their daily expenses; in some places the best general hospital and outpatient psychiatric resources are employed by those who are knowledgeable, not by the most needy. The picture is blurred, however, varying among countries (some countries give all college students maintenance grants or salaries) and among regions in the United States.

To turn to personal social services, the field of special inquiry in this volume, data about redistributional effects are very scarce, but there is a significant body of research about limited service utilization by the most disadvantaged, their high dropout and failure rates, and their general lack of access to the more sophisticated services.[5] In general, a program that is sharply selective, focused on a deprived group or depressed area, or available on a means-test basis, will have considerable redistributional impact (Head Start, public housing, Title XX services in states with low income ceilings for eligibility). It will transfer resources, in the the form of services, from "haves" to "have-nots."* A universal program, whatever its

*But if it spends a large proportion of its funds as salaries to nonpoor professionals or sales commissions to middlemen (shopkeepers who handle food stamps), the effect is tempered.

other merits, may or may not be redistributional, depending on its attractiveness to the poorer members of the community (take-up) and on the system of information and access that affects the actual pattern of utilization.

It is this knowledge, as suggested in the discussion of "creaming" in the section on universalism versus selectivity in the preceding chapter, that led adovcates of redistribution to favor such selectivist programs as the U.S. antipoverty program and to urge more jobs in social service programs for local, uncredentialed, poor people. Proponents of these measures were prepared to risk the disadvantages of stigma and the allegation that programs for the poor are poor programs, in order to ensure access by the underprivileged and a greater likelihood of redistributional effect.

Those who would argue for universalism in social service and who accept the redistributional goal must, in turn, consider ways in which guarantees of access by the most underprivileged may be built into such programs for redistributional effect. Just as redistribution, if that is a goal, may be achieved by passing new tax-wage-subsidy legislation, by enacting new policies, and by launching new programs, "one also achieves redistribution . . . by arrangements to facilitate access to the established rights, benefits, services, entitlements and to assure the actual delivery and use of intended services.[6] This makes relevant the entire subject of organization for service delivery at the local level (see page 147). It makes immediately salient such matters as (a) advice and information services, usually on a neighborhood basis; (b) case advocacy services; (c) complaint machinery; and (d) legal services.[7]

The specific techniques available to ensure access, and the supporting developments in service organization and staffing, are discussed subsequently. Here we note only that the proposals are logically convincing but are not backed by hard research data on a significant scale. Evaluative studies are awaited.

At this point we must recognize, again, that the implied premise of the entire discussion — the desirability of utilizing social service programming for its potential redistributional effect — is also subject to the broad differences of opinion that prevail about all social policy, differences that have already been pointed to as going well beyond social service policy. The objections come from two wings of political opinion. There are those who would offer social services to ensure equality of opportunity, not of condition (status). To them, social service per se need be only modestly redistributional. Their purpose is to facilitate personal mobility by providing a foundation of capacity and skill. Others, who would utilize social services rather than jobs and market mechanisms to decrease inequality and to guarantee adequate levels of living, would go further in evaluating the redistributional effects of social services. Inevitably, then, this more fundamental issue of social policy must be resolved before social service policies are fully confronted.*

Investment versus Consumption

The redistributional effect of a service could be long-term and indirect, thus not visible in the calculations cited.

During the early 1970s, Congress and the Department of Health, Education, and Welfare initiated a variety of measures that emphasized a utilitarian concept of social services. Programs would be financed and developed to "overcome barriers" to economic self-maintenance among the unskilled, handicapped, or unmotivated. Measures would be promoted if they gave promise of removing people from institutions or increasing their capacity for self-care while living in the community. Program evaluation would focus upon barriers overcome, in a progression from institutional care to community care of an intensive kind, to self-care, to partial self-support, to self-support.

Measures of this kind, later stated in modified form as goals for state social services under Title XX of the Social Security Act, are attractive to many people who consider most social goals diffuse and social service programs to be of questionable value. They are regarded as too constricted by critics who would also emphasize the developmental, socialization, and enrichment missions of the personal social services. In a modern form of the residual versus institutional debate in social welfare, these two opposing views represent what might be considered "investment" versus "consumption" positions.

American planners or programmers of social services seldom talk of policy issues in terms of an investment-consumption dichotomy, yet the distinction appears frequently in the international literature on development planning.[8] The policymaker will find these concepts tricky, but not to be ignored.

In a sense, the tradition of social services in relation to private charity's benevolence or the humanitarian's social minimum would seem to support the notion that the service is good in itself; it provides funds or supplies for needed consumption by the disadvantaged or offers useful personal help. Yet brief exploration shows that, in fact, this has never quite been accepted as the sole mission of general social services.

---

*Theodore J. Lowi has formulated the relevant social policy options as distribution, redistribution, and regulation. See his "American Business, Public Policy, Case-Studies, and Political Theory," *World Politics*, 16, 4 (July 1964), 677–715.

Something more has been sought. Elizabethan poor law demanded a work return from the able-bodied adult and child, whether he was given outdoor aid or assisted in an institution. Private charity, at least that segment of it in the nineteenth century that evolved into family service agencies and child welfare programs (perhaps, in a sense, some settlements, too), clearly differentiated the "worthy" from the "unworthy" poor. The former clearly were seen as morally virtuous — or at least as salvageable; the assistance or combination of assistance and concern was clearly an investment in their rehabilitation. Their failure to follow the rules, to take advice, to reform was a cause for redefining them as unworthy of the aid of voluntary social agencies. They would be left for the more punitive and controlling poor law authorities.

Child welfare literature, for example, quotes Charles Loring Brace, a pioneer, to the effect that a childless farm couple taking in young, homeless children would be assuring themselves at a future time both of a loving responsiveness and help on the farm. Earlier indenture arrangements ignored sentiments entirely: training an apprentice was an investment.

Settlement houses were focused on environmental ills as much as on individual adjustment problems. However, to the extent that they offered citizenship courses, woodworking training, dental clinics, child care, cultural activities, and boys' clubs, they often went beyond a desire to enrich people's daily experiences (consumption). Indeed, many of the pioneering settlement leaders spoke of the services as facilitating more rapid Americanization, promoting community adjustment and harmony, encouraging self-support, and decreasing deviance (investment).

In the world of Keynesian economics, another line of analysis appeared. Social service and income maintenance expenditures, if related to the state of the economy, could be an important instrument of demand management. A government would want some authority over the elasticity of consumption. (In recent years it has become clear, however, that expansion to spur demand is easy, but contraction to counteract inflation is politically difficult.)

In short, social services have a tradition of both consumption and investment motivations. The rhetoric has favored consumption, while the latent, or unexpressed, motives were perhaps most often investment. There have been few who have supported noninstrumental social services.

Two developments have brought the policy issue — consumption or investment? — to the fore in recent years: the experience in organizing social services for developing countries and the antipoverty program in the United States. The poor country that is seeking to industrialize and modernize finds itself facing very difficult choices. Should it rapidly make universally available the health protection and services that are technologically possible, because people have a right to them, and ignore the consequences (lower infant mortality in a country with major food shortages, for example, thus shifting the age and cause of death!). Or should this consumption approach be discouraged in favor of a strategy that says, "Let us target and time the new health services in relation to educational, feeding, and housing programs tied to the economic plan for an area?" This latter, the investment approach, which receives its rationale from the need to allocate scarce resources, forgoes humanitarian impulse for allocative efficiency.

Similarly, should universal elementary education be offered at once, to all children, because literacy is desirable and democratic, thereby commanding all resources that might be assigned to intermediate technical education and advanced training, or is an investment strategy to be developed for education? In the latter approach, resources are rationed among educational ventures on the several levels in accord with the personnel demands posed by economic development — and to ensure a gradual increase in the reservoir of teachers for the eventual universal system.

From these illustrations it becomes clear that at a given instant it may be difficult to determine whether the program is actually conceived in investment terms, or only so presented. In a sense, consumption and investment may become evaluative categories or public relations instruments that are politically employed in some contexts. Shifts in the definition of goals have political effect. Many of the proponents of stronger social service programs began in the 1950s and 1960s to talk of "investment in human resources," and they advocated social service programs as good development strategy.

To the social service planner the entire issue poses a serious dilemma. Conceptually, social services are goods and services made available on the basis of other than market criteria to facilitate socialization and individual development and to cope with problems. Why should one, therefore, distinguish some services as better "investments"? If a decision as to whether the offering of access to service is a good investment for society (a "market" question) must be introduced into the equation, this would appear to be contrary to the very function of social services. On the other hand, the planner knows that resources are always in short supply.

Much of the debate is confused by semantic difficulties as economists meet politicians and both deal with social welfare advocates. As Myrdal notes,[9] much talk about education and health as investment is naïve and uninformed, especially in developing countries, where the effects of expenditure vary with whatever else is done about the institutional context in which expenditures are made. Politicians sense this, but also fluctuate between a rhetorical and precise employment of the investment term. Social welfare personnel, for their part, too often tend to ignore the fact that any given society must weigh its priorities and has a right to an instrumental view of social services. In this sense, however, criteria of desirability need not be derived solely from the marketplace. Societies attend to more than economic growth, productivity, and other such objectives if they would be just and humane — or be politically viable.

A social service policymaker may find his way with such a posture. He may at a given time favor setting up a program and giving it priority because it meets urgent societal objectives (opening opportunity to minority groups), reflects the resource picture, and promises large payoffs (investment criterion); however, he may still consider the notion that allocative priorities within the program should be assigned to eligible individuals or groups in accordance with means, needs, and social justice concepts (consumption criterion). This is not to deny the constant pressure he will face to give service priority to those best able to fit into the program, since payoff will then be highest (again, creaming). But, in social welfare, optimum output should not supersede the need for and ability to *use* a service (diagnostic criterion).

In short, since money, materials, and skilled manpower remain in short supply, it is legitimate to introduce the investment issue among other criteria for choice. While few societies can afford large amounts of consumption that are not in some sense instrumental, it is hardly wise to contend that any consumption of services is good since it leads to economic growth. Developed and underdeveloped countries are inevitably focused on urbanization, industrialization, modernization, or specified problem solving. The notion of investment may be more broadly conceived in relation to societal goals relevant to these processes.

Developments in the United States in the 1960s may be viewed in these terms. Several of the youth-opportunity mobilizations of the early 1960s, precursors of the antipoverty program, turned away from the more traditional approaches to delinquent young people. They decided not to expand personal counseling, group therapy, residential treatment, or Big Brother efforts. Instead, they would concentrate on education, job guidance and placement, and training — and on those aspects of role training that would prepare young people for the job market. The rationale was clear: working on the premise that many young men became delinquent because of lack of access to legitimate or illegitimate means of success in the world of work and money (they had neither jobs *nor* rackets as sources of income and social status), these mobilizations concluded that the primary mission was to open opportunity. In fact, they often called their social services "opportunity programs." These were visibly intended as a social investment in offering legitimate channels for the activities of young people who might otherwise choose the illegitimate or "cop out." Program success was to be gauged, not by the insight, happiness, or "adjustment" of the participant — or by whether similar investment in *others* would have better payoff — but by the participant's attainment of skill and his employment of that skill in the world of work.

This type of thinking, translated into the subsequent antipoverty war, tended to make the policy choice as between investment and consumption strategies more visible and more legitimate in a non–market-oriented social welfare. Indeed, the antipoverty war represented clear preference for investment-type programs: skill upgrading, small business development, agricultural loans, job preparation and placement, child care services, and education. Cultural, character development, therapeutic, personal enhancement, and recreational offerings were given low priority, if acknowledged at all. It is therefore hardly a surprising matter to observe that the arrival of such an approach coincided with the introduction of an efficiency approach to planning and policymaking in the public social welfare sector (see page 121 ff.).

The issue currently appears in several forms. Community support systems for the aged may be justified and assessed by whether they avoid and are cheaper than the nursing home alternative (investment). Or services may be developed out of a conception of the quality of life the society can and should provide its elderly, as a good thing in itself (consumption).

Day care may be promoted as freeing welfare-recipient or other mothers to work, thereby adding to economic production and cutting public costs, or as being a questionable approach because good child care is more expensive than the welfare budgets that will keep mothers at home. On the other hand, compensatory child care (Head Start) may be favored as an excellent way to break the cycle of deprivation and ensure long-term self-support. (All this is investment thinking.) Still other analytic perspectives state that in our kind of society a more satisfying life pattern for children, mothers, or families may be achieved if child care programs are seen as valuable per se (consumption), without the need for extraneous justification.

Obviously each of these orientations suggests criteria by which the policy may be tested in relation to its objectives. And each raises the question: Is the proponent merely marshaling what he thinks is a good or acceptable argument, or is this how he makes choices? Indeed, it may be the evaluative criteria as much as the internal program preoccupations that differentiate investment from consumption approaches. The program planner will consider both.

This exploration tends to suggest that the policy planner concerned with social services will not be able to avoid the investment-consumption formulation in looking at proposals; but it is in the very nature of social welfare, and therefore of social services, that people of different value stances or time perspectives will classify the same program differently and that in some cases one should define investment in noneconomic terms. Particularly as human gains or human benefits are included in the cost-benefit equation by which potential investments are evaluated, the boundary between consumption and investment becomes very vague. On the other hand, in the more extreme instances of developing countries, or of deprived areas or neighborhoods in developed countries, the hard choices involved in allocating scarce manpower and money may be helped by focusing on expected outcomes of competing programs. Then it may at times be useful to pose the issue of "the program as an end in and of itself" or "the program as a means toward a series of high-priority ends." And, "which program has the largest payoff?"

At this latter point, the substance of the last two sections comes together: personal social services focused on "take-off" (a firm foothold on social mobility) by disadvantaged citizens may have long-term redistributional impact. The operative policy could be investment in the disadvantaged through redistribution. Yet the public rationale may be social justice or an improved quality of life.

Formalization versus Participatory Administration

The previous two sections have discussed the connection between one's perspective on goals (redistribution? consumption? investment?) and the specific objectives of large and small social service programs. The present section asks how objectives are arrived at and protected. It examines the balance between citizen-client participation in program control, on the one hand, and bureaucratization, on the other.

As already noted, to some observers, participation is, per se, a goal of personal social services. Our own view is that, while often true, this would hardly distinguish the personal social services from other institutions in a democratic society. For most citizens who are not politically engaged, participation as volunteers, committee members, or officers is a direct means to affect the quantity, quality, and particular objectives of all service programs.

Most social services have been dominated by the professions and semiprofessions: medicine, education, social work, vocational rehabilitation, physical education, counseling, and so on. In recent years, the combination of ethnic separatism, interest in participatory democracy, and disillusionment with large organizations has created interest in decentralization and community control as vehicles to ensure increased service responsiveness and improved quality. These forces have also encouraged interest in noncredentialed personnel and in less bureaucratized systems of organization and service delivery.

Decentralization as a programming strategy has implications for both more and less bureaucratized programs. However, when bureaucracies create local outlets without relaxing control, the term "dispersal" (or "localization") is more appropriate, since the outlets may all be cut from one pattern. There are exceptions, but a prerequisite of most authentic decentralizations is the offer of local options, to be exercised by staff or community (that is, less bureaucratization). We here consider one aspect, but a major aspect, of current policy approaches to greater program responsiveness: the search for a balance between bureaucratization and what we would call "participatory administration."*

Most professionals (doctors, lawyers, and so on) do not work in bureaucratic organizations. In the general social services, however, they do. And the complaint is that rigid, formal organizational patterns shield staff from feedback, weaken consumers, and lead to a predominance of organizational maintenance goals where there should be an emphasis on service to clients. The alternative posed is a locally shaped and controlled organization, with few guidelines and directives from higher levels, employing local people where possible, with local administrators (and/or line staff) hired by and subject to approval of "the community." Community control and decentralization become mutually reinforcing.

Others disagree. They would stress professional responsibility, competence, efficient organization, standardization, and accountability for funds. Thus emerges the policy issue: What balance is to be sought in development of a specific public social service between formalization, hierarchy, centralization, large organization, and economy of scale — on the one hand — and the variability, informality, uniqueness, experimentalism, and independence attributed to true community involvement and control — on the other?

Since evidence is limited and mixed, both as to whether the alleged attributes actually characterize community involvement and as to whether the advantages assumed really do follow, there is no empirical way to make the decision. Furthermore, the issue may be transitional or false, no matter how vital it may seem. In a sense, the development of comprehensive services of any kind — day care, homemakers, individual help, substitute care, protective programs, or therapy — appears inevitably to lead

---

*This section should be read in conjunction with the discussion of general versus separatist services at the end of the previous chapter. On the limits of decentralization, a topic beyond the scope of this section, see Henry Cohen, "The Changing Role of the Planner in the Decision-Making Process," in Ernest Erber (ed.), *Urban Planning in Transition* (New York: Grossman Publishers, 1970), pp. 180–181.

to formal organization. Funding from higher to lower levels (most communities, especially poor communities, cannot fund their own social services), as well as standard setting and accountability, demand hierarchy for rule making and enforcement. Professional service requires layers of hierarchy for supervision and consultation. Diverse skills and specialties need to be meshed simultaneously and sequentially. Program units require policy coordination. Qualifications for various positions demand definition and publicization to avoid excessive nepotism, and promotional rules must be announced. Administrators cannot be held accountable unless they (rather than the community) evaluate, hire, and fire. Reporting of several sorts, internal accounting, and various communication channels demand standardization.

In effect, social services tend to be professional activities of a special kind: unlike professionalism in the marketplace (private medical or dental practice, private law practice), social services generally are carried out in and through organizations. The normal dynamics of formal organization tend to generate the consequences described above, among others. Rather than bureaucratic "pathology," these developments may be defended as the vehicles for the objectivity, rationality, efficiency, and accountability that can be the contribution of modern organization. These latter impulses, in turn, tend to encourage consolidation and a search for both monopoly and economy of scale. Formal organization, thus, often becomes large-scale organization.

Why, then, the countertrends of the 1960s and the attempts in the 1970s to find a new balance? Several factors appear to have operated. Initially, the issues of relevance and adaptability were raised. Were social services in deprived areas focusing on what was most needed, or on the processes of interest and priority to the agency staff? Were services taking adequate account of the life styles, cultures, predilections, concerns, and modes of coping of consumers in deprived areas — particularly the poor, and ethnic and racial ghetto minorities? Could the professions continue to ignore evidence that people make more use of services that are close by? The case for diversity, adaptability, accessibility, and relevance became the case for decentralization. A pluralistic society, it was argued, could do no less.

Now the issue was escalated: First, the demand was made that organizations have local outlets and end the tendency toward large district or central offices. Smaller offices were proposed for natural neighborhood groupings, reflecting ethnic-racial-economic clusterings. Such offices would be more accessible, geographically and socially, and could reflect population diversities. Second, the call for decentralization and adaptability, a goal compatible with large-organization structure, since it could be met by a high degree of centrally directed localization, was joined to a call for decentralization of power — community control. Here the objective became political: The local group must control the local agency if it is to be truly adapted to the program priorities and to the service-using styles of the local residents.* A third ingredient was also in the picture: the "new careers" emphasis on the employment within local social services of indigenous paraprofessionals — both to ensure service responsiveness and to create jobs for the poor.

Some observers see the political demand for community control and employment of local paraprofessionals as the natural consequence of the neighborhood need to assert its own program priorities and delivery modes. Others believe that the political objectives came first and that the program rationale has been used to bolster the case. Since one may cite illustrations of each type, it is probably true that the community control and staffing demands of the late 1960s stemmed from both sources. There was no firm empirical basis for either argument as the demands shifted from education to health, mental health, and public welfare in the late 1960s. However, the issue had become so salient that no new programming could be seriously considered without attention to the question — at least insofar as poverty areas were concerned.

Political jockeying about community control may long confuse the social service policy issues. But the political decisions will be made in terms of stakes and factors that go well beyond the social services. We assume that American society, or any large, interdependent nation, cannot frequently, consistently, and in many fields reject the position that Lincoln took in his rebuttal to Douglas: the sacred right of self-government of the few cannot be permitted to override the concerns of an entire nation. A sensitive nation, however, will wish to employ decentralization, sometimes as local control and antiformalization, and sometimes merely as service localization, when comprehensive analysis of its interests suggests it. There can be neither a fully centralized nor a fully decentralized strategy.†

---

*Advocates of community control and of the employment of indigenous personnel implicitly reject Banfield's analysis and its alternative policy implications. It should be recalled that early Head Start programming emphasized the cognitive deficits of children reared in "culturally deprived" environments. To remove them from such environments was to open new opportunity. Banfield argues, along similar lines, that the urban problem is the problem of a social underclass and that theoretically the most effective intervention would require separation of "lower class" (which he distinguished from "working class") children from parents and environment. We might extrapolate from this a policy that favors domination and staffing of institutions serving lower-class children by working and middle-class boards and professional personnel. This is quite contrary to American social policy of the past decade. See Edward C. Banfield, *The Unheavenly City* (Boston: Little, Brown, 1970), especially Chapters 3 and 11.

†A rigorous analysis shows that no central body can survive without information; and information, in turn, is never fully separate from authority. This sets parameters on decentralization,

Social service planners will wish to identify those program types or *social situations* that require far more flexibility, adaptability, unorthodox staffing, and community involvement than is possible for the local outlet of a centralized service. In such instances, funding mechanisms and accountability devices must be sought or invented that will allow the maximum of program decentralization, community control, and staffing experimentation. Such programs would avoid excessive formalization and structuring and would be small enough to carry it off. Most programs can tolerate more standardization than this, while allowing for adaptability and localization (that is, decentralization without community control, or what is called administrative, as opposed to political, decentralization). In many programs the technology is quite standardized or the options scientifically engendered (health services, employment placement, public assistance). Often the outcome variables are standardized and measurable (secondary education). Generally, higher levels of government have a commitment to legislative bodies about the quantity or quality of service that is being offered and for ensuring its delivery without the imposition of additional requirements on local citizens (separatism, participation). We may therefore expect that formalization and bureaucratization will continue in social services, as in most modern enterprises, despite consciously protected exceptions. What is also to be expected, however, is that *organizational* solutions will be sought for many of the problems that do seem to flow from the bureaucratization process as it affects social welfare — such as complexity, case discontinuity, lack of accountability, disappearance of diversity, and decline of consumer initiative and responsibility. Some of these matters are discussed in the final section of this book, where programming is emphasized.

Finally, we might predict that the issues — decentralization, local control — will be with us as long as there are closed-out groups or consumers who consider services unresponsive and inflexible. The demand for what we have called participatory administration will recur as long as organization maintenance seems to dominate service delivery. A satisfied consumer will find higher priorities on his time than the monitoring and

---

according to Julius Margolis, "Decentralization and Urban Problems," in Anthony H. Pascal (ed.), *Thinking About Cities* (Belmont, Calif.: Dickenson Publishing Co., 1970), pp. 49–68. However, local variability and complexity demand some degree of decentralization, Margolis adds, arguing for a mixed system. Many authors caution that the decentralized decision-making bodies are more often than not oriented toward land values, not "population" values — or fail for other reasons to deliver the desired, responsive services. See Irving Kristol, "Decentralization and Bureaucracy in Local Government," in Pascal (ed.), ibid., pp. 69–80, or "Decentralization for What?", *The Public Interest*, No. 11 (Spring 1968), 17–25. See also Howard Hallman, *Neighborhood Control of Public Programs: Case Studies of Community Corporations and Neighborhood Boards* (New York: Praeger, 1971).

"control" of local social services. Even where his is the formal control (the suburban school board), he will under most normal circumstances delegate responsibility to administrators — whom he can remove for poor performance.

It may be noted that the New Federalism of the Nixon and Ford administrations favored a form of general and special revenue sharing in which states received block grants for large program domains and were encouraged to plan in accordance with their unique needs. Some transferred such options in turn to local government, facilitating their initiatives in policy and programming via their own direct operations or subsidy to traditional voluntary social agencies or newer community corporations. Such approaches, encouraging decentralization and even consumer control, were variously applied to education, employment programs, community development, and several of the personal social services. Title XX opened the option both for personal social services and for related programs. This approach continued into the early years of the Carter administration, although one could also discern, in and out of government, renewed concern with national policy. By the late 1970s, while responsiveness was still articulated as a generally sought goal of social service programming, thus implying some decentralization and consumer participation, there was simultaneous emphasis on the protection of federal policy initiatives. The latter faced both the legislative and the executive branches toward regulation, more program requirements, and efficiency-effectiveness, objectively measured. Participation would not substitute for performance. Thus the inevitable and continuous swing of the pendulum in modern social policy between the poles of organizational rationality and responsiveness, between expertise-leadership and participation. Each place and time would continue to seek its optimum balance points.

Notes

1. The classic and pioneering study is by Richard M. Titmuss, *Income Distribution and Social Change* (London: Allen and Unwin, 1962); see also his "The Role of Redistribution in Social Policy," *Social Security Bulletin,* 23, 6 (June 1965), 1–7. For the United States, see S. M. Miller and Pamela Roby, *The Future of Inequality* (New York: Basic Books, 1970); also, Herman Miller, *Rich Man, Poor Man* (New York: Crowell, 1971).

    Robert J. Lampman has produced the most significant U.S. analyses thus far: "How Much Does the American System of Transfers Benefit the Poor?" in Leonard H. Goodman (ed.), *Economic Progress and Social Welfare* (New

York: Columbia University Press, 1966), pp. 125–157, and "Transfer and Re-distribution as Social Process," in Shirley Jenkins (ed.), *Social Security in International Perspective* (New York: Columbia University Press, 1969); see also his *Ends and Means of Reducing Poverty* (Chicago: Markham Publishing Co., 1971).

An international overview with specific reference to social services is found in United Nations, Department of Economic and Social Affairs, *Social Policy and Distribution of Income in the Nation,* ST/SOA/88 (New York: United Nations, 1969).

2. Congressional Budget Office, *Poverty Status of Families Under Alternative Definitions of Income,* Background Paper No. 17 (Washington, D.C.: Government Printing Office, 1977), p. vii.

3. Robert D. Plotnick and Felicity Skidmore, *Progress Against Poverty: A Review of the 1964–1974 Decade* (New York: Academic Press, 1975), pp. 54–57.

4. Ibid.

5. Miller and Roby, *The Future of Inequality,* Chapter 6.

6. United Nations, *Social Policy and Distribution of Income in the Nation,* p. 15.

7. Alfred J. Kahn, "Perspectives on Access to Social Services," *Social Work* (London), 26, 3 (July 1969), 4; also published in *Social Work* (New York), 15, 2 (April 1970), 97.

8. For a review of the tradition and an informed critique, see Gunnar Myrdal, "Investment in Man," being Chapter 29 of his *Asian Drama* (New York: Pantheon, 1968), Vol. 3, pp. 1533–1551. The American debate is illustrated in Martin Rein and S. M. Miller, "Poverty, Policy, and Purpose: The Dilemmas of Choice," in Leonard Goodman (ed.), *Economic Progress and Social Welfare* (New York: Columbia University Press, 1966), pp. 20–64, reprinted in Rein's *Social Policy: Issues of Choice and Change* (New York: Random House, 1970), Chapter 12.

9. Myrdal, "Investment in Man."

Policy
Meets Program ◄◄◄◄ 6

We have already noted the distinction between concrete services, such as day care or an escort program, and relationship services, such as counseling or guidance. Some prefer to talk of these as "hard" and "soft" services. We have described the difference between money-granting programs of several kinds and personal social services in our sense. We have yet to face the question of how one may formulate the choice between giving a person a benefit directly (food, an apartment), or giving him an entitlement (voucher) for the particular benefit that he may redeem at one of a number of places, or providing him cash for the purpose — or for his own purposes. In short, we have yet to discuss one of the oldest policy questions in the social services field: cash or benefits-in-kind? It will soon become clear, as it has in the previous section, that policy options formulated as dichotomies or trichotomies are not necessarily resolved through absolute rejection of specified options. This discussion also serves to introduce a more fundamental question, already touched on briefly in the previous section and to be approached in several ways in subsequent sections: To what extent and in what sense does the market and its mechanisms or concepts, in the economics sense, belong in the social services field?

Cash, Vouchers, or Benefits-in-Kind

To most people, services are concrete things. Policymakers may debate the mix between hard, practical services and counseling or guidance; but the question gains validity only as users, too, perceive the issue.

Genevieve Carter notes that studies of social services have shown consistently that users and potential users of social services in public welfare (generally very poor people) always list money as their first need and consider jobs and employment services as closely related to the money picture. Medical services are highest on the list of services, with assistance in getting money as the next priority. Poor people also see themselves helped (priority order) by having special needs granted (school clothing, housing equipment); by being assured quick response in an emergency (check loss, child care during mother's hospitalization); by a social worker's intervention with landlords, teachers, police, and others who make major decisions affecting them; and by supportive referrals for or procurement of such resources as food stamps, camps, Medicaid cards, and so on. There is far less recognition of counseling or advice about child care as service and little visibility for — if not negative re-sponse to — help with household management, parent-child relations, marital problems, and other issues involving personal change.[1]

The preference listing, which may not be either up-to-date or applicable to all groups and locales, does include what we have called liaison, ac-cess, and information services. Moreover, recognition of the need for personal help as service by even a small percentage may imply significant case totals for a geographic area. Other studies show appreci-ation for interpersonal and behavioral help among persons higher in the economic scale — and when basic food and shelter needs have been met. Certainly, relationship and guidance should not be offered as sub-stitute for or prior to food, shelter, medical attention, or clothing. But, when there is to be a benefit, whether concrete or relationship, the question remains as to how it should be conveyed to the user.

It has already been noted that services are part of the "new property." This does not relieve the policy analyst or the social services programmer of the need to consider just when the provision of money is preferable to the guarantee of service, when service is preferable to money, or when vouchers are a desirable intermediate recourse. Are vouchers, in fact, the equivalent of cash or of benefits-in-kind? The issues are as old as social services, and the resolutions vary with societal concepts.

Several policy considerations are embedded in the general topic. Where the service is an indivisible public good (clean air, a park, sewage disposal, a community center) no issue arises; the service cannot exist except as a benefit-in-kind created by the community, independent of consumer market behavior — even though user charges may be levied in some instances. Where real choice regarding means remains open — a circumstance for all but indivisible goods — there is, first, the matter of the better buy for the community. Where the policy planner can choose between cash or direct service, benefits-in-kind in the form of public social utilities or case services appear to enjoy the advantages of economy of scale. Although data are limited, it is a reasonable hypothesis that at a constant service volume, the benefit-in-kind approach is cheaper.

Public officials can buy food in bulk more cheaply than can a customer in a supermarket. Standard rental rates, negotiated en masse, are visible and (in the absence of corruption or gross inefficiency) likely to reflect the real market situation. (Besides, the cynical might add, benefit-in-kind products are often identifiable, perhaps increasing stigma and decreasing applications. This, after all, was poor-law strategy.)

However, this issue is not simple. The inauguration of a benefit-in-kind may in fact increase the volume of provision under some circumstances. The unit cost may be cheaper but not the total expenditures. There is some tendency, perhaps only in some fields, for grants of materials or services — whether the obsolete turkey basket for Thanksgiving, the medical care program, or the school lunch — rather than cash, to result in a quantitative increase in provision. It is not clear whether this is the result of service standardization (the recipient knows what to expect), organizational dynamics (the administrators of a program increase their "customers" and thus their constituency), or the imposition of community rather than consumer priorities. Some benefit-in-kind services become near universal, or at least quite general in some areas; Medicaid services approached this situation in some parts of New York City in the early 1970s before a congressional clampdown; food stamp participation increased from 400,000 to 18 million between 1964 and 1977. Even between 1972 and 1977 there was a 7 million increase.

Thus, the issue is not resolved by reference to economy of scale and remains open to empirical exploration: Does benefit-in-kind provision increase or decrease volume of service? Do only specified types of benefits-in-kind lead to increased utilization? Do public bureaucracies increase utilization rates for their own purposes? Do economies of scale really appear; if so, when? Do they balance increased demand?* Are public services inevitably so inefficient as to dissipate economy of scale?

Opponents of benefits-in-kind have argued, usually, that whatever the

*Before the recent explosion of take-up, which is not fully understood, Steiner explained rather low participation in food stamp programs as perhaps due to administrative requirements for regularity in purchase and for certain purchase minimums. Stigma also operated. Yet surplus commodity programs, involving more visibility and less consumer choice, had far higher participation in some circumstances. There is obviously much yet to be learned in this field. Gilbert Y. Steiner, *The State of Welfare* (Washington, D.C.: The Brookings Institution, 1971), pp. 193–213.

specific case implications, social services are self-defeating if under-privileged members of the population are offered in-kind provision while everyone else utilizes cash. Here, then, is the heart of the matter. Whether focused on development-socialization or therapy-remediation, the purpose of the social service is to engender or to restore and enhance competence. If the recipient is given a "protected" benefit, that is, a service in kind, *in those instances where consumers in the free market would employ cash,* the agency is demonstrating "no confidence" and perpetuating dependency. Thus, when the country moved toward economic underpinning in certain circumstances after the Great Depression of the 1930s, social workers and others urged cash payments rather than food vouchers. It became and remains regressive social service practice in well-staffed agencies to offer Thanksgiving turkeys, Christmas baskets, food vouchers, or food stamps where people require and are perfectly competent to utilize cash. Indeed, benefits-in-kind in this sense — employed as a substitute for cash where the general consumer uses cash — are regarded as an avoidance of responsibility for adequate income maintenance.* (However, the complexity of the matter is illustrated by the almost universal support of massive food stamp program expansion from the mid-1960s to the mid-1970s, while welfare reform initiatives were stalemated!)

This is not to say that the phrase in the previous paragraph, "where people are perfectly competent," should be ignored by proponents of maximum use of cash. Dependent children need guardians. Some old people reach a point of requiring protection. There is considerable experience in the United States that, while abuse is possible, even cash assistance programs need a procedure permitting "protected payments" where proven necessary, with a third party handling the cash (or service could be offered or categorical vouchers substituted). Benefits-in-kind are important for "less competent people" — meaning people who are found, through carefully specified procedures, to be incapable of managing money to purchase what is needed and spread it over the appropriate time horizon.[2] In all other instances where consumers in the free market, that is, people who do not ask for public aid, employ cash, one would favor cash.

This rule of thumb does not settle all issues, however, for in a universalistic and rights context a benefits-in-kind approach would not need to involve stigma and might offer economy of scale and standardization of services. Public education is a prime illustration. Other illustrations are some health programs, libraries, cultural endeavors, and community

---

*Ibid. Steiner documented the unsatisfactory status of several benefit-in-kind programs in the United States in the early 1970s: surplus commodities, food stamps, public housing.

centers. In a basic sense, a society's policies, as reflected in tax laws and other related legislation, as well as in collective bargaining agreements and wage policy, set the balance between wages and occupational welfare (including in-kind fringe benefits), between communal provision of communal goods and what the consumer must purchase for himself, and between cash and in-kind public entitlements. These are analyzable, debatable, and changeable decisions, although they do become somewhat fixed in community mores. To pose the issue of cash or benefits-in-kind in relation to universal services is therefore to seek relevant anchor points.

Major considerations appear to be whether or not an indivisible good is involved (if a public playground is to be created, it cannot depend on individual decisions and, once created, it exists for all) and the degree of community determination that a specific service should be available to all and be utilized ("merit goods"). The presence of potential consumers, even consumers able to pay fees, is no guarantee that *enough* schools or hospitals of the required *quality* will be made available. The technical "adequacy" of family's budget does not ensure that the children will purchase nutritious school lunches. Currently, for example, housing for low-income people could not profitably be produced by the market; most education could not be paid for in a market economy. By creating a benefit-in-kind, sufficiency and standards are, or could be, guaranteed. Access may also be improved. In addition, the program may be organized to achieve universality, integration of population elements, and lack of divisiveness (for example, if *all* pupils eat lunch at school). This arrangement avoids the problem of whether a consumer who is aided financially will actually spend his resources to purchase the specific services deemed essential by the larger community.

Were communal benefit-in-kind provisions always accompanied by automatic guarantees of sufficiency, quality control, and assured access, the issue here under discussion would seldom arise. However, both bureaucratic dynamics and communal factors creating differential access by some population elements have challenged these premises. Ghetto schools have been found inferior despite formal legislative guarantees of equality or comparability. Professional interest groups and narrow constituencies have led institutions to avoid responsiveness to new circumstances and needs. Bureaucratic rigidities and civil service protections have nullified efforts at quality control in communal services. As a result, increasing numbers of advocates from the left and from the right have urged a departure from in-kind provisions and the assurance of cash with which consumers may buy access to services. The proposals have related both to case services and to universal public social utilities.

To illustrate, there are those who propose and continue to urge that parents be provided with tuition money to purchase their children's elementary and secondary education in the marketplace. The assumption is that competitive market forces will enhance quality. In the housing field there has been some shift to subsidization of the low-income renter and buyer (rent supplements, mortgage supplements, and, most recently, housing allowances), rather than of the builder or public housing authority, to bring market components into the picture. Many health planners urge that individuals be aided in purchasing health and hospital insurance, as an alternative to a national health service.

To the charge that this approach leaves the naïve consumer unable to judge quality, at the mercy of providers, the response is that standard setting and inspection can and should be strengthened. Reference is also made to the fact that a free market and its competitive forces generate quality improvements. Again, we must point out that this is true only if the consumer can judge quality — something very difficult in education, medicine, counseling, and so on. There is no escaping the need for improvements in enforced licensing, standard setting, and inspection. It is far from clear that a community or state not capable of organizing and implementing these essentials would be capable of carrying out successful and more economical direct service operations of its own.

To the point that the granting of money does not ensure the desired pattern of expenditure by individual recipients, the proponents of a free market in welfare respond in two ways. First, as already noted, they assert that the consumer's judgment as to his family priorities should prevail — unless he is judged by the courts to be incapable of exercising family responsibility. Second, to the persistent rebuttal that a community has an obligation to define and protect access to some basic educational, health, and related services for all citizens, or at least for all children, whatever the personal judgments made, the idea of the categorical voucher is introduced. Medicare and vocational rehabilitation are cited as precedent.

A categorical voucher is thus definable either as benefit-in-kind (a way to provide a service the community deems essential) or as cash equivalent (the consumer may use it in the market and have the advantages of the competition generated by the bidding for his voucher). There have been numerous calls in recent years for systematic experimentation with vouchers for social services to see whether market dynamics might improve the quality and quantity of service. It has been proposed that non-profit voluntary agencies, profit-making groups, and public agencies all be eligible to compete for the vouchers. As in the instance of cash, the naïve consumer with a voucher to spend will need to be protected by licensing, inspection, and certification arrangements as he shops. There must also be provision to ensure that a professional monopoly that is superagency does not eliminate the benefits of competition that should accrue when competing agencies enter a market.

Apart from the issue of whether it is sound to use vouchers in a *particular* program is the question of the extent of their use in a diversity of programs. Whereas it may be possible to make a case for vouchers in a specific context (housing or medical care or day care or education or prosthetic devices), the employment of vouchers for several different purposes at a given time and place would appear to infringe considerably on consumer autonomy and self-reliance.

In effect, the interim conclusion must be that the superiority of cash, voucher, or benefit-in-kind is contextual. It depends on a variety of community, agency, professional, and consumer factors that will vary with time, place, and milieu. Democratic values and many observations create a bias toward cash or vouchers, yet social realities and the real — if overrated — need to protect both social objectives and some people lean favorably toward benefits-in-kind. Each of the approaches can be made to work if the value hierarchies can be specified and the contexts analyzed. Conclusions vary, depending on whether the intent is to render a social service or conduct a publicly operated business.[3] This is a field in which scholars face several major research challenges.

There is yet another aspect of the cash-voucher-kind issue to be highlighted. It is a generic issue for all government and has particular implications in the decision as to whether a service program is to be sponsored or operated, or a benefit voucher is to be granted the consumer. The issue may be stated as *demand* subsidy or *supply* subsidy. Which is the better buy once the service need is acknowledged? Which approach ensures the quantity, quality, and location of services needed, in the best time frame? Clearly there is no one answer: place, time, field do make a difference. The questions are amenable to analysis as and when decisions need to be made. Readers who wish to pursue the implications of the topic may ask: What will occur if we subsidize agencies to offer day care, as contrasted with giving mothers money for fees; what are the consequences of creating a publicly funded homemaker–home health aide program — either publicly or privately operated — instead of reimbursing for the consumption of those services? While market enthusiasts stress the demand subsidy as strategy, the record of experience is mixed: one needs to ask about consumer sophistication, supplier monopolies, and service standardization, if one would predict results.

The Performance Contract and Accountability

Market behavior provided one of the points of analysis of the cash, vouchers, or benefits-in-kind issue. The market and its dynamics are also cited in relation to another strategy (largely untried) that joins policymaking with programming — the performance contract. It enjoyed almost faddist popularity in the late 1960s, suffered a major setback when a critical experiment in the educational field reported failure in 1972,[4] but recurs regularly in programming discussion.

The performance contract is congruent with the economy-efficiency strategies of policymaking. It risks the possible unplanned, unanticipated consequences and side effects of encouraging service purveyors to emphasize output where others have been content with process. Social services, we have noted, have a history in charity and poor law. Intent, motive, and social control are their own justification in the tradition from which social welfare arises. Recipients belong to an underclass and should not raise too many questions about the quality of goods and services. It is such tradition that, when joined with the inherent complexity of the measurement and research control problem, makes social service evaluative research so unsatisfactory — and rare.

The current era of operations research, cost-benefit and cost-effectiveness analysis, and consumerism has seen increasing challenges to this state of affairs: social service resources are scarce. The public should ask about effects and effectiveness. There is greater pressure for program evaluation that inquires not only about *process* (what does the professional do?) but also about *outcome* (what are the results of the doing?). If government would use the services of voluntary nonprofit or proprietary agencies, many who are concerned with output would urge that government pay fees for *delivered* (or effective) service, rather than grant general subsidies. Perhaps the consumer should pay directly when he knows the service has been delivered to his satisfaction, even if he requires a publicly provided voucher for this purpose. In the instance of publicly delivered services, in this view, there should be routine output measures as a way to ensure accountability: tests of the progress children make in their reading and writing, ratings of the cleanliness of city streets, statistics on criminals apprehended and convicted, reports on air quality, and data on consumer satisfaction with community centers or aftercare programs.

In this context, experiments with performance contracts were launched. In the most widely publicized of performance-contracting experiments, the Office of Economic Opportunity (OEO) sought to determine "whether a private educational firm could teach academically underprivileged children to read or write better than the local public school could." OEO also wanted to learn how successfully a "pecuniary incentive system operates in education. If firms — or teachers — were paid more as their students learned more, would they do a better job of teaching?"[5] By 1972, negative findings were obtained and publicized. Since that time there has been debate as to whether a less defective research design and a longer time span would have yielded different results. The failure has served for the moment to deflect any major new public initiatives of this kind, however.

Since there has been little personal social service experience with such approaches, an experimental posture toward performance contracts, as toward related market strategies, remains warranted. The dangers are visible and easily described: (1) Some performance contractors in education used operant conditioning strategies and rewarded the children for performance in turn (candy, trips) — the children learned skills but may not have had balanced educational experiences. (2) If, in any program, there are agreed outcome variables that become the basis for payment, the specified goals may be achieved at the cost of many undesired side effects. (3) Market-oriented contractors want to take on only "promising" tasks, thus ignoring the very point of the social service system.

If the performance contract approach is to persist, its advocates will need to demonstrate ability to develop acceptable criteria for success in service delivery. The measurement of a narrowly defined service output or result will not be enough for most social services. But, of course, criteria for effectiveness must be formulated and measured whether or not there is to be performance contracting. Sophisticated outcome formulations and sound measurements should be possible where services have validity. The issue of whether the performance contract, per se, actually achieves better and cheaper results than other accountability approaches in the public services is an empirical one, still worthy of exploration.*

But, for that matter, a case may also be made for greater attention to results in some pure market services as well. Except for lawyers in negligence suits, it is rare for doctors, teachers, psychiatrists, psychologists, counselors, or rehabilitation specialists in private (market) practice to agree to fee scales tied to the effectiveness of the effort.

Policy Choices by Efficiency Rating

Many economists and political scientists would find the discussion to this point quite incomplete or even irrelevant. The policy issues posed involve various combinations of value choices and empirical assumptions. Except where market strategies were referred to (vouchers, performance contracts) there has been little attention to the actual review, within the

---

*A no-birth bonus scheme tested in southern India offered a performance contract of a sort to individuals. A tea picker who joined the scheme earned significant increments by avoiding pregnancy — under a contract developed by the United Planters' Association of Southern India but implemented by plantation managements (*New York Times*, July 2, 1972), p. 2.

decision process, of data regarding economy and efficiency. Yet much of policy analysis in other fields gives highest priority to these latter considerations.[6]

Thus, a debate about income maintenance strategy is resolved by a federal commission and by other analysts on the basis of expert research that shows that — if efficiency is defined in its economic sense as involving the proportion of expenditure reaching the "target population," the poor — negative income tax approaches are more efficient than family allowances.[7] No weight is given in the final debate to the universalism-selectivity considerations and the fact that means-test approaches may stigmatize while universal methods reinforce "solidarity."[8]

The same analysts, we have noted, argued against expanded public day care as part of a reform of public assistance, on the grounds that the payoff was too small — it would cost more to provide good day care than the mothers could earn. Family planning services, on the other hand, yielded high cost-benefit ratios and were readily recommended for expansion in another study.

In short, major centers of policy analysis, both in and outside of government, ask questions about efficiency and economy. They employ the tools of the market expert. Sometimes their conceptual point of departure is welfare economics.[9] This class or family of methods has become important to social service planners and policymakers as pressure has increased for better results and more efficient use of resources. Where resources are in short supply, objective evidence is asked about the payoff potentials of competing opportunities for expenditure or investment. The very pressures that have pushed governments toward program budgeting approaches that require cost-benefit analysis have also encouraged use of efficiency criteria in other policymaking circumstances. Even where results cannot be quantified or monetized, they ask for an analysis that compares potential payoff with risks incurred and with social costs. The potential or helpfulness of such methods is hardly to be questioned.

This family of methods (operations research, systems analysis, efficiency and effectiveness studies) *does not yet involve one standard set of procedures*. The studies are characterized by specification of goals, careful attempts at quantification, formulation of alternatives available, clear definition of criteria, and the employment of either "best buy" for a given expenditure unit or "cheaper price" for a given desired effect as the decision-making base. Goals and means are mutually adjusted until an acceptable balance of resource requirements and expected results is achieved.

Why, then, the discussions of policy options in the earlier chapters? Why the value and preference debates we have summarized? Why not an expansion of cost-benefit and cost-effectiveness studies as the *sole* strategy to improve policymaking? Alice Rivlin has summed up her experience as assistant HEW secretary in charge of planning and evaluation at a time when there was an all-out governmental attempt to introduce analytic quantitative thinking, cost-benefit studies, and program budgets:

First, such approaches can and do produce useful, quantitative answers to such questions as what the problems are, how they are distributed, and in whom they reside.

Second, such approaches can and do add considerably to the knowledge of who might be helped by specific programs and at what cost (who benefits and who pays).

But, third, such analytic work, in the absence of application of other values or political considerations, cannot tell one how to choose among programs with different objectives (developmental services for young children, community centers for the aged).

Nor does such work, per se, tell the planner how to improve services.[10]

Rivlin found, as had Charles J. Hitch, who introduced much of the federal government to PPBS, that "systems analysis is simply a method to get before the decision maker the relevant data, organized in a way more useful to him." She also concluded, with her predecessor, William Gorham, that analytic methods like cost benefit do not shed light on the large program options and on balancing the investment among a variety of public objectives, since legislators and members of the executive branch prefer to trust their political intuition above cost-benefit ratios derived from debatable assumptions. However, as Gorham has noted, once the large choice is made, programming decisions within a given field or project can (or should) be improved through such analytic work. Systems analysts cannot help one to decide between more elementary school educational support or more investment in manpower programs. After a selection is made, they can help choose among programs or specify details within the selected field.

The efficiency approaches may sometimes shed light on the consequences of choosing decentralization or centralization; vouchers or benefits-in-kind or cash; universal or selective strategies. They can specify the costs or benefits of funding voluntary programs, as opposed to public operations. They may help identify where the taxpayer will get the most for his money. The decision maker will — or should — therefore seek out researchers able to produce such findings. To the extent that evidence of an objective kind, derived from economic premises, can be helpful, he or she obviously cannot ignore such evidence. We have suggested in the earlier discussions of policy options where it would be particularly helpful to have objective data of particular kinds, relevant to choices.

And, even where assessments of political realities or dominant value configurations introduce forces that are critical to the decision making, the objective, analytic data about costs and benefits are essential. Decision makers need to know the real price of a value preference, a popular demand, or a political requirement. Cost will at times sway the decision, outweigh a pressure. If not, the more costly or less efficient choice should at least be knowingly made. It can, perhaps, be consciously faced as an essential trade-off and should condition expectations as to program outcome.

Ultimately, of course, it must become clear that in specified circumstances some of the "other value" oriented options can or should be adopted with full understanding that they contradict or are in tension with efficiency approaches. Arnold Gurin has noted this in an analysis of a variety of social service policy issues. He points out that sometimes efficiency criteria will lead to the choice of service unit sizes and geographic boundaries for programs that negate the push (from other value perspectives) for greater decentralization as a contribution to increased democracy.[11] Gurin does not make this a firm, universal generalization but notes that it *may* hold in some circumstances, thus illustrating the tension between the efficiency criterion and others. Similarly, amid the rush toward decentralization he notes that "considerations of equity lead inevitably toward centralization." Only central initiative and power can ensure coverage, resources (fair quantity), and standards — the preconditions of equity.

Bauer and his collaborators have also shown how economizing, if this is taken to mean the various policy-development models in normative economic theory, may be in tension with other value hierarchies and/or may be differently interpreted and employed as other values are introduced. A project may be worth undertaking, for example, given zero results in cost-benefit efficiency terms, if it nonetheless has redistributional impact. Administrators and policy board members may wish to reject choices that would appear to follow from market-efficiency models because other values are dominant.[12] Participation, especially the variations on "maximum feasible participation," has a pace and reaches conclusions that are often in tension with, or even quite opposite from, those derived from operations research and cost-benefit studies.[13] There is a convergence (Bauer) that states that although people have more complex approaches to utility preference than does a market-efficiency model, the decision maker has need to know what the efficiency approach has shown. Furthermore (Stokes), since "analytical skills are for sale," community participation in its more sophisticated stages may employ analysts who share the "other" values that are central both to monitor the output of governmental planning and to develop plans and proposals in areas where the locality makes the decisions.

In introducing the problem of tension among policy options, we arrive at the question of whether there is an identifiable hierarchy among them. Are there some choices that should always be made first? Do some decisions lead to resolution of a broad range of issues? Is there a general paradigm that orders these and related policy issues and is applicable to all or most social service policy matters?

The Lack of a General Paradigm

The answer is simple, direct, negative. Nobody can offer one well-developed social policy paradigm, proven in its applicability to all decision making in social services. Nor is it clear that a paradigm will or should evolve. Some of the dimensions outlined appear to have greater weight at one moment than at another. Any hierarchy that is established among the choices is contextual, or dependent upon both reality assessment and a balancing among values. One cannot announce which questions must always be settled first or how a decision about one policy issue should influence decisions about others. The issue hierarchy shifts with general fluctuations in preference and in the power of competing decision makers and with changing times. Economizing or optimizing models lead in one direction, social welfare or sociologizing in another.*

Nevertheless, students of social services have increasingly been able to conceptualize their roles in society and to clarify the potential consequences operationally and philosophically of different choices from among the options. And, reporting of experience and employment of an understandable vocabulary about social service policy matters does sharpen issues and permit decision makers to act with far more insight than ever before into the significance and potential consequences of what they do.

In short, although the social service programmer or policymaker does not have access to clear operational rules for selection among all of the following options (nor is it clear that all are relevant in all circumstances), he is less likely to proceed blindly if he is acquainted with the thinking and experience relevant to such opposing approaches as consumption or investment; formal organizational structure or participatory administration; redistribution or nonredistribution as the primary goal;

---

*Martin Rein illustrates in detail how the policy analyst's ideology and values affect his assessment of policy process, policy research, and the hierarchy of policy dimensions. This extends to the weighing of economy-efficiency and of other policy targets. See "Social Policy Analysis as the Interpretation of Beliefs," *Journal of the American Institute of Planners*, 37, 5 (September 1971), 297–310. See also the discussion of economizing versus sociologizing on page 70.

public social utilities or case services; rights or non-rights as the basis of entitlement; general or separatist services; cash, vouchers, or benefits-in-kind; public or voluntary services — and so on. Many of these issues and several others that they suggest are translatable into general programming strategy or detailed operational guidelines.

A final word about policy: ideally, policy choices are based on an exploration of their empirical and value consequences and analysis of their compatability with other strongly held values and goals. The premise therefore always is that if one adopts the given policy, certain desired consequences will follow. Some of the assumptions may not be correct; research would be useful in this connection. Often, policy choices are made in the belief that specific policies implement favored values, yet the empirical base for the assumption proves to be flimsy. Are decentralized services truly always more responsive to local priorities and better able to adapt delivery system to subgroup circumstances than centralized programs? Is it true that, in many fields, means-tested programs are stigmatized and have more trouble in ensuring quality of program than universal programs? Do the assumed advantages accrue to consumers who can spend money for services in the marketplace, as contrasted with those who must utilize publicly provided in-kind services? Do so-called investment-type social services pay off for societies that are modernizing more rapidly than do consumption programs? Does community control enhance program responsiveness? Does selectivity increase or decrease take-up, add to or diminish disincentives?[14]

Dimensions usually discussed separately may be or are in tension: equality and decentralization, integration and decentralization, efficiency and local control (or subsidization of small voluntary agencies). These, too, are matters for further analysis and research. A decision maker cannot forgo full understanding of where his choices may lead. Therefore, there is need for more case studies of the policy correlates of various choices in social service, with special focus on the interrelations among the dimensions discussed in the past several chapters.

The efficiency-economy school of policy analysis has become quite central to this exploration. Premised on the notion that "least cost," "best buy," "greatest efficiency" are high or highest values, such approaches have been absorbed into the decision process even though sometimes political considerations may give equal or higher priority to other value perspectives. Here, too, then, there is need to study and examine the interplay among efficiency and some of the other values posited by those who debate policy questions. Policy analysis cannot be assigned completely to systems analysis or operations research ruled only by marketplace criteria, but it is obviously impoverished without it. Nor can social workers and others merely proclaim rejection of efficiency approaches while adopting other stances — unless they do more to elaborate and clarify their unique orientations and the feasibility and consequences of the alternatives they propose.

The policy issues discussed earlier in this section do not comprise the totality of possibilities. When values confront social realities in a given historical context, there are many dilemmas. At a given moment, particular issues enter the debate as matters of high policy. Special attention has therefore been directed at choices currently highlighted in the personal social services. Others will, at other times, seem more urgent; any particular paradigm will be short-lived.

Related to the major policy items are others that are intermediate between high policy and programming strategy. Elsewhere I have called these "parameters of programming."[15] For example, a provision about the degree of centralization-decentralization might help in choices about assignment of program operations to a given level of government, one of the intermediate policy questions. A decision about rights would require specification of type of accountability mechanism. Efficiency criteria would mandate choices in favor of provisions for case integration and responsibility.

A clear goal relative to redistribution could provide guidance in specifying program benefits and the method of financing. The latter issue would also be helped toward resolution once there is a point of view about introduction of or freedom from market strategies in social welfare programs.

No all-purpose and all-time policy paradigm, perhaps. Yet, for any given purpose, a policy frame must be developed. The social planner or policy scientist (the term varies with the analytic model) cannot ignore the issue of policy coherence, lest what begins as policy clarification emerges as policy "sprawl." This demands, in turn, some clarity about task or goal. It calls for operational criteria to implement empirical and value "screens," and a political assessment. Projection of alternatives and their consequences is essential to discover both complementarities and tensions.

Approaches to a Paradigm

While none could ever be universally accepted or found permanently useful, a standard approach to policy analysis for a specific field has much value:

· It guides the analysis of the alternative options posed with reference to a *proposed new* law, policy, program, program element, or implementation strategy.[16]

· It guides the analysis (evaluation) of *current* laws, policies, programs, program elements, or implementation strategies.[17]

At some point the various options and alternatives we have introduced in this and earlier chapters need to be ordered and placed in hierarchies. Choices must be made. Those considered important should become criteria. Even where policymakers and researchers disagree about criteria proposed, the availability of one or more paradigms and their use sharpens the debate and clarifies issues. The paradigm, after all, is a standard set of categories for assessment in a given field (applicable to proposed or current policies). Each category calls for translation into specific criteria: What (under this category) is to be regarded as "good," what as "acceptable," what as "not acceptable," and so on? If answers are forthcoming, the entire process may be advanced.

In the public assistance field, the work of the last decade has generated substantial research and policy-analytic work. It has created significant consensus on behalf of the following categories of analysis for welfare reform proposals:[18]

· Economy (is the price acceptable?)
· Adequacy (enough to meet needs)
· Target efficiency (the bulk of the benefit to intended beneficiaries)
· Administrative efficiency (and feasibility)
· Horizontal equity (equal treatment of individuals or families in similar circumstances)
· Vertical equity (redistribution between individuals or families with different levels of living)
· Work incentives
· Family stability incentives
· Independence incentives
· Coherence and control

There is by now much experience in translating these categories into operational criteria. It will be noted that, while dominated by economy-efficiency and self-support items, the listing by no means ignores other values. The independent analyst will of course observe that the weighting in any specific study is affected by broad political and contextual considerations.

A similar paradigm requires refinement and testing for personal social service policymaking. Perhaps separate paradigms are needed for state/local government and on the national level.

In an analysis of *proposed personal social service policy* I would suggest categories such as the following (translating each into operational criteria)·

- Appropriateness (to task or function)
- Economy (is the price acceptable?)
- Adequacy (enough to meet needs)
- Target efficiency
- Quality (state-of-the-art service level)
- Administrative efficiency (and feasibility)
- Horizontal and vertical equity (in relation to decisions about universalism, selectivity, or a mix; adequate redistribution; fairness to people in similar circumstances)
- Coherence and control (in relation to other personal social services and human services)

This listing does not have behind it the long series of exercises that have tested the welfare reform categories. It does, however, derive from some experience and has face validity. Along with colleagues, I have also employed the following more ambitious outline when the objective was to *characterize or assess a complete policy system* already in place:

- Current issues and debate (why is change proposed?)
- Legislative, policy, and organizational frameworks
- Program models
- Available research and evaluation (all research relevant to economy, adequacy, target efficiency, quality, suitability, administrative efficiency, equity, coherence, control, and service-specific client impacts)
- New proposals and insights (all sources)
- Hypotheses, conclusions, recommendations[19]

I would assume that experience over the next several years will test and refine the categories while operationalizing the criteria.

Notes

1. Genevieve W. Carter, "The Challenge of Accountability — How We Measure the Outcomes of Our Efforts," *Public Welfare*, 29, 3 (Summer 1971), 271.
2. For a rationale for the employment of benefits-in-kind for the "incompetent poor" on a relatively large scale, see Edward C. Banfield, *The Unheavenly City* (Boston: Little, Brown, 1970), p. 246 and Chapter 6. Banfield feels that cash harms those whose poverty has "inward" causes since it maximizes disincentives.
3. Gilbert Y. Steiner, *The State of Welfare* (Washington, D.C.: The Brookings Institution, 1971).

4. Edward M. Gramlich and Patricia P. Koshel, *Educational Performance Contracting* (Washington, D.C.: The Brookings Institution, 1975).

5. Ibid., p. vii.

6. For example, see Raymond A. Bauer and Kenneth J. Gergen (eds.), *The Study of Policy Formation* (New York: Free Press, 1968); Anthony H. Pascal (ed.), *Thinking About Cities* (Santa Monica, Calif.: Rand Corp., 1970); Joseph A. Kershaw, *Government Against Poverty* (Chicago: Markham Publishing Co., 1970); Philip M. Morse (ed.), *Operations Research for Public Systems* (Cambridge, Mass.: MIT Press, 1967); Harry Hatry et al., *Programs Analysis for State and Local Governments* (Washington, D.C.: The Urban Institute, 1976); and Alan Williams and Robert Anderson, *Efficiency in the Social Services* (Oxford and London: Basil Blackwell and Martin Robertson, 1975).

7. *Poverty Amidst Plenty,* Report of the President's Commission on Income Maintenance Programs (Washington, D.C.: Government Printing Office, 1969).

8. Alvin Schorr, *Poor Kids* (New York: Basic Books, 1966).

9. Richard Zeckhauser and Elmer Shaefer, "Public Policy and Normative Economic Theory," in Bauer and Gergen, *The Study of Policy Formation,* pp. 27–102; or, for an illustration, see Kenneth Arrow, "Criteria, Institutions, and Function in Urban Development Decisions," in Pascal, *Thinking About Cities,* pp. 41–48.

10. Paraphrased and summarized from Alice Rivlin, *Systematic Thinking for Social Action.* (Washington D.C.: The Brookings Institution, 1971).

11. Arnold Gurin, "Responsiveness and Control of the Social Services: Some Issues of Decentralization," unpublished lecture, 1970. Adams argues that "purely economic solutions will not do. Yet, the economic value set is likely still the best place to begin a policy analysis . . . by starting with economic values and a production model, he [the policy analyst] can often . . . 'flush out' the professional values and goal structure . . . ." This case illustration deals with rehabilitation. See Harold W. Adams, "On Economic Values in Policy Analysis," *Policy Science,* 1, 2 (Summer 1970), 214.

12. Raymond A. Bauer, "The Study of Policy Formation: An Introduction," in Bauer and Gergen (eds.), op. cit., pp. 1–26.

13. Geoffrey C. Stokes, "Maximum Feasible Participation Confronts New Management," *Trans-action,* 8, 11 (September 1971), 4–10.

14. On the latter, see Mike Reddin, "Universality Versus Selectivity," in William A. Robson and Bernard Crick (eds.), *The Future of the Social Services* (Baltimore: Penguin, 1970).

15. Alfred J. Kahn, *Theory and Practice of Social Planning* (New York: Russell Sage Foundation, 1969), pp. 208–211.

16. For the uses and limitations of policy analysis in government, see "Symposium on Policy Analysis in Government: Alternatives to 'Muddling Through,' " *Public Administration Review,* No. 3 (May–June 1977), 221–263; or *Policy Analysis,* 2, 2 (Spring 1976).

17. A systematic conceptualization addressed to social work is offered in Neil Gilbert and Harry Specht, *Dimensions of Social Welfare Policy* (Englewood Cliffs, N.J.: Prentice-Hall, 1974).

18. Although there are variations in the lists and weightings, the commonalities are considerable. The categories were applied under Presidents Nixon and Ford, by the Griffiths committee, and in the Carter 1977 welfare reform proposal. For example: Consulting Group on Welfare Reform, *Report of the 1977 Welfare Reform Study,* Supplement No. 1, Vol. 2 (Washington, D.C.: U.S. Department of Health, Education, and Welfare, 1977), pp. 229–234; Michael C. Barth et al., *Toward an Effective Income Support System: Problems, Prospects, and Choices* (Madison, Wis.: Institute for Research on Poverty, 1974), pp. 40–42; and Subcommittee on Fiscal Policy, Joint Economic Committee (Martha W. Griffiths, chairman), *Income Security for Americans* (Washington, D.C.: Government Printing Office, 1974).

19. Sheila B. Kamerman and Alfred J. Kahn, *Social Services in the United States* (Philadelphia: Temple University Press, 1976); and Kahn and Kamerman, *Social Services in International Perspective* (Washington, D.C.: Government Printing Office, 1977).

III

▶▶▶▶▶▶▶▶ **Programs**

The Programming
Model Reflects
a Policy ◀◀◀◀ 7

The citizen or the public official must not withdraw from policy exploration at the level of high abstraction. If he would influence programs and would monitor output from the perspective of policy goals, he must also consider the relationship between policy and program. These final sections are devoted to the topic; but, since research into policy consequences and complementarities is limited, one can say little that is firm. Much of what follows has face validity, at most. Much of it poses research tasks but cannot rest on research evidence.

Although there is some inevitable tendency in these chapters to be prescriptive, the objective is to introduce analytic habits for those who do or should care about the interplay of policy and program. The materials are deliberately fragmentary and illustrative. The objective — of creating concern with policy alertness — would be lost were we to offer a complete manual of social service administration or a checklist of policy guides.

Interested citizens, public officials, and students should know that the social service administrator or program planner finds some of the policy choices outlined in the previous section relatively clear-cut; his implementation mission then is not ambiguous. A program may be public or voluntary; federal, state, or local; sectarian or nonsectarian; more or less decentralized in administration; financed one way or another. There may be many details to be worked out, regulations to be formulated, organizational structure to be designed. Yet the nature of the choice to be made is specified in the policy issue, and its operational referents are identifiable in practice.

Other policy issues are far less readily translated into program specificity. For example, when we go beyond a decision to assign a program to either the public or the voluntary sector and express a preference for a mix, complex questions of quantity, coordination, and client rights are introduced. The solutions may advance or undercut basic objectives. Or a decision to add flexibility and options, where a basic program structure is legislatively specified and bureaucratized, faces the administrator with many decisions that can, in effect, make new policy.

The complexity involves more than just developing details where there are only objectives or direction. Since policy thrusts are often chosen because of their assumed compatibility with overall political goals or value stances, their empirical basis may be meager. The formal policy choice does not in itself imply clarity as to how it is to be implemented. The programmer may find it necessary to experiment with alternate means to realize a policy or may choose the most likely route and monitor it carefully. For example, a universal social utility demands a series of easy entry points, and the planner must provide them, without knowing whether the particular scheme set up actually achieves general access. Any attempt to use social services for redistributional objectives must be quite experimental, since a series of unknowns about access, utilization rates, alternatives as defined by consumers, financing, and so on, are involved.

None of this is easy; the charity derivations of many of the social services and the close relationship of many personal social services to religious and humanitarian programs with long tradition ensure that any programming effort begins with a large component of conventional wisdom and what might be called conventional practice. An act of will and a spark of creativity is often required to appreciate that the intended program does not carry with it an "obvious" or "clearly appropriate" approach, and that it is useful to pause to consider the means by which policies may be most effectively realized.

As he thinks about implementation, the program developer or administrator has the following among his reference points:

1. General or "high" policy objectives
2. Values and standards that are dominant in our ethic
3. Administrative principles
4. Experimental strategies

And he operates in a highly political environment. In addition, to facilitate his intellectual tasks and administrative activities, he is offered systems of concepts that would organize the relevant variables and sharpen his choices. Those who care about policy do well to note that even the choice of a model has consequences. Especially relevant to social services, and not necessarily always mutually exclusive, are:

1. Public health conceptualizations
2. Systems approaches
3. Market strategies
4. The concept of network (a "partial system")

Public Health Conceptualizations

Public health concepts have been very useful to social service programmers over the years, particularly as they have concerned themselves with case services. Some elaboration of public health concepts is needed for this purpose, but the approach has proven merit.[1]

Public health theory and practice have been developed on the basis of early preoccupation with three elements: *agent, host,* and *environment.* Traditionally, prevention consists of eliminating agents (eradicating the mosquitoes), strengthening the host (immunization and general health measures), and improving the environment (putting up a screen, draining swamps). Treatment, in turn, requires detecting those infected, preferably early, and eliminating the disease from the host. Rehabilitation involves maximizing functioning of those affected, whose treatment would not completely eliminate the condition but who can benefit from retraining, prosthetic devices, and encouragement.

For reasons not immediately relevant, public health personnel have developed a rhetoric of "prevention" to describe such activities: primary prevention (changing the environment, strengthening hosts, eliminating agents), secondary prevention (early detection and cure before there is impairment), tertiary prevention (treatment), and rehabilitation. The concepts have been refined and their use improved by the addition of epidemiology (study of the distribution of pathology in the environment), the recognition that health is more than the absence of disease and is probably part of another continuum, and the insight that treatment and rehabilitation often require positive "inputs," not merely the counteracting of agents and of negative factors.

Notions of this sort (grossly oversimplified above) have been of considerable use to organizers of social services: prevention, treatment, and rehabilitation have been differentiated and have often been assigned to different agencies and personnel. When there is individual, family, or group trouble, it is "diagnosed," so that a focused treatment or rehabilitation plan may be made. Much of the medical delivery scheme has been translated into social service analogues: inpatient and outpatient services, diagnostic process, treatment unit, general practice and specializations, patterns of treatment, and social worker–client relationship.

Three types of limitations have been noted:

1. For all its talk about prevention, public health tends to be oriented to pathology. Environmental improvements are considered in relation to avoiding illness; the "medical model" of intervention targets is on "disorder." The theory of enhancement of functioning is poorly developed, since public health people are basically expert clinicians undertaking a broader mission than the individual doctor. For social service programmers this is a serious problem, since most public social utilities are inventions intended for universal access. They seek to enrich communal living and to promote individual development and socialization. They need a broader framework than the mere avoidance of pathology.

2. The public health model works best where the problem concerns contagion. Public health conceptualizations applied to social situations may tend to overdo the disease and contagion analogy, with the result that victims are blamed ("Why didn't they practice good hygiene or avoid the bug?") or isolated ("Let us not permit it to spread."). Public health thought patterns in international relations led to the concept during the 1930s that international crises could be resolved by "quarantine [of] the aggressor."

The social service planner deals, in his case services, with acute conditions and also with some states and conditions that are dysfunctional for the victim but "normal" to the system (poverty, relative deprivation, personal incompatibility, and so on). He needs a broader model of intervention lest he try to cope with all societal malfunctioning by treating victims and blaming their inadequacies for all system failures.

3. Whereas in some social services it may be useful to think of the service event as social worker treating or helping a client (doctor-patient relationship), this model of service may be dysfunctional for other social service realms where the issue may be one of the following: (a) access to a concrete service in which the worker is an intermediary but not an agent of personal change; (b) self-organization for mutual aid; (c) staff and users together creating new services or seeking political or policy answers not known at the outset to the practitioner (some urban community development, for example). For social services often deal with problems for which there are no answers, in the sense of scientific "cures," but actions based on group interests and preferences. For example, community control and client participation in decentralized services create dynamics inconsistent with rational implementation of a public health model, which suggests the linear sequence — diagnose-treat-cure.

One concludes with the view that public health approaches and categories are useful for alerting the administrator and planner to many important issues and programming possibilities, particularly in relation to case services; but they need to be supplemented by other concepts, particularly where case services are not the focus or the sole focus. Even with regard to case services, where the medical model is at its best, there is need for inventive adaptation to the personal social service context so as to take account of the following: social service components are less clearly interrelated than medical specialties; more social services carry stigma, are "protective"; there are patterns of competition and overlapping among professions and agencies rendering services; there are aspects of poor law and charity heritage that complicate the service design; sectarian and voluntary services carry much of the responsibility in some parts of the country and in some fields, but not in others; and public information and acceptance of social services and social services expertise do not compare with public searching out of medical services for many conditions.

Systems Approaches

A public health approach is a form of systems analysis. Systems approaches are analytic policy-making or planning efforts that seek to take account of the range of major interacting variables relevant to the field in focus. In general, because of the number of factors deemed relevant and the complexity of relationships, research application for such approaches have become possible only as computers have become available. While many systems tools have been standardized, each piece of work is in some sense creative and different. System conceptualization and problem formulation are faced anew each time.

For present purposes, there is no need to clarify the several meanings of systems analysis.[2] Among the major ideas here relevant are the following:[3] A variety of components are interrelated, by some connective force (which may be real or an analytic construct), so that performance of one component is affected by performance of another component. By studying such relationships, learning how the system is influenced, and arranging for signals (feedback) from components, it is often possible to exert a measure of control. The control is oriented to the "big-picture payoff," in Boguslaw's terms, that is, the goals chosen for the system, rather than to performance of components, except insofar as the latter are oriented to the former.

The policymaker may choose a systems approach because it is essential to effectiveness-efficiency, a way to be most responsive, or a planned way to interrelate many elements (public-voluntary). His concern may be to relate his policy or programming efforts to the real-world environments in which they will be implemented, so as to consider constraints and consequences. Or he may choose a systems perspective because those who observe his performance do. To quote Rivlin:

the history of the Family Assistance Plan also illustrates another point about analysis: the importance of looking at the whole problem rather than just a piece of it. In developing the Plan the analysts had enough problems handling the interrelations between the old welfare system, Family Assistance, the tax system and food stamps. They appear literally to have forgotten that some other income-tested benefits were available to the poor, such as public housing, rent supplements and Medicaid. When these other programs were brought into the picture it turned out to be at least theoretically possible for a family on Family Assistance to lose all monetary incentive to work. Such a family might be better off on assistance than working for higher wages and losing their income-related benefits. This spectre, raised in the Senate Finance Committee, sent the Administration analysts back to their computers to devise a more comprehensive proposal that would preserve incentives to work.[4]

The systems approach is organic yet avoids false organismic analogies. Total situations are to be characterized and overall goals and directions kept in mind. Yet, in a sense, at some levels, all things are parts of systems involving larger things, so there is a degree of arbitrariness in deciding what to include, where to stop. The real world sometimes sets the limits: a city may operate elementary and secondary schools, but not colleges; a state may be responsible for juvenile institutions, but not youth police. If not faced by political or legal systems definitions initially, the planner must seek them out in relation to what he wishes to achieve and what is conceptually sound. He considers medical care, recreation, housing, education, and so on, as operating systems and stops to ask whether it is conceptually wise and politically feasible to join them — or some of them — with welfare and manpower in a human services system, for example.

The application of a systems approach (and operations research tools) to a local government's social service decision making is illustrated by the following summary and flow chart.[5] (See Table 7.1 and Figure 1.) It will be noted at once that the relatively arbitrary decision to exclude voluntary parental placement and many adoptions, the failure to address prevention strategies, the elimination of income maintenance as an approach, and the questionable assumption that volume of need would remain unchanged, all add up to a considerable compromise with the systems concept. Occasionally (see the quotation from Schon on page 143) there is a comprehensive approach, although action recommendations are

Table 7.1   Costs and Children Served in Four Short-Term Program Combinations

Program	First Year[a] No. of Children	First Year[a] Cost ($000)	Second (and each later) Year No. of Children	Second (and each later) Year Cost ($000)
Alternative I				
24-Hour Screening	90–200	11	180–400	12
Emergency Caretaker Service	12–25	2	25–50	5
5 Emergency Foster Homes	36	9	73	18
30 Homemakers[b]	126	110	252	219
Reduction at Richland Village	162[c]	−25	325[d]	−75
TOTAL COST		106		179
Alternative II				
24-Hour Screening	90–200	11	180–400	12
Emergency Caretaker Service	12–25	2	25–50	5
13 Emergency Foster Homes	89	24	179	47
15 Homemakers[e]	73	55	146	110
Reduction at Richland Village	162[c]	−26	325[d]	−75
TOTAL COST		66		99
Alternative III				
24-Hour Screening	90–200	11	180–400	12
Emergency Caretaker Service	12–25	2	25–50	5
5 Emergency Foster Homes	36	9	73	18
4 Homemakers[f]	47	14	94	29
Reduction at Richland Village	83[g]	−17	167[h]	−51
TOTAL COST		19		13
Alternative IV				
24-Hour Screening	90	11	180	12
Emergency Caretaker Service	12–25	2	25–50	5
Reduction at Richland Village	18[i]	−1	37[i]	−1
TOTAL COST		12		16

[a]Based on 6 months program development time and only 6 months operating.
[b]24-hour, 7-day per week service.
[c]Amounts to 17 child-years (one child-year is equivalent to 365 days care for one child).
[d]Amounts to 34 child-years.
[e]24-hour, 7-day per week service.
[f]8-hour, 5-day per week service.
[g]Amounts to 10 child-years.
[h]Amounts to 20 child-years.
[i]Amounts to about one child-year.

SOURCE

Reprinted by permission of The Urban Institute from *Options for Improving the Care of Neglected and Dependent Children* by Marvin R. Burt and Louis H. Blair.

Figure 1: Flow of Children Through Neglected and Dependent System, 1969

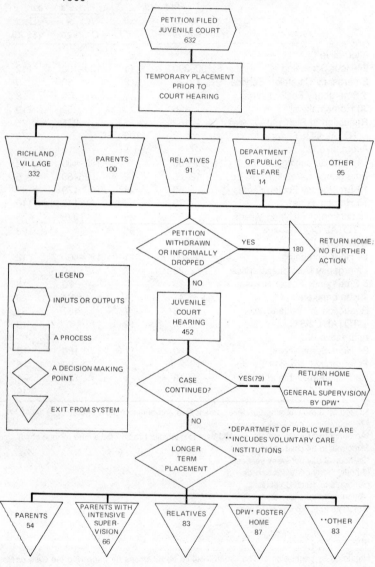

Reprinted by permission of The Urban Institute from *Options for Improving the Care of Neglected and Dependent Children* by Marvin R. Burt and Louis H. Blair.

then only on large issues. If we would give specific programmatic guidance by "costing out" alternatives, arbitrary delimitation is essential and a rationale for such delimitation must be sought. Then one approaches the "local network" analysis, a minisystems perspective, which is dealt with in a later section, and introduced here by Burt and Blair.

Sometimes in defining policy and often in specifying programming details, systems analysts employ tools of operations research. Operations research is constantly preoccupied with field tests of alternative approaches, in cost-benefit terms and from other perspectives; it is alert to trade-offs; it permits specific programming; it seeks feedback. It supports an effectiveness-efficiency policy and tends to be more consistent with centralization than with dispersed authority. It favors formalization.

Since there are now a considerable number of experiments with systems methods,[6] increased utilization in the future in planning social services is predictable. In general, effort, costs, and time would suggest likely application to major, not to small, policy and program questions. One recent study suggests the broader horizons that are opened. A *total* presentation of the blindness system, according to Donald A. Schon, involves:

that interrelated network of people, organizations, rules and activities which includes: (1) *all persons with severe visual impairments;* (2) *all agencies and groups that serve these people;* (3) *the training and research that affect these services;* (4) *the laws and policies under which services are provided.*[7]

Figure 2, dealing with one aspect of this, merely shows the resources expended in this system and their points of origin.

Any attempts to employ such models encounter lack of data, serious problems in setting widely acceptable boundaries, urgent need to curtail scope so as to make the approach manageable, and major political and administrative obstacles. Yet the analytic and practical advantages appear clear, if the problem requires a wide lens; even if there is no political sanction, the analysis of a system yields valuable insights and important proposals. It guards against too many unanticipated consequences, too frequent unacceptable spin-offs, too many ignored variables.

Thus, at present, any broad planning effort in the social services should be expected to define a systems strategy on some appropriate level of generality and scope. Proponents of decentralization, community control, and participatory administration could find their activities in conflict with a systems emphasis. Legislators and executives will need to make choices. Advocates of other policy strategies with strong value justification but little empirical emphasis will also find themselves sharply questioned by systems proponents.

Figure 2: National Resource Flows Related to Blindness

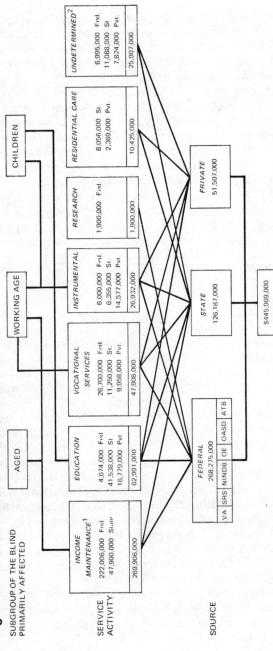

SUBGROUP OF THE BLIND PRIMARILY AFFECTED

AGED   WORKING AGE   CHILDREN

SERVICE ACTIVITY

INCOME MAINTENANCE[1]	EDUCATION	VOCATIONAL SERVICES	INSTRUMENTAL	RESEARCH	RESIDENTIAL CARE	UNDETERMINED[2]
222,006,000 Fed.	4,674,000 Fed.	26,700,000 Fed.	6,000,000 Fed.	1,900,000 Fed.		6,995,000 Fed.
47,900,000 State	41,538,000 St.	11,250,000 St.	6,355,000 St.		8,056,000 St.	11,088,000 St
	16,779,000 Pvt	9,958,000 Pvt.	14,577,000 Pvt.		2,369,000 Pvt.	7,824,000 Pvt.
269,906,000	62,991,000	47,908,000	26,932,000	1,900,000	10,425,000	25,907,000

SOURCE

FEDERAL 268,275,000 — VA | SRS | NINDB | OE | OASD | ATB

STATE 126,187,000

PRIVATE 51,507,000

$445,969,000

[1] This figure included $118,130,000 of Veterans Administration funds which are allocated on the basis of visual impairment and are not limited to legal blindness.

[2] This category includes funds which could not be assigned with confidence to any other service category.

From Donald A. Schon, "The Blindness System," *The Public Interest*, 18 (Winter 1970).

Market Strategies

The market model is familiar. It assumes that competition produces a better mousetrap, at a lower price. It is premised on the idea that the meeting of supply and demand in an arena in which consumers, producers, and middlemen are all seeking to maximize their own interests produces the best type of coordination and the most responsive system of production and distribution of goods and services. Market proponents prefer to "cash out" social services and in-kind benefits. We have already seen also how vouchers and performance contracting have been introduced into the social service field of late so that these advantages may follow. The evidence is not yet in; preconditions essential to the strategy and possible dysfunctions have been cited (pages 113 ff.).

The market model may be seen as an alternate model for service planning. The "invisible hand" replaces the detailed design. Governmental agencies enact policies and broad programs. They vote appropriations and set up guidelines. The profit or nonprofit groups bid for contracts to deliver services. Or consumers are granted cash or categorical vouchers (for rent, food stamps, prosthetic devices, tuition, transportation, and so on) for which private (and/or public) agencies compete in the marketplace of services. In short, the market strategy, when introduced to social service planning, involves use of monetary incentives — rather than laws, policies, and detailed program specifications alone — as the way to achieve public objectives.[8]

Who would have predicted in 1960 that a society with increasing social welfare commitments would, a decade later, be giving major attention to market models? Bureaucratic insensitivity, a desire to encourage service diversity, and a demand for more access by ghetto populations to public resources, have joined to create this new interest among long-time proponents of government action. Market strategies have also become attractive to some professionals and entrepreneurs who have recognized the opportunity for profit as the social services become large scale and are backed by the tax dollar.

The policy-conscious citizen will recognize, of course, that market models need to be kept under control in the social services. A market may reflect effective demand without measuring all need. Consumption rights should not be limited to what the individual can command in the market, even if the market is utilized as a service *delivery* mechanism. The citizen-observer will also note that monopolies, vendor conspiracies, supply shortages, and consumer ignorance, if present, can make the social service market as unlike the ideal type as the commercial market is often found to be.

During recent years, nursing home scandals, Medicaid cost inflation and service abuse, and similar experiences have introduced a note of caution into the market discussion. However, there are still those who favor market approaches because they want social services to be integrated into the economy with minimum impact on the work ethic (a value choice) and wish to avoid extensive development of centralized planning, large public systems of service delivery, or service standardization throughout the country.

A market strategy in social welfare is defensible if so implemented as to either (a) enhance coordination or (b) promise the kind of competition that will benefit the consumer. Always a potential source of values contrary to the social welfare ethic ("access to service by nonmarket criteria"), market approaches will need careful observation. In a brilliant comparative study of methods of providing blood needed for transfusions under different systems, Richard Titmuss has concluded that altruism may ensure a higher quality product than do market incentives.[9] Using both economic and value criteria, and contrasting the British system, which depends largely on volunteer donors, and the American, which depends significantly on paid donors, he argues that the nonmarket system produces a more reliable supply of blood for transfusions, with less waste and less administrative complexity, than does the market system. Moreover, American blood available for transfusions is of lower quality, more often carrying infection. Other analysts have disputed some of the specific Titmuss conclusions in this field, but his broader argument remains relevant: Noting that freedom requires "breathing space" for altruism and decrying the "Philistine resurrection of economic man in social policy," Titmuss argues against a totally utilitarian concept of the welfare state. He believes that altruism enriches society, in this sense, whereas market approaches may impoverish it.

Neither System nor Market: Independent Services

Systems approaches lend themselves to policy analysis and planning. Market strategies are offered as alternatives to planning and control measures. Categorical, fragmented, and segmented agency-oriented services are seldom regarded as an option with administrative advantages or as a vehicle of efficiency. However, they are the common pattern. They assume that humanitarian commitments and professional ethics replace the invisible hand of the marketplace and the rationality of the system.

Many personal social services are operated by small churches or voluntary nonsectarian agencies. Others are initiated and run by ethnic or racial groups responding to constituent needs. Still others are encouraged, supported, sometimes regulated, often kept apart and visible by various categorical federal grant programs, which insist on uniqueness of administrative agencies, delivery systems, staffs, or interventive approaches and require their own visibility and special imagery.

What results is not a model, to be compared with the market or the network. This is not quite laissez faire, since the units operate under constraints or directives (and often with a good deal of public money). However, despite vague rhetoric to the contrary, there are no significant demands for coherence, coordination, efficiency, standardized access, equal take-up and coverage, and so on.

The detailed picture inevitably varies with state and locality, since each has a unique mix of local public and voluntary resources, traditions, staffs, public policies, and political forces — which mesh with whatever comes down from the national level.

The nonsystem has advocates: they hold that any imposition of planning, any search for coherence, any effort to *organize* service delivery threatens pluralism, diversity, freedom to innovate, ability to attract volunteers. They occasionally also argue that planning of social services threatens freedom generally.

Thus there are those who oppose social service policy development and planning, and prefer nonorganization. They do not debate about alternative models. They will be backed by the supporters of the *status quo* (for that is really what they offer) or the *status quo ante* (it is not clear what era they would consider attractive), considering almost anything to be superior to public intervention. Our own view is that anarchy, laissez faire, or only minimal efforts to apply rationality and deliberateness to social services are by now dysfunctional. Such approaches may serve a variety of organizational maintenance, political, and personal objectives — but not the cause of improved service provision and access for the public at large.

The Local Network

A local network model is less grandiose than the full systems approach. It notes the complexity, when programming, of dealing with everything at once, yet it tries to establish a *system* of services as an alternative to the isolated agency. A local network model, therefore, may deliberately ignore many dimensions that would be addressed by a full systems analysis of a field of service: some aspects of the relevant law, sanctions, finance, prevention, boundary maintenance, personnel administration, and so on. Sometimes the program planner or administrator who wishes to operate direct services efficiently, in a fashion consistent with a series of policy choices and responsive to user needs, lacks sanction or facilities to take on all aspects of a field under any circumstances. More often, delimitation is accepted in order to deliver services within a reasonable period of time. The limited local service network conceptualization is useful to such purposes. It is oriented to effectiveness and efficiency, but may be made compatible with decentralization and much employment of the voluntary sector.*

A local network constitutes the service component of a system and the most immediate administrative supports for such a component. Requirements for such a network are identifiable.[10] The premise introducing a network model is that social services have a socially assigned task and are accountable to users and to the broader society. Whether conceived as universal or selective, such social services wish to deal with people considerately, respectfully, responsibly, and with equality. Whether public or voluntary, sectarian or nonsectarian, case services or utilities, therefore, they cannot be conceived as independent islands, as private principalities. It is appropriate to view them as responsible *for working in relation to one another* to accomplish socially defined tasks — and as needing to be evaluated in relation to goal achievement.

What topics does this introduce to the planning agenda? How does one size up a network, or plan one? What are a social service network's major dimensions, given such general policy?

Definition of Boundaries: One cannot organize an integrated service system without some agreement as to what will be encompassed. For the personal social service planner, this requires a decision as to whether mental health programs are part of the medical system or belong within its sphere. What of drug programs, services to the aged, programs for delinquents? Among the matters relevant to resolution of the boundaries issue are: what network boundaries will facilitate public understanding and use; what network boundaries will be efficient for the professions involved; what network boundaries are essential if the task is to be achieved, that is, if service efforts are not to be defeated by unmanageable fragmentation?[11]

The observer will note that boundary decisions involve policy. If personal social services are administered along with income programs, relief recipients have a separate means-tested program (selectivity). If juvenile probation is handled within child welfare, there may be more emphasis on treatment than if it is separated (and stigmatized, perhaps) by a relationship to the correctional system.

---

*Our view is that comprehensive systems analysis is probably most relevant to macropolicy development. The local network ("local" could mean state, region, city, neighborhood) is a systems approach to programming as used here.

Access Provision: Provision for access is a basic requirement for all service systems. Access machinery is especially important for the personal social services insofar as they deal with people under stress and disadvantaged populations and adopt a rights concept. People do not categorize their lives or classify their needs in social service language or dimensions.[12] Universalism increases the urgency of access programs, but selective programs cannot forgo them. Citizens require *information* about rights, benefits, and services. When the information alone does not ensure access, they may need more formal *referral*. If obstacles appear in their way, interfering with access to rights, they may require *legal assistance*. If the problem is abuse of administrative discretion or poor service, the need may be for *complaint machinery*. These access components are realizable in a variety of ways and in different relationships to one another, varying with both service and user characteristics. The quality of the access machinery determines whether personal social services are rights, whether they may have redistributional effect, and so on.

Assessment of Eligibility: Some public social utilities are available at user option, and there is no need, within the system, for any assessment of eligibility to draw upon it (some community centers, recreation programs, educational programs, and so on). Many other utilities are available by user status (over sixty-five, three to five, blind, physically handicapped, teen-ager, and so on). In most of such instances a simple registration procedure establishes eligibility. Services, if universal, may be free or may involve uniform user charges. Should there be differentiated fees, varying by income or family size or residence, more elaborate machinery must be set up.

In the instance of case services, the machinery must be even more extensive. Case services are assigned on the basis of illness, diagnosis, problem, need, and so on — that is, a category deemed as classifying people into groups whose members require a particular intervention. Such classification has traditionally been the responsibility of "intake machinery" in social agencies. Tests, examinations, interviews, observation, and other assessment devices may be used. Case services may also need to incorporate means tests, residence tests, and so on, as well, to allocate costs or control user populations — depending on the overall policy thrust.

For case services, the eligibility assessment thus merges with the specification of the intervention, the "prescription." General social services are committed to individualized assignment of service components, as appropriate.

The assessment takes place at the doorway of the entire personal social service network (if it is so organized) or at the doorway of individual agencies that may have their own "intakes" (is this is be a coordinated system or a marketplace?). In most systems, the general network doorway will be responsible for channeling, but the case service agency will need to do some case assessment to connect the user with appropriate service modality. The utility, by contrast, will do much simpler classification — grouping in day care, selection of a compatible homemaker to visit an older person, introducing a teenager to a group in the local center.

Provision of an Interventive Repertoire: A network of utilities and case services is concerned with offering a range of resources, services, facilities, and benefits that will coincide with user needs and preferences, on the one hand, and the state of knowledge and professional skill, on the other. It is not a network if the repertoire is thin, outdated, offering few options and choices. Selective services will be less sensitive to this. Programs with little consumer participation will not enjoy the evaluative advantages of good feedback.

The implications of this requirement necessarily vary with the service category. It implies such notions as the following:

1. A child-care system that offers foster homes, large institutions, small group homes, agency apartments for adolescents, services for children at home, after-school centers.
2. A training school system for adjudicated delinquents that offers many types of settings, among which are some offering general education, vocational training, psychiatric individualized treatment, group social psychological treatment approaches, differential security and degrees of integration of services with the local community.
3. A program to help families in trouble that encompasses group education, casework, individual and group psychotherapy, supportive resources such as vacation facilities and homemakers, protective services.

Case Integration: If social services are to be task-oriented — that is, are intended to enhance functioning or to solve personal problems, not merely to satisfy those who "give" or "do" services — a network must seek to maximize effectiveness through provision of case integration machinery. More specifically, devices are necessary to ensure meshing of sequential and of concurrent case interventions into a situation. For example, if a child comes to the attention of the police, goes through juvenile court, spends time in an institution, and is helped by an aftercare parole service while back at a public high school, a device is needed to ensure that these several steps are additive, resulting in consistent help and a community responsiveness that strengthens conformity and adjustment. Similarly, if at a given moment a family is receiving service from a number of agencies, it is urgent that their efforts be mutually supportive. This is illustrated by the instance in which financial aid is being rendered by a public assistance department, a voluntary family agency is assisting the mother with a marital problem, the father is reporting regularly to a veterans administration mental health clinic, one child is of concern to a school social worker and another to an attendance officer. If the family is not seen as a "whole" and addressed (at the minimum) with a mutually consistent service strategy or (even better) by an overall approach consisting of mutually reinforcing components, little that is constructive can happen.

Program and Policy Coordination: This network component might have been listed first. The very notion of a network is premised on availability of specific instruments to ensure the coordination of policy and program elements of the agencies that are part of the network. This does not mean that the network precludes competition, some inefficiency, diversity, or other devices that will keep it responsive and effective. The issue is how to guarantee that degree of coordination adequate to specified objectives, not perfect coordination and completely uniform policy. Enthusiastic advocates of the market would underplay coordination and encourage competition. They do not seek to construct networks.

Similarly, beyond coordination, there is the opportunity, where desired, for a measure of *program integration* as well. Agencies may wish to mesh components administratively and to move beyond mere case by case integration.

Reporting and Evaluation: A range of instruments is needed to assess the output of the network as a whole and of its components and to propose improvements and departures:

1. Periodic large-scale evaluative research (measuring effectiveness)
2. Consumer feedback
3. Staff self-assessment
4. User boards or advisory committees
5. Experiments with alternative intervention repertoire components
6. Cost-effectiveness analysis

These reporting components are part of the accountability and public responsibility of socially established and supported community services. They are also important administrative, planning, and knowledge development tools. Without them, there is no network.

The Scope of the Network: State and Local Levels

Local planning for a service network will be affected, perhaps even determined, by decisions in Washington and state capitals. Statutes, regulations, manuals, guidelines, and organizational structures may govern. Critical boundary decisions will affect the range and content of services within a delivery system, the types and ratios of professionals and other staff elements, and the way in which the network is constituted.

Near the end of the 1970s, federal legislation and regulations, historical traditions, the preferences of state governors and legislators, professional concepts, and interest-group actions had created the following different state-level approaches to the organization of social services, each with different implications for the delivery network level:[13]

A state umbrella agency that does not interfere with categorical service delivery patterns in the various human services. This has been a very common pattern in recent decades. State government may find ways to consolidate somewhat, but not fully, for programming, coordination, planning or budgeting (and may even encourage integration in delivery without requiring it). Separate programs often operate locally for child welfare, services for the aged, youth services, corrections, health, mental health, housing, and so forth. No two state umbrella agencies are exactly alike. Local service systems report to and depend upon specialized state functional programs for financing and backup. Thus delivery systems are not changed in any basic sense.

A state umbrella agency that maintains some functional identity for the separate human services, but only centrally. This provides a structure for specialized planning, budgeting, program development, and technical aid — a structure that meets federal categorical requirements. However, the representatives of the several human services operating at the client-contact level are not administratively responsible to state personnel in the specialized fields. Service delivery covering some, many, or all human services is implemented at the local level, under control of a district manager. In Florida, the one state that had gone this far by 1978, the next step has not been taken: while the district manager controls all services, service delivery to the case is not integrated. There is no common intake or provision for case integration or case accountability in our sense. In short, Florida achieves the many advantages of local-level co-location and administrative consolidation, without as yet discovering the range of service consolidation possible. Florida neither proves nor disproves hypotheses about personal social services or human services as the strategic range for service delivery integration, since the reorganization and the assessments have not yet addressed this issue fully. The issue is on the agenda, however, and its experience in Florida will be followed.

State human services administered as several different systems, with the components of the personal social services also continuing as several semi-independent categorical services. This, too, is a common pattern. The states reflect federal organizational and legislative patterns. Even though there may be some administrative consolidation (health and mental health, child welfare and youth services, employment and adult services, for example), there is no one umbrella agency. Personal social services are somewhat fragmented. The separate commissioners report to the governor, legislature, or board(s). At the local level the personal social services appear as several quite separate or as partially integrated delivery systems. Many localities have service systems for the aging, child welfare, day care, employment-related social services, community care for the mentally ill, social services to alcoholics or drug addicts, services to recipients of public assistance, homemaker and home health aides. No two patterns are alike. Because this approach offers neither coordination nor integration at the state level, nor delivery-level consolidation or integration, improvements are sought. A first step is usually creation of the state-level umbrella structure described earlier. Simultaneously there are often efforts at service co-location, shared management information systems, or common access services — whether or not in multiservice centers.

Personal social services organized as a partially integrated, freestanding system at the state level, relating to other parallel human services: employment, health, education, housing, income maintenance, corrections. This is a subset of the previous category, highlighted for present purposes. While there may be some consolidation for planning and delivery, each human service system has its own local delivery outlets, state operated or supervised. Under this pattern, in which the "old" public welfare social services slowly evolve toward a broader mission and more comprehensive coverage (family and child welfare, the aged, youth), the local delivery system is most often categorically organized (child welfare, aging, youth). New efforts are being made in a few local jurisdictions to develop a more integrated, freestanding delivery outlet for personal social services locally, staffed by generalist social workers, in the English pattern. All of this is rare, incomplete, and dwarfed by the previous pattern.

The wisdom of this latter pattern is debated. Are freestanding personal social services a good idea? Would categorical networks not be wiser? Does integrated delivery not decrease choice and throttle voluntary agency and sectarian diversity? Could integrated service and accountability for all human services not be achieved in multiservice centers?

Exploration of these matters in the remainder of this chapter and the next illustrates the policy-practice connection. Clearly, the issues will remain open, at least for some time to come.

Should Personal Social Services Be Integrated? Categorical? Freestanding? Adjunctive?

Social welfare legislation has tended to be categorical, since legislators and the executive branch respond both to interest-group pressures and public concern at a given moment with a specific problem. Therefore, there are programs for veterans, children, refugees, flood victims, the aged, the handicapped, drug users, and so on.[14]

Friends of categorical programs argue that they increase access. Veterans feel that they have a right to their own programs; old people know that certain programs exist for them. It is also argued that it is possible to obtain better public funding and to raise more voluntary funds for categorical programs than for general programs, since the former tend to concentrate sentiments and to engender more interest-group activity. Finally, advocates of special services in this sense often hold that there are distinctive needs that are well served only by unique networks. In short, there are here questions for both policymaker and programmer.

Obviously, no matter how convincing the data about interrelations among needs and problems, no one can define an undifferentiated, accessible, and efficient delivery system for the full variety of high-quality social services, broadly defined. Imagine one neighborhood service unit that is school, medical clinic, housing authority, employment agency, social insurance office, day center for the aged, and so on. The volume of need and the range of service is so great in all but the smallest communities as to create chaos if all is put into one operation. There can be one or more related buildings, perhaps, but several administrative bodies are needed. While appropriate linkages among such services are deemed vital, there is also general recognition that different programs enjoy varied public evaluations, are subject to differentiated professional dominance, and involve quite distinct patterns and delivery system requirements. Indeed, as previously noted, these factors have led to the separate growth and institutionalization of health, education, employment, income, and housing services. Where these separately institutionalized services employ social workers and related personnel, their tasks are seen as adjunctive.

However, even if the independently institutionalized human services or social sector services are eliminated and the focus is narrowed to what we have here defined as personal social services, the problem of designing a viable delivery scheme is still present. Is one unit to deliver probation, child guidance, school social work, family counseling, day care services to the aged, home helpers, abortion counseling, and services to several categories among the handicapped? Are there ways of packaging and interrelating services that entail more (or less) likelihood of accessibility and effectiveness? Do some of the choices have favored, others undesirable, policy outcomes?

Social services experts have noted that it can be extremely harmful to those in need of case services to have the presence of a specific handicap deemed the critical basis for assignment of service responsibilities in all realms of a person's life.[15]

The crippled, blind, palsied, defective, and so on, have needs for medical care and rehabilitation services specific to their maladies and handicaps. But they also need housing, education, recreation, and work opportunity. There is some evidence that, if segregated by handicap for these other purposes, handicapped people tend to maximize what psychologists call "secondary gain." The handicap becomes the dominant life element, and community integration is more difficult. This issue of service integration versus segregation by handicap, only recently recognized, has wide ramifications. The Joint Commission on Mental Illness and Health called for a complete restructuring of services to the psychiatrically ill when it came to realize that their being "cast out" from community life and segregated in isolated hospitals reinforced the illness. Several scholars have documented a similar process among blind people, with resultant new emphasis on integration of the blind in "normal" institutional systems.

Special age groups (aged), problem categories (blind), and status groups (veterans) may need specialists or special services at some point. Nonetheless, wise policy would begin programming strategies on the assumption of a maximum role for the personal social service system and an interpretation of that system as organized around service integration, rather than segregation. This would not preclude construction of a system that could tap specializations when and as needed, constantly coming back to and referring to the generalists, who constitute the spine of the service network at the local level.[16]

Some exceptions will be necessary for administrative purposes or because of public preference and pressure. One would find it difficult to convince veteran lobbies that the policy of minimizing special services is wise, for example. Nor can the separativeness of correctional programs be wiped out very readily, even though the clientele of courts, police systems, and other correctional programs share many or most of their needs with those who come to general social services from nonauthoritative channels. Wherever possible (that is, whenever it is not absolutely essential that the public intervention involve the actual or potential deprivation of freedom) it is desirable to refer people out of correctional services into the general social services. However, since the degree of control and the exercise of public authority in some interventions must be considerable, the introduction of protections for due process is inevitable.

A separate correctional system, albeit a reformed one, must remain. Recent Supreme Court decisions tend to make juvenile courts more, rather than less, like criminal courts, as formal protections are introduced.

Social service systems for migrants or a rural welfare system may be separately recognized in some places as solving specific problems of access and adaptability to clientele but belong to and require integration with other general social services. Child welfare programs, services to the aging, physical and social rehabilitation are all well developed, but their separation out from other personal social services destroys the network and promotes dysfunctional fragmentation. The same may be said about counseling services for adolescents; such public social utilities as homemakers, home help, day care, and meals-on-wheels; group treatment facilities of many kinds; a diversity of community centers; and general public multipurpose cultural and socialization resources.

In short, what is needed is a universal policy thrust, a concern for socialization and development as personal social service functions — along with direct helping through case services — and all of it part of an integrated delivery approach. Experiences with the need for specialization, and external constraints mandating some categorical organization, will place some limitations on this approach, however. One can conceive of an integrated personal social services network with some categorical specialists or units.

Still to be considered is whether an integrated personal social service network will best deliver services through a freestanding system or by creating outlets in other social institutions. The final answer should of course be empirical. The history of social services is of a peculiar and accidental mix of some freestanding services (child welfare, family services, services to the aging), generally categorically organized, paralleling personal social services based in other systems (schools, hospitals, settlement houses, factories, social insurance offices, trade unions, etc.). A major effort to develop and expand personal social services, to make them visible, accessible, competent, and accountable, and to provide a locus for case integration, would appear to require a freestanding system and one that is relatively comprehensive and integrated. This is the direction chosen by the British.

Also on the side of a freestanding personal social service is the claim that personal social services placed within systems that have other primary missions may become the handmaidens of such institutions ("speed his return to work," "get him to behave in the classroom"), rather than focusing primarily on the client and his welfare, to the point of becoming his advocate. In other words, the organizational decision not to "stand free" could support a questionable policy.

Such freestanding systems, of course, could still outpost staffs to hospitals, clinics, or schools — while providing them a home base. The relationship would be similar to that of the public health clinic doctor outposted to a school several days each week. Similarly some of the advantages of categorical programs might be achieved by staff specialization or creation of specialized units for specific tasks. A system of contracts for specialized services by voluntary sectarian and nonsectarian agencies could also guarantee diversity and protect against monopoly and monolithic networks.

This is not the place to go beyond broad outlines and elaborate program specifics; the point for emphasis is that policy clarity can be translated into experimental delivery networks that can be monitored. Alternative views of human services, their similarities and differences, do not lead to major conflict about the urgency of some measure of delivery-level service integration. The differences that emerge have to do with the range of services to be joined. The following are the three major proposals that are current:

· A local, comprehensive human services outlet, providing for case integration
· Categorical delivery outlets operating locally from the various human services, with some within-system consolidation (employment, health) and some categorical separateness (vocational rehabilitation, child welfare, the aged, youth, etc.)
· Organization of personal social services as a local system network, relating to other human service systems

Each approach may be regarded as an operational hypothesis. I have proposed the last of the three as worthy of particular attention and careful assessment.

Notes

1. For example, see Alfred J. Kahn, *Planning Community Services for Children in Trouble* (New York: Columbia University Press, 1963); Eileen Younghusband, et al., *Living With Handicap* (London: The National Bureau for Co-operation in Child Care, 1970); Catherine King, *Preventive Child Welfare: The Feasibility of Early Intervention* (Melbourne, Australia: Melbourne University Department of Social Services, 1971).
2. For example, see Roland N. McKean, *Efficiency in Government Through Systems Analysis* (New York: Wiley, 1958); Robert Boguslaw, *The New Uto-*

pians (Englewood Cliffs, N.J.: Prentice-Hall, 1965); Anthony Downs, "The Coming Revolution in City Planning," in Edward C. Banfield (ed.), *Urban Government: A Reader in Administration and Politics,* rev. ed. (New York: Free Press, 1969), pp. 596–610; and, especially, Alice Rivlin, *Systematic Thinking for Social Action* (Washington, D.C.: The Brookings Institution, 1971). Also, Stanford L. Optner (ed.), *Systems Analysis* (Baltimore: Penguin Books, 1973); Jack W. Lapatra, *Applying the Systems Approach to Urban Development* (Stroudsburg, Pa.: Dowden, Hutchinson, and Ross, 1973).

3. Boguslaw and Downs are the bases for these summary sentences.

4. Rivlin, *Systematic Thinking for Social Action.*

5. Marvin R. Burt and Louis H. Blair, *Options for Improving the Care of Neglected and Dependent Children* (Washington, D.C.: The Urban Institute, 1971), pp. 7, 33.

6. For a recent public welfare attempt, see Jack C. Bloedorn, et al., *Designing Social Service Systems* (Chicago: American Public Welfare Association, 1970). Also Lapatra, *Applying the Systems Approach to Urban Development.*

7. Donald A. Schon, "The Blindness System," *The Public Interest,* No. 18 (Winter 1970), 24–25; or, see Robert A. Scott, *The Making of Blind Men* (New York: Russell Sage Foundation, 1969).

8. For the rationale, see Anthony Pascal (ed.), *Thinking About Cities* (Belmont, Calif.: Dickenson Publishing Co., 1970), pp. 82–90.

9. Richard M. Titmuss, *The Gift Relationship* (New York: Pantheon, 1970).

10. Alfred J. Kahn, "The Service Network as Heuristic and as Fact," in William Ryan (ed.), *Distress in the City* (Cleveland: The Press of Case Western Reserve University, 1969), pp. 163–172.

    Network studies employing different network dimensions, may be illustrated by Elaine Cumming, *Systems of Social Regulations* (New York: Atherton, 1968); D. V. Donnison, *Welfare Services in a Canadian Community* (Toronto: University of Toronto Press, 1958); Margot Jefferys, *An Anatomy of Social Welfare Services* (London: Michael Joseph, 1965); Margaret Purvine and William Ryan, "In and Out of a Child Welfare Network," *Child Welfare,* 48, 3 (March 1969), 126–135; and Jean Packman, *Child Care: Needs and Numbers* (London: Allen and Unwin, 1968).

11. For a more formal discussion, see Alfred J. Kahn, *Theory and Practice of Social Planning* (New York: Russell Sage Foundation, 1969), Chapter 5; or Kahn, "The Service Network."

12. Linda Winiecke, "Self-Determination of Need for Social Services Among OAA Recipients," *Welfare in Review,* July–August, 1971.

13. Robert Agranoff (ed.), *Coping with the Demands for Change Within Human Service Administration* (Washington, D.C.: American Society for Public Administration, 1977); National Academy of Public Administration, *Reorganization in Florida* (Washington, D.C.: 1977); "Services Integration," a special section in *Evaluation,* 3, 1–2 (1976), 53–154. Also see Harold Hagen and John E. Hansan, "How the States Put the Programs Together," *Public Welfare,* 36, 3 (Summer 1978), 43–47.

14. For illustration, see *Encyclopedia of Social Work, Seventeenth Issue,* 2 vols. (New York: National Association of Social Workers, 1977).

15. Younghusband, et al., *Living With Handicap.*

16. Ibid. This is the strategy of the United Kingdom's local authority social service departments. Detailed U.S. proposals appear in Alfred J. Kahn and Sheila B. Kamerman, "The Course of Personal Social Services," *Public Welfare,* 36, 3 (Summer 1978), 29–49.

Practice
Enacts Policy ◄◄◄◄ 8

If models reflect and affect policy, specific programming decisions are even more critical in this regard. This chapter offers illustrations of how the administrator or programmer utilizes program specification to advance goals — and of how less deliberate approaches to programming may defeat fundamental objectives.

To keep the presentation in reasonable focus and related to current social service realities, all of the illustrations are kept in the frame of a network approach to personal social services at the local level, as specified in the previous chapter.

Again, the objective here is to illustrate a way of thinking, not to close out other possible solutions. We do not know how many jurisdictions will establish personal social service networks or the degree of program integration likely to appear if the step is taken.

Access as Service

Access services are part of personal social services. They are essential to such other social services as medical care, employment, education, housing, and income maintenance — as well as to the more specialized and ongoing general social services. As noted earlier, access services include:

1. Information, advice, referral
2. Case advocacy
3. Class advocacy
4. Legal services
5. Complaint machinery

A so-called service network without provision for entry and channeling would obviously not deserve the designation, nor could it function effectively. Yet — for lack of adequate conceptualization and organization — many of the social services leave access to happenstance. The consequences have been documented in a library of studies and tracts; they affect both universal and selective programs:

1. Many agencies keep their caseloads to manageable proportions by avoiding publicity and serving only those who reach them through word of mouth or other limited devices.
2. Since access requires mobility, information, and initiative, some agency services are reserved for the more fortunate or "competent" among potential clients.
3. For lack of efficient channeling mechanisms, many people who need help suffer considerable buffeting until they reach a proper source of help, if indeed they ever do.
4. Many citizens never learn about rights, benefits, or entitlements that would ease their lives, enhance their routines, or enrich the development of their children — benefits ranging from social insurance, to educational programs, to vacation resources.
5. Consumers may fail to find adequate means of redress when mistreated, discriminated against, or closed out unjustly by administrative agencies controlling important services, by landlords, or by unscrupulous merchants or salesmen.
6. For lack of a place to turn in a personal emergency, especially a generalized emergency not clearly requiring firefighters, police, or an ambulance, many people suffer irreparable consequences.

These are consumer-related consequences, the most important of all to a social services system that considers itself humane and whose very raison d'être is the meeting of urgent personal, group, or communal need.

From the point of view of agencies and of the public at large, additional consequences must be mentioned:

1. For lack of adequate access machinery and channeling provision,

social services involve tremendous wastage. People in need of advice or service go from place to place, sometimes never getting to the right place, sometimes getting to the right place after inordinate expenditure of "steering time" by personnel in a series of agencies, sometimes getting good service but misusing personnel where more "parsimonious" provision is possible.*

2. Since people in need of services will seek them wherever possible, a social services system without adequate channeling provision tends to provide biased access. Each agency to which a person comes by chance or recommendation to ask for help has a stake in the outcome. Some want more cases; some do not want any; some want particular types of cases. More formal access machinery, although not free of stereotypes and subject to the perceptual and prescriptive biases of the system it serves, is less likely to be tied to the stakes and limited perspectives of given agencies, their characteristic vantage points, and the unique assessment about the superiority of their service modes — which are normal for agencies.

In sum, whether one is concerned with making the system work more humanely and effectively for the user, or more efficiently and parsimoniously in view of communal stakes, a service network requires well-planned and appropriate access machinery. A policy of charity, focused on donors — rather than recipients — and not committed to efficiency, can ignore access. A "participation" strategy that favors encouraging people to "get theirs" by self-organization and confrontation will not want to regularize access, since assisting people to find services and benefits has been found to facilitate organization (as in the welfare rights movement of the late 1960s). Proponents of market strategies may not wish to have standard routes into service systems, since this may constrain competition.

Where access machinery is to be developed as congruent with a network's philosophy and mission, it must command personnel whose com-

---

*Under the principle of parsimony in treatment, the following obtain:
1. The least disruptive intervention is the first treatment of choice.
2. The least separation from family and job will be sought.
3. The least expensive treatment will be used first.
4. The least extensive treatment will be used first.
5. The least trained intervenors will be used first.

  "This means that most people will be cared for in their homes or job settings. Most will be cared for by caretakers and frontline agencies, except for acute emergencies. It means clinical personnel will be more involved in diagnosis and supportive consultation and training. It also implies that we will be using time trials of minimum, low-key interventions first, then picking up failures for more expensive and intensive forms of care." See William G. Hollister and Quentin Rae-Grant, "The Principles of Parsimony in Mental Health Center Operations," as abstracted in *American Journal of Orthopsychiatry*, 40, 2 (March 1970), 277.

mitment is to the effectiveness of case channeling into and within the network and whose professional discipline leaves them unbiased as to the direction of channeling: all services should have equal chances of receiving referrals, the determinant being the client's situation and needs, professional knowledge, and community policy.

Policy Questions for Access Services

A decision to provide universal services and to encourage and facilitate utilization — rather than to shame users and hide resources (the poor-law strategy) — calls for a general-purpose entry point to the network as well as for information and referral competence at the doorways of many organizations and institutions to which citizens might turn. The universalism policy, oriented to seeing user as citizen, focuses on efficiency and effectiveness in organization of the network, since it assumes the right to information and to service.

One attractive way to achieve the desired imagery and other qualities, but not at all offered as the only way, is through establishment of what I would call a *neighborhood information center*. Objections to this approach are described subsequently, as are some alternative approaches. The term "neighborhood information center" is here employed for the all-purpose entry point to the total human services system, whether education, housing, public assistance, recreation, social insurance, consumer guidance, homemakers, or any other specific field. The center would have to be a general, unbiased, easily accessible, visible, unstigmatized, universally usable facility. Its basic function would be information, advice, and referral. If it could be set up so as to lead to public social utilities as well as case services, universal services as well as selective services, public services as well as voluntary, fee-charging agencies as well as free ones, sectarian programs as well as nonsectarian, agencies involving more or less authority and control, agencies suggesting client capacity as well as problem — the information center would be truly accessible to citizens and would affect their access to services.

While there are circumstances under which such information centers could not be decentralized or need not be (sparsely settled countryside; rich suburbia, in which all potential users can drive to a shopping center or a town center; areas of low-volume demand), under normal circumstances accessibility would be enhanced by decentralization to the immediate neighborhood: "within pram-pushing distance" or "where people get off the bus and shop" or "the most accessible point in every natural community of 50,000 to 100,000" or "in or near the post office or public library." Depending on local factors and the imagery sought, information centers might be freestanding or based in town halls, libraries, shopping centers, settlement houses, or other locations.

If the goal is to serve people, not to regiment them, a center, of course, is a *resource,* not a *requirement* when seen from the citizen's perspective. He is and must remain free to avoid channels and go directly to any agency or program that seems right to him, and that agency must be equipped for considerate response, service, or referral. Anything less converts the network into a constraint upon freedom.

Neighborhood information centers and their equivalents would not eliminate the need for adequate doorway services — information, screening, and steering — in all agencies to which many people come of choice or necessity. The latter category would include health services, income maintenance programs, police stations, and libraries. Nor would such universal information centers preclude the development of specialized centers that have "natural" constituencies, centers whose existence would improve access for specific groups. The targets of more specialized centers might be conceptualized along several dimensions, the classification's validity and the center's specificity varying with time and place. Such centers, for example, might include those specializing in ensuring access for old people, young drug users, veterans. Because certain groups and geographic areas face particularly difficult access problems, there has also been a tendency in recent years to make information, advice, referral, and case advocacy a major component of multiservice neighborhood centers.

The creation of access agencies (information centers or "hot lines") or access functions (doorway services in many agencies) does not, of course, relieve any given service organization of the responsibility to enhance the accessibility of its own specialized offerings. This may involve considerations and activities as diverse as publicity, public education, office location, office furnishings, provision of child care arrangements for mothers who bring children with them, office hours, and the training of doorway personnel.

Even the specialized neighborhood information center might take one of several forms. Local social service programmers will find it necessary, within this framework, to make locally appropriate policy and administrative decisions about the specific delimitation of functions for each neighborhood information center. This, too, represents a protection for diversity and freedom. Each choice involves a price, the sharpening of public image and agency response, community feeling about the service, client view of himself. Each possibility has validity, but all are not compatible, and local choices are inevitable.

We have noted elsewhere, for example, that some elements are basic in any information and referral office, whereas some are optional —

varying with resources, other community provision, policy thrust, and the readiness to accept a given public image. This imagery, in turn, apparently affects who comes to the service and how agencies upon which the service calls respond to it.[1]

The neighborhood information center as presented thus far would be a special unit within a personal social services network assigned a doorway mission for all human services.

Essential Elements in a Neighborhood Information Center Program

1. To provide simple information, such as where something is located or how to get there
2. To provide information about more complex matters, such as the provisions of a law or an agency's function
3. To clarify the significance of a statute or of provision for a specific person (one aspect of the advice function)
4. To give advice on how to proceed — not only clarifying the possible but suggesting a course of action
5. To steer the inquirer to an agency or service able to help, merely telling him what and where the service is but doing nothing to help him get there
6. To refer the inquirer to the right agency, going beyond steering to arrange for an appointment, or to send a referral letter or summary, facilitating the transition from inquiry to service
7. To provide a supporting, friendly relationship for those people whose continued welfare requires an occasional dropping in for a friendly chat, often supplemented by information and advice
8. To help the inquirer with the contact — or to make it for him. (Sometimes the inquirer is helped to make the contact with a telephone referral or a letter. At other times the action required involves a letter of inquiry from the information service itself or an attempt to achieve a solution by mail.)

Optional Elements in a Neighborhood Information Center Program

1. To go beyond the presenting problem in helping people. (In general, social work services stress the need to see beyond the presenting request and to offer information, advice, referral, or help related to the real problem.)
2. To carry out formal diagnostic study
3. To carry out continuing counseling and treatment
4. To follow through (aggressively if necessary) until the inquirer has his needs or his rights recognized (case-oriented advocacy)

5. To seek program and policy changes in agencies (class advocacy)
6. To conduct general community education, where inquiries reveal widespread need for information
7. To recruit potential clients (outreach)
8. To monitor and report one's experience with human need and public provision. (A well-functioning information and advice service is, indeed, a window on the man in the street.)
9. To facilitate the self-organization of people with common problems. (The intent may be sociotherapeutic, group education, institutional change, or political action.)

The packaging of elements for the program of a given access service will derive partly from an estimate of the capacities of other local services already operating and partly from an estimate of the user population and the help it needs (are most of the people who will want service basically self-steering, able to use information, or are they people who need sustained support?). But it will also reflect the planners' sense of the local culture and the need to protect privacy, demonstrate outreach and concern, involve users as volunteers or policymakers for the center, employ the access service as a vehicle for service reform or expansion, and initiate social action.

Each decision along these lines involves a price. Diagnostic acuity in the information service may frighten away potential users who want requests taken literally. A lack of outreach may signify no interest to other potential users. One must set priorities among potential local service consumers. One must estimate the burden of community need in making such decisions or, perhaps even better, find ways for potential consumers to help shape the definitions.

The definition of function thus carries wide implications. This is illustrated even more sharply with reference to whether an information center should carry out case and class advocacy or how such activities are to be provided otherwise in a network that assumes that social service access is a right that may sometimes need defending.

Case and Class Advocacy in the Access System

Case advocacy is an essential component in dealing with particularly deprived people who cannot themselves manage to cope with service networks, even if given information and steering. As defined in the above listing, it is quite compatible with an information-advice-referral service. Information center staff need to be equipped to know whether their suggestions work out and their referrals "take." If not, there must be provision for persistent follow-through with the service and follow-up with the client so that rights are implemented and needs met. A substantial literature on the philosophy, technique, and ethics of advocacy of this kind is developing among helping personnel, particularly in social work.[2]

Sometimes community circumstances and agency structures may result in removing case advocacy from the neighborhood information center and placing it in other case services, such as child welfare units or family counseling agencies. Sometimes the function is discharged in both settings. The issue is, which agency has the capacity and freedom for persistent follow-through, the more competent and responsible staff, and a community image that will bring in the clientele needing the service. And, which agency will be able to absorb advocacy without changing in an undesirable way or giving up entirely other essential functions?

The location and implementation of another essential function, class (policy) advocacy, poses an even more difficult and controversial question. At times an information center, multiservice center, or specialized agency learns that its referrals never "take." The service that should be available, the benefit that should be paid, does not materialize or is inadequate to its purpose. When this happens, some combination of the following is required: changes in laws, revised budgets, new procedures or adjustments in their application to the circumstances of some categories of individuals, reassignment of personnel, and so on. Under these conditions, case advocacy may help a given person, sometimes. Or it may be blocked by policy and provision. In either case, class advocacy promises larger payoff. Its techniques range from court challenges to laws and practices, to petition writing and traditional efforts to meet with responsible officials and "negotiate" changes in policy and provision, to the more recent forms of "confrontation."

Obviously, this is one field in which choices must be made deliberately. Some class advocacy focuses on policy, some on program; some is oriented largely to aiding its immediate clientele, some to larger social objectives. Therefore, such advocacy sometimes considers it legitimate and appropriate to recruit clients to serve broader objectives than the solution of such clients' immediate case needs. How one (or how an organization) regards this depends on the decisions made about goal priorities. Such issues of function and priority are not easily ignored in the structuring of neighborhood information centers (or, for that matter, multiservice centers or any other social services that are oriented to redressing inequality, unfairness, and lack of access as experienced by minority and other deprived consumers).

Where class advocacy is not encompassed within the program of the neighborhood information center or multiservice center, it is generally assigned to either or both of two interrelated outlets: (a) a community organization agency that undertakes social action and class advocacy (sometimes as a program component of a multiservice center or local antipoverty agency); (b) a legal services agency.

Legal services, thus, are an important element in the community access system. In the past, when privately funded, such services pursued class actions in a few major policy fields (for example, the work of the NAACP on segregation). Individual situations were not served per se, except where individuals could afford their own lawyers. Legal aid and similar services were employed largely to help poor defendants in criminal cases.

Since the advent of neighborhood legal services under the U.S. antipoverty program, which, in turn, inspired a number of related efforts, legal services have been available to poor individuals on a variety of civil matters, ranging from matrimonial actions to utilization of administrative appeals machinery and court process in relation to public assistance, housing, school suspensions, and so on. The result has been both a considerable strengthening of case advocacy and an expansion of class advocacy. Inevitably, major victories in court or before public boards are translatable into new rights for many additional clients. To illustrate, we cite decisions in public welfare on residence laws and "man in the house" rules, or juvenile court decisions related to due process and proof. More recently, new law has been made with reference to the "right to treatment" for institutionalized patients.

Middle- and upper-class individuals are able, themselves, to afford and to introduce legal talent where case and class actions are sought. For the poor, it is now widely affirmed, there should be available free or income-scaled neighborhood legal services. Some major programs in community action and consumer protection employ staff counsel in such roles. Experience with British Citizens' Advice Bureaus and U.S. local social services suggests that, although neighborhood information centers can and must refer to neighborhood legal services, and although both are absolutely essential to the implementation of access, a strong case can be made for the separation of the two (however, there are differences of opinion about this). They involve different professional disciplines, different public imagery and acceptance, and different responsiveness by the service agencies that are their objects. A complete merger of information and advocacy may not in most contexts provide maximum access.

In sum, Cumming's[3] finding for Syracuse may be generalized: the differential flow of clients to various services probably reflects agency characteristics and the social system more than it does client troubles. Nonetheless, there is a movement from gatekeepers — people regulating access — to support and control services. Agencies tend to be either professionals' agencies (screening to produce a population suitable for the treatment in which the agency specializes and wishes to specialize) or clients' agencies (responsive to client troubles). An effective access system may rationalize the client flow if such is the community policy, may serve to increase agency responsiveness to client needs or lead to the creation of more services responsive to client troubles, and may even promote planning and the more efficient employment of scarce resources. All of this is more likely to occur if the general policy is one of universalism and if the social service system includes a reasonable range of both public and social utilities and case services.

None of this solves the service quantity problem in the many jurisdictions in which social services are in short supply. Indeed, it often seemed in the late 1970s as though access programs were being expanded as substitutes for the ongoing help needed! However, active work in an information center does make it more difficult for agencies to solve shortages by making access difficult; it may improve the estimates of need; and it avoids solution of shortages by reserving services for those personally capable of achieving access without help. To summarize, the access function in a social service network is a critical factor in institutionalizing rights.

The Case Against a Neighborhood Information Center

The above scenario may be inaccurate or may be only one of several possibilities. This at least is suggested by the role of the British Citizens' Advice Bureaus following the creation of an integrated personal social services system in which they had no formal part. The CAB has become a place for consumer information, advice, and complaints; its referrals are to all social services (human services), and it is not a major doorway to the personal social services per se. Those people in need of personal social services go directly, or are referred by one of many possible sources, to the local personal social services office. They are seen by an intake social worker. If the personal social service unit will not undertake the requested or needed service, it may make any type of referral needed.

In the British experience, the local personal social service office outlet is the service core of that network (which also does include shelter, detention, day treatment, senior centers, specialized residential and nonresidential units, homemakers, staff for chore services, etc.). The functions of the local office include information, advice, and referral, but *also* ongoing counseling, case integration, delivery of concrete aid, and ensuring access to certain group services, specialists, or social utilities. In other words, the office is more specialized than the neighborhood information center, offers ongoing help, carries the imagery and structure for *case* services, and is something like a "family practice center" in medicine — a social "health maintenance organization."

By contrast, the neighborhood information center as described earlier offers all citizens information, advice, referral, advocacy, outreach — without being identified as part of any particular ongoing service. A personal social services office, as the hub of its own network, sees its major responsibilities as including case integration, case accountability for specified cases and situations, and ongoing direct help, as determined by community policy.

In short, these are two alternative models, each carrying a different overall view of human services, their likelihood of integration, and the relationship of a personal social services network to other service systems.

Decisions About Case Integration

Here we look a bit more closely, if briefly, at another personal social service network task, case integration, to suggest other policy issues facing planners and programmers. The various professional role aspects of the topic are not explored.

Complex human problems and the multiplicity of needs in an urban-industrial society demand a multiplicity of specialized, or at least separated, social services. Where individuals or families are in considerable difficulty, help to them inevitably involves the mutual reinforcement and additive effects of services from a number of agencies and programs. Some of these services must be smoothly meshed in a sequential order, lest the intervention effects at any given stage be wiped out: from acute hospital for the mentally ill, to the longer-term hospital, to community day group, to individual aftercare help, and so on. Some of the services are simultaneous, and their meshing is essential if they are to be mutually supportive rather than cancel one another out: the father's attendance at the veterans' psychiatric clinic, the family contacts with the public assistance worker, the mother-child visits to the school social workers, and the older brother's supervision by a court probation officer.

The segmentation of the social services is in fact a reflection of legitimate specialization. In part, too, it reflects the diverse motives that created an undifferentiated and punitive "poor law" for those unable to cope without help with society's daily requirements, and then allowed subgroups to be differentiated out from the mass as changing social evaluations and deepening knowledge invalidated the earlier moral judgments. Simultaneously with the latter process, competent — or at least charitable — help was specified. Fragmentation of services is also, of course, a reflection of tendencies both among professions and among bureaucratic organizations to retain and strengthen their own identities and to protect themselves by developing unique and loyal constituencies.

There is utility and validity in program specialization, relating as it does to the protection and development of uniqueness and expertise. But there is also in it a reflection of needs and motives not necessarily or solely related to the promotion of service goals and meeting of needs. The result, known wherever social services exist, is a pattern of service fragmentation, gaps, and failure to interrelate simultaneous and sequential service efforts for optimum effect. Many service failures, much wastage, and considerable client disillusionment grow out of these facts.

Thus, a personal service network must seek to provide for case integration, defined here as the sequential and simultaneous meshing of interventions directed toward a given client or user (individual, couple, family, group). Case integration is distinguishable from, although obviously related to, program and policy coordination as between agencies or among groups of agencies, and from agency-level service integration. The former focuses on the consumer of services. The latter relates to policy, provision, procedure, and agency interrelationships in terms of general principles and overall planning.

How, then, is the case integration function to be discharged in the personal social services network? To a small degree, the staff of the neighborhood information center, where one exists, may be concerned with such matters, referring people with complex needs to a variety of places and managing the interconnections. However, most people given referrals or information at an information center are able to manage the next steps on their own: they use the information, apply for the social utility, and pursue the benefit. Those with larger and more complex problems or less personal capacity require more help.

The transition, then, is to the case service category — helping services that are individualized by diagnosis or case evaluation. Here one must ask about possible provision for case integration. Social service programmers have been seeking structural provision for case accountability, a fixing of clear professional responsibility to serve or guide a client, even if in the process there is also need for a specialist's assistance. There is widespread interest in the suggestion that the core case service in the personal social service field be a generalist social work service, which would have the same relationship to the more specialized social services as does the general medical practitioner (GP) to the remainder of medical practice.[4] People who need individualized help, as contrasted with social utilities, would come to or be referred to such a personal social work service.

The prototype is the general medical practitioner, the family doctor (with full recognition that the continuance of this role in the United States required its definition as a specialty, guarded by an Academy of Family Practice!). In the instance of the personal social service local office, the general practice would inevitably be team or group practice. Medicine, too, is moving in such a direction in the United States. The pattern is now being established in the United Kingdom.

It is assumed that a generalist would be prepared to employ both individualized and small-group methods in work with clients. He/she would be prepared to span several of the fields of practice that are central to the personal social services (family and child welfare, aging, youth), at least at the level of basic counseling and assistance. This would not preclude having on the team staff members specialized in fields where technical expertise or special knowledge or skills were required. While the latter need to be "discovered," not proclaimed, the possibilities include: intensive work with young children, adoption law and procedure, and the availability of nursing home and adult home facilities.

The Basis for a Network

State-level organization patterns have been described. What are the available local service systems, if any, out of which a personal social service network might emerge, a network with capacity for case integration, direct services, and some of the other functions already described? These become immediate questions for social service programmers. Having clarified the state statutory, regulative, and administrative possibilities and constraints, they might emerge with the following "candidate" systems:

1. Local public welfare departments, now often called local social service departments, as they shed public assistance eligibility functions and are free to reconstruct themselves as several categorical subsystems or as integrated personal social service agencies.[5]
2. Voluntary family agencies and settlement houses, under contract with public departments and held to specific performance requirements (For family agencies, this must involve a major shift in functions; for settlements that are multifunction agencies, it requires creating a subunit for the role; for both it must mean acceptance of more public guidance of voluntarism.)
3. Local community action (antipoverty) service units or units created for the express purpose by antipoverty neighborhood corporations (This would require clear separation of social action and class advocacy from the service function, as well as more professionalism and a

greater readiness to employ and utilize professional personnel than
has characterized most such groups; but it would increase selectivity
and community variability.)

4. Local community development, community school, neighborhood re-
    newal, or community mental health agencies. (Each of these suffers
    major disabilities because, in total, the units do not add up to com-
    munity coverage, have other primary missions, and may not be able
    to attract all users needing the service because of existing imagery.
    But such an approach does integrate personal social services with
    other institutions — an investment perspective.)

The analysis in earlier chapters along several policy-relevant dimensions and the values I have highlighted throughout lead me to the following views. Other observers offer different conclusions.

· There is a case for a universal strategy, since the need for personal
    social services reaches all social classes and groups, and univer-
    salism promises a qualitatively better service network for all.
· A personal social service network must be characterized by geographic
    coverage and accountability; it requires coordination with other
    human service systems; otherwise its mission will not be fulfilled.
· It therefore is essential that the personal social service network be a
    statutory (publicly operated) system. However, while local outlets
    and baseline services (which need specification) should be statutory,
    there is a strong case on the U.S. scene for tapping available exper-
    tise, encouraging pluralism and diversity, and avoiding monoliths by
    continued contracting with voluntary agencies and through third-
    party payments to proprietary vendors. This can be accomplished if
    the public system has strong planning, administrative, and profes-
    sional capacity and is held accountable for the network output.
· A reconstructed state and local (public welfare) public social services
    system is the core upon which a personal social services network
    may be constructed. Title XX of the Social Security Act is the major
    funding component. Also to be considered, depending upon local
    circumstances and federal developments, are programs funded
    under the Older Americans Act; federal and state community mental
    health programs (except for their psychiatric services); federal and
    state-funded child welfare programs (including Title IV-B of the So-
    cial Security Act); child abuse and neglect programs; social services
    funded federally under community action, Law Enforcement Assis-
    tance Administration, employment, community development, run-
    away youth services, and so forth — insofar as the real mandate is

for personal social services.* While political, interest-group, and regulatory obstacles are recognized, current experience suggests that they are not prohibitive. Regulations and guidelines from diverse programs create problems and cannot be ignored, but they are not overwhelming obstacles to determined local and state leadership.

For those not prepared for so large a step, we turn to a periodically favored alternative model, the multiservice center.

Storefronts and Multiservice Centers

The interplay of policy with administrative strategy (in this instance the conception of the functional requirements of a local social service network) are well illustrated in a discussion of a far more modest subject than just how or where a personal social services network might be developed. Here we ask whether or how storefronts and multiservice centers should be planned as part of the network. Periodically, storefronts and multiservice centers enjoy popularity with the media, federal funding agencies, and the professional journals — all of which see them as an essential component of decentralization of services.

The development of such facilities should be seen in the context of a widespread revolt against prevailing patterns of social service organization, as the failures of traditional patterns to facilitate access and ensure delivery of services to all population elements and all parts of the city became apparent. Throughout the 1940s and 1950s, social service organizations had tended to centralize and their delivery modes had been increasingly standardized. Then, in reaction, came a move that stressed diversity, local policy flexibility or control, indigenous staff, informality, easy access, one-stop service, a mixture of service receipt and one's own involvement in the rendering and changing of services. Storefronts and multiservice centers became major vehicles during the 1960s. New variations on them were being launched or proposed even late in the 1970s!

Storefronts and multiservice centers are and can be many things, and an assessment of their potential and desirability in a social service network must depend upon what they are designed to be and become in a given place at a specific time. There is danger, as Edward O'Donnell has noted, that such centers will become an "organizational Twiggy," temporarily capturing the public imagination and causing disregard of the

*This type of listing is inevitably soon outdated. The reader will want to consider as well any recent congressional or Administration action.

merits of other useful models and long-term experience. On the other hand, storefronts and multiservice centers can be shaped to fill specific gaps and to play needed roles in a network in which other components are strengthened and utilized.[6]

The storefront's major merits are informality and locale. If the goal is to localize or decentralize (the former implying central control and the latter some decentralization of policy or programming authority), there is need for a comfortable and convenient outlet. Poverty areas and racial ghettos have many empty, visible, convenient stores. Neighborhood information centers, centers offering generalist social work services or such specialized programs as job placement are easily set up in these locations because they require little more than desks, files, phones, typewriters, and simple partitions. Especially if indigenous personnel are to be employed, a storefront location may represent convenience and comfort.

There is, however, a negative argument that cannot be completely ignored — with the decision perhaps ultimately resting with local people. There are those who resent the dreary and shabby storefront, even if it is cleaned up, reasonably furnished, and supplied with a coffee urn and milk bar for the convenience of parents and children in the waiting room. Why, they ask, should facilities not be better than the level prevailing in the poverty area? Why poor surroundings for deprived people? Why not good buildings, more conventional offices, more privacy? There is obviously need for a trade-off and balancing point, reflecting prevailing preferences: familiarity versus improvement, convenience versus equality.

But *function* is more important than the type of housing for the office. Storefronts may be specialized or multipurpose, information centers or places to organize social action. They are part of the decentralization strategy. The decision to use or not use them is independent of planning with reference to multiservice centers, despite the constant joining of the two in discussion and analysis. The question remains: where *does* the multiservice center fit in relation to the series of functions that belong in the personal social services network?

First, the multiservice center is often a place where several networks meet for service delivery: visiting nursing, employment placement, family counseling, housing complaints, neighborhood legal services, or public assistance intake. The center may play this role whether in a neighborhood storefront or a downtown office building, but the more recent linking of storefronts and multiservice centers is motivated by the conviction that a multiplicity of social services and other communal functions should be joined for one-stop convenience in the immediate neighborhood.

Its more expansive proponents see the multiservice center as a neighborhood base that combines information–advice–referral–case advocacy with decentralized service outlets for a variety of voluntary and public social services — meaning by the latter both personal social services in our sense and services belonging to other human services systems. The argument is that this kind of service organization increases access and facilitates case integration. (The latter is referred to generally as coordination, but the function intended is case integration, in our sense, or program integration.) Seldom identifying the general practice social service role per se, these proponents tend to see the information–advice–referral personnel (often local case aides) serving as "social service" or "urban" brokers and as case advocates, helping disadvantaged people (to use their language) "to negotiate the complex bureaucratic systems that deny them service." While not formalized or professionally specified, there is some implicit assumption that the broker is a case integrator. He is seen as offering expertise and advice about services, but not as a skilled personal counselor. For the latter type of help, one uses a family service agency, adult psychiatric clinic, and so on.

Conceptually, then, the multiservice center may be defined as an attempt to create a relatively broad human services network in one location. It would be a complete one-step social services "department store," a shopping center in which one has a guide (an urban broker or case aide). All the functions deemed essential are provided, and there is convenience of location — whether the poverty area storefront, the downtown office building, or office space in a commercial shopping center complex. This ideal model is logical and attractive. Its rarity as an operating entity in the world of daily service operations must be seen as a caution sign for social service programmers. Are the limitations that are widely identifiable indigenous to the model or idiosyncratic to the local circumstance? One tends on the basis of available research, consultant reports, and observations to suspect the former; but the case is not closed.[7]

Multiservice centers are seldom equal to the promise implied in the name. For example, they generally do not provide for the critical generalist social work practitioner coverage, which is the anchor point for case services. This is no occasion for surprise: the "first contact" role is often relegated in multiservice centers to information and referral personnel, who are not equipped for ongoing counseling. Or the general practice task may be assigned to family service agency personnel, who are more · specialized casework therapists and do not ordinarily assume the full general practitioner responsibility.

Nor would one wish information-referral services to carry the imagery of or demand the professional qualifications and control for, personal social practice. Most users of information-referral services are likely to be in need of facts about rights and entitlements (consumer rights, social security benefits, and so on), to be in need of referrals to or application forms for public social utilities (day care, homemakers, community centers, and

so on), or to require services in other than personal social service programs (housing, income maintenance, employment, and so on). This
would not preclude the sharing by information-referral services and
others of building space or the joint participation in a multiservice center if
circumstances permitted the projection of an image encouraging broad
usage, even by people who did not consider themselves as having personal "problems."

Multiservice centers also have difficulty in becoming true local outlets
for many specialized human services, such as job placement, housing
application processing, well-baby clinics. Any such effort confronts
counterpressures quite familiar to students of organizational dynamics. A
health department may agree to place a well-baby clinic in a multiservice
center, but in fact soon finds that it cannot provide the necessary
specialized equipment and personnel for several such centers, even
though the pledge may be fulfilled for a major "demonstration" project.
The usual substitute arrangement is a public health nurse, available at
specified times each week, who renders simple services and channels
most users to the health department or hospital clinics.

Employment and housing offices respond similarly: they find that they
cannot manage either the needed specialized personnel or the complete
duplication of job or housing files and coordination mechanisms that are
indispensable if the same core services, utilizing the same resources, are
delivered at two locations. The solution is usually the assignment of a
partial service outpost — rendering what is simple service (usually referral and information) and routing the inquirer to the main office for the core
service.

When this occurs, the multiservice center has become an information–advice–referral–case advocacy location at the doorway of several of
the human services, whose services are strengthened by the presence of
specialized liaison personnel from a number of agencies whose services
are in high demand. The latter are to be seen largely as enhancing the
information center function — their expertise and contacts presumably
ensuring more accurate advice and more potent referrals.

The obstacles to delivering an agency's full service through multiservice centers under shared administrative authority or under new local
auspices go well beyond the problem of setting up a complete service
requiring specialized personnel and equipment. One could invent solutions to such difficulties. Also operating is an organizational-political tendency that must be recognized. Agencies receive public support, staff,
equipment, and authority as they become visible and develop consumer,
staff, and political constituencies. Whether correctly assessing the importance of the phenomenon or not, most departments consider themselves better off if they have visible, local outlets that are clearly identifi-

able, employ significant numbers of people, and are valued by citizens. Therefore, when asked to sacrifice some of their visibility and to share a facility under *other* auspices, they are hesitant and may take half measures. Or, if their units remain in multiservice centers, they often tend to become independent enclaves.[8]

Nor do multiservice centers guarantee the program coordination and case integration that is always part of their rationale. Their doorway personnel undertake a measure of information–advice–referral–case advocacy. But, without a general practice unit or a tradition of case accountability in any of their subunits, they do not typically offer the service to the average run of cases. The organization offering initial auspices and housing for the center tends to conceptualize the unit as enriching its own offerings and supplementing its own coverage (antipoverty, health, mental health, housing, employment), not as meeting all of the neighborhood's social service needs. Nor does the governing or administrative structure of such units allow for remedying the gap once it is acknowledged.[9]

Most multiservice centers seem to manage to implement a *few* fully specialized services, however, reflecting the center's auspices, special local needs, and unique motivations. A number may, for example, conduct youth training or employment programs. Some house very effective and complete neighborhood legal services. Others offer consumer counseling that is comprehensive and of high order. Many carry out child care and Head Start program mandates. When the job load becomes heavy, they act as does any agency: they become "legalistic" and find ways to limit their caseloads.

The typical multiservice center, then, is not really the comprehensive, one-stop, department store for all the human services that is often discussed. It is, rather, a conveniently located facility (which may be anything from a neighborhood storefront to an elaborate central building) that combines the access function with a limited number of specialized services from among several systems.

All this is stated by way of description, not criticism. Multiservice centers, set up as described, may be very useful. They currently suffer because the interdepartmental or interagency arrangements that must accompany their establishment do not ordinarily include sufficient surrender of sovereignty or guarantee of power to provide for an administrator or board capable on a day-to-day basis of weaving even the limited components into an operating network. For the most part their subunits report to different organizations and are supported and evaluated by different boards. The parent agencies may have different views of clientele and their needs, and even independent agenda for the multiservice centers. This should not be expected to change significantly unless there is real insistence on development of a local delivery network — with the corresponding sacrifice of some sovereignty. Given such a development, four possibilities emerge: the multiservice center as a human services outlet; the local personal social service office; the multiservice center as an access facility; the multiservice center as a network for one categorical service or problem group. Each of these alternatives has been previously introduced.

1. First, state-level umbrella *human service agencies* provide a base for successful local multiservice center operation where the line of administrative control does not run from a functionally specialized state unit within the human services system (community mental health, child welfare, employment, etc.) to a local staff component of a multiservice center. As experience in Florida in the late 1970s seemed to suggest, multiservice operations create opportunity for true integration only where the local administrator has effective control of the several human service staffs whose work is to be integrated in the district. (Florida had not yet attempted to organize for integrated delivery to the case.)

None of this fully settles the delivery question for the human services multiservice center. Is the intent to create convenience of *place* (several human services in one building and sharing an information clerk) or integrated *operations*? If the latter, which human services can so function together and which components really do belong back at the home base (diagnostic equipment? job banks? housing location inventories? day treatment services? remedial reading?)? Despite long experience and new experiments, the cumulative multiservice research and monitoring offer no firm guidelines.

2. An alternative possibility sees the local *personal social services* center, part of an identifiable personal social services network, as a multiservice center or storefront. To create an integrated generalist team that brings together several categorical personal social services (aged, child welfare, family services, youth services, mental hospital aftercare, day treatment for certain handicapped, etc.) is an enormous task. There is some hope for integration, given the centrality of Title XX funding, even though there are categorical counterpressures and traditions. True, the multiservice center is a delivery mode that could be employed by any one of the human services. However, the health, income maintenance, and educational systems by now have quite standardized delivery modes. It is the employment and personal social services systems that need most to improve their performance. Each might experiment with its own multiservice forms, and there might be collaborative efforts as well, particularly insofar as employment and training efforts targeted by legislative mandate at the poor and long-term unemployed require personal social service supports.

3. A third option is to return to the *neighborhood information center* model as discussed previously. It would be freestanding, serving all human service systems, and it would emphasize *access* — information, advice, referral, case advocacy, and related educational and mutual aid efforts. It thus would be multiservice and could function well in a storefront location to ensure easy availability and participation.

4. Some experiences with drug control programs, rehabilitation, and work with the retarded suggest another possibility: the multiservice center that offers all network *elements related to one problem or group.* Here the motivation, power, and conceptual clarity necessary for a network in one location may be brought together. For the community, it would mean a continuation of the confusing, overlapping, and fragmented multiplicity of categorical programs. But for some groups of clients it could ensure a rational delivery system.

Thus, the multiservice center is probably, as O'Donnell states, a Twiggy — but it has its possibilities. A community needs service *networks,* providing for all network function, and multiservice centers can contribute if well conceptualized.

We have yet to turn to the question of user participation in policy and service delivery in such centers or elsewhere within service networks, and to the related matter of the wedding of direct service with social protest and social action, a pattern that expands from time to time and then declines again.

Direct Service and Social Action

To begin with the latter, the issue has an interesting recent history, although there have been earlier and in some ways similar developments in American social work at several points over the past one hundred years.

In the early and mid-1960s social workers and aides working in local antidelinquency and antipoverty neighborhood service centers,[10] imbued with an accountable ideology of reaching out,[11] pioneered in what we now refer to as case advocacy. Where agencies did not deliver the announced or legally prescribed services, these new-style workers followed through. Where clients could not themselves cope with the complexity of procedures and requirements standing between them and the help needed, the social workers or aides went along and assisted whenever necessary. Later, if it appeared that unfair agency practice, questionable rules, or arbitrary judgment deprived needy citizens, these social workers or aides teamed up with the new and emerging neighborhood legal services to challenge decisions before appeal boards and in the courts. Given the needs of the groups served and the program focus of the day, these actions tended to select for their targets public welfare departments, housing authorities, and school boards.

The action to this point, it should be noted, was oriented to serving the individual client. One went from application, to advocacy, to legal action because of the obstacles discovered en route.

The escalation from these measures to class actions in the legal sense, and to social action generally, was natural and probably inevitable. Follow-up with an agency, one case at a time, is time consuming and frustrating. One might achieve some positive results for the given case, while knowing that there were hundreds of others like it. Why not change the policies or administrative practices affecting everybody? Why not amend the laws that bind the hands of agency personnel? Why not reform staff practices? Shared responses of this kind, affecting the dedicated staffs of these new programs, led to a buildup of class action cases through the legal services — cases that sought rulings affecting many people by showing procedures, requirements, and provision to be inequitable and unconstitutional.

At the same time, the various outlets for social action were pursued to obtain better legislation relating to public assistance, housing, health, and schools. Where the issue was not the statute but procedure, administration, professional practice, or budget levels, these became the targets. The methods eventually ranged from delegations to officials, petitions, letter writing, and lobbying, to sit-ins, mass demonstrations, rent strikes, and public confrontations, to office vandalism and destruction of facilities.[12]

We have described this as a development growing out of experience in case advocacy and commitment to serve people in need. In one sense, from the perspective of the direct-service practitioner, it was. In another sense there is a broader explanation: antidelinquency and antipoverty programs of the mid-1960s began with what are essentially *service* strategies, even though they carried out innovations within such strategies. Basically, their goal was to offer training, access, and motivation as a way to remove inequality that blocked opportunity. True, they placed less emphasis on personal treatment and guidance and more on job training and education than had earlier service programs; nonetheless, their object was the victim and his reform or retooling.[13] Slowly, a number of leaders in local community programs, their academic consultants, and even their governmental and foundation supporters, began to question such strategy, particularly as it affected the black population. Diagnosing the core problem as communal powerlessness, they saw little likelihood that individual help could pay off (or even be well done) except in the context of institutional reform. And the latter was seen as requiring local mobilization of, and political action by, deprived neighborhood people. Here, too, there was a shift from initial interest in social action directed at improving schools, welfare departments, and housing authorities, among other institutions (class actions and policy advocacy) to a demand for either community control of or participation in control of such institutions. "Maximum feasible participation" had become the slogan. Clearly, the major vehicle was now social action merging into political action. If the former sees program change as its objective, the latter seeks political power. Case services become secondary.

We need not trace the evolution of the process through the 1960s and 1970s for present purposes. Poverty areas, ethnic and racial ghettos, Indian reservations, and even prisons became politicized. Social action escalated both in volume and in militancy. While there has been some deescalation in response to the national mood, the experience has been important and the pattern periodically recurs. Thus, what is now confronted by the social services programmer is an organizational question of the relation of direct services to case and class advocacy and to social action in a service network. The issue is a real one, and must be faced even by the most sympathetic advocates of the entire process here described.

Although the evidence is limited and opinions vary, it appears that the client in need of service does better in a neighborhood information center, personal social service office, specialized agency, or multiservice center dedicated to case service, up to the point of case advocacy and — perhaps — policy advocacy, but not undertaking the social action aimed at wider objectives as well. Where the one organizational entity assays both functions, people in need of direct service may be recruited for demonstrations and protests, or as class action "documentation," to the sacrifice of their personal needs.* Social action strategists, given their tasks, cannot avoid converting service needs into social action "ammunition." But to the programmer or administrator whose focus is on service, not on social action, such an approach represents unreasonable exploitation of people who enter an agency seeking immediate personal help. From this perspective, it is not inappropriate for a social action organization to utilize the circumstances, needs, and testimony of those who freely join it in order to attain its objectives, nor is it inappropriate for such an organization to go out to seek evidence and witnesses to advance its goals. What is questioned by those who would protect direct services is only the conversion of a request for personal help to what is publicly

---

*Systematic data are limited. The findings may be different for child advocacy programs, which combine case and class approaches focused on improved service delivery, than for other programs whose political goals are central. See Kahn, Kamerman, and McGowan, *Child Advocacy: A National Baseline Study.*

perceived as a direct-service agency into a recruitment device and use of the applicant, thus diverting or converting the appeal.

The joining of the direct-service task with the social action role within one organizational unit has another undesirable consequence — unless one's commitment is only to political action. Agencies to which neighborhood information centers or multiservice centers refer for benefits and specialized services have found it confusing to receive service requests from an organization at one moment and be picketed by it at another. They have become suspicious when case developments are used against them in administrative hearings and in court actions. The result is that where social action, case and class advocacy, and direct service are combined, a kind of inevitable process operates: it becomes more and more difficult to obtain services for clients through other agencies if such agencies know that they may also be attacked for policy and practice by the referring group.

Grosser sums up as follows:

The separation of services and action functions into discrete organizations is suggested because the two functions are frequently in disharmony . . . and because the dispensers of public agency services are congenitally and organizationally unable to distinguish between the protest and service function when practiced by the same organizations.[14]

If the policy is to ensure service availability, then a local service network planner should probably not attempt to organize social action and social protest through the agencies that channel people into or render direct services. Indeed, despite a continuing debate, most service agencies have apparently arrived at such a decision. However, service agencies as well as specialized units may be able to contain a measure of case and class advocacy.* Nor does a limitation on such development or on broader social action in service agencies necessarily signify a failure to recognize the need for consumers, clients, and citizens to organize in order to affect policy and programs. It may involve taking an alternative approach, giving support to the creation of special social action outlets (community assemblies, administrative boards, advisory committees, client organizations, neighborhood groups). Or it may involve efforts to make social policy and program concerns visible within the general political system. Social provision and social services are important enough to modern society to be at the center of public policy debate and advocacy.

Participation was listed in an earlier section as one of the proposed objectives of social services. Some multiservice centers organize clients

*I am not yet prepared to generalize about the boundary between class (policy) advocacy and social action with broader goals than service system change or reform if they are located in a nonservice agency.

for self-help that falls far short of social action and protest. Included are tutoring, cooperative child care, clean-up campaigns, giving "advice" to staff, implementing a new service. The goal is the strengthening of the individual participants and encouragement of local leadership. Such programs, basically sociotherapeutic, can be contained within direct service agencies without undermining the core function. They do not seem to thrive because deprived population groups find this kind of activity unfamiliar, based as it is essentially on a middle-class self-help ethic. Those who seek more aggressive social action define it as a diversion.

Between the latter self-help and the generalized social action described earlier is a category of activity that may be effectively implemented by a service agency, however difficult it will be to keep on the appropriate "middle" path. Clients and workers may join for service reform and innovation directly related to the client's need and clearly the responsibility of staff responsive to such need. The client is thus not recruited to general reform but engaged in self-help out of personally experienced need.

In addition to all of this, one would not wish to overlook or fail to appreciate the impressive record of many self-initiated self-help groups, often the parents of children with a handicapping condition (mental retardation, cystic fibrosis, muscular dystrophy) but sometimes adults in a common plight, who come together and simultaneously do several things: organize a direct service, advocate better public policy and provision, provide mutual support and aid.[15] These initiatives often do not depend on professional staffs or formal agencies, but they have launched major new programs and service systems.

Who Represents Consumers?

The rationale for neighborhood information centers, localized personal social service offices, multiservice storefronts — and the like — emphasizes *responsiveness* of services to diversity and preferences. However, the concept of network and of formally organized accountability, case integration, and a balance among service components that reflects objectively weighed priorities and needs also assumes analytic *rationality* and *expertise.* The tension between these values is never quite resolved. Title XX of the Social Security Act, the major personal social services funding source, has imposed upon the states a planning process requiring exposure of plans to citizen evaluation (responsiveness), and many of the categorical programs also stress citizen participation. However, the record thus far suggests that the specifications and substantive output may be too small (rationality). Our discussion has offered possibilities to take the planning further.

In short, the social services programmer and policymaker will need to develop a point of view about consumers and their role in shaping or controlling social services, as well as about public officials, administrators, and professionals in their appropriate roles. Some of the questions are introduced here. The discussion should be read in connection with the earlier coverage of participatory administration but goes a bit further since service delivery options have now been specified.

In the search for program responsiveness and "relevance," there is widespread interest in and support for considerable user-client-citizen involvement in the planning and assessment of social services. Historically, legislative bodies, public officials in the executive branch, and paid staff, in their development of policy, creation of programs, and delivery of services have often displayed shocking lack of sensitivity to the problems, priorities, and realities faced by disadvantaged community members. The latter high-rate utilizers of some services (public assistance, public general medical programs, public psychiatric facilities, courts, and police) often found themselves offered programs in which they were major consumers and the advertised beneficiaries, but that were in no way attuned to their needs. The civil rights and antipoverty "revolutions" of the 1960s and 1970s therefore included, along with their many other elements and a stress on decentralization, some components designed to bring the traditionally disadvantaged consumer into a position to influence policymaking, programming, and service delivery.

To the extent that they are identifiable as serving poverty areas and districts, or disadvantaged ethnic and racial groupings, therefore, neighborhood information centers, multiservice centers, and specialized public or voluntary programs, have introduced "the community" to positions of influence as members of governing boards, policy committees, and advisory committees and as indigenous service volunteers or paid aides. Similar practice has been followed in local antipoverty community corporations and other comprehensive programs that operate or contract for a range of services. The scale is significant but the practice is not nearly as prevalent as professional literature might seem to suggest. Although operational problems are many and conflict among competing local groups considerable, this trend to decentralize power and democratize the advisory, administrative, and policy functions is in the spirit of the social service network and its assigned mission in the sense of our discussion. It is consistent with the notion that human services must be responsive to users and subject to their reactions. We would expect individual agencies to be enriched and improved by the process, and there is anecdotal reporting that says that they are. Problems and obstacles are also visible, however, and obviously require attention if the full potential of consumer involvement is to be realized.

The two major identifiable issues may be formulated as follows:

1. What is the boundary among administrator, professional, and consumer prerogatives in agency governance and administration?
2. How should those who are legally responsible resolve competing claims of citizens to represent "communities" served by agencies?

We take as point of departure the premise that there are some services that for reasons of substance or of history operate locally on the basis of policy developed at higher levels, often in statutes, and whose staffs are controlled within structures of bureaucratic organization. Local committees are, then, advisory and focus on program. At the other extreme, there are some social services that allow very substantial local policymaking, as well as programming. Here local bodies may become governing or administrative boards. Where such boards have statutorily defined rights with relation to significant aspects of budget, staffing, or administration, the phrase "community control" may be said to apply. In between are most agencies, allowing some local policy options and some local programming, and capable of sustaining a variety of degrees of consumer involvement, depending on how the power relationships emerge.

Here the two questions posed above appear salient. Professional practice is interlaced with value and preference components, with judgments as well as with scientific knowledge. If there is interest in that consumer involvement which does not undercut service quality, it will become urgent during the next several years to identify the realms in which members of the several professions must be permitted to render professional judgment and to make decisions for which they are accountable. It will also be urgent similarly to delineate when they may be subject to lay boards and their decisions. The difficulty of this question is best appreciated if one considers the types of choices inherent in curriculum development in elementary school, recreation programming in after-school centers, the operating of a residential treatment center, counseling approaches in a family agency, or the choice of substitute care arrangements for an abused child. Contrast the value components among such options with the expertise-value components in an engineer's decisions in planning a bridge or a surgeon's in deciding whether to operate. Because the social services rest on quite limited validated knowledge, have in many instances only vague notions as to their own effectiveness, and rely for implementation on non-, pre-, and paraprofessionals as well as on fully qualified and licensed practitioners, social services find it difficult to make a case against considerable consumer involvement even in the details of programming. Such involvement, while obviously desirable since these will always remain services in which value choices are central, must not be so defined and implemented as to discourage and inhibit the development of knowledge and strengthening of technique. Otherwise, there will be no basis for improvement in practice; there may even be a true decline in quality. The issue is urgent; the solution, long range.

The second question is essentially political: How is a decision to be made about who is the "community" to be represented on local administrative boards or policy or advisory groups? Even in minority communities and deprived areas one finds what Norton Long has called an "ecology of games."[16] In a bid for a voice in local institutions and services, or for what is locally referred to as "a piece of the action" — to express the notion that one is dealing with jobs, business, and power — neighborhood residents find themselves wooed by competing local racial, ethnic, and political groups. Or the group identification and ideologies may be secondary to the personal rivalries of different aspirants for careers of leadership.

Particularly in the past two decades, the results have often been irrational, wasteful, and of little apparent advantage from the point of view of services per se. The positives, too, are readily identified in the sense that new political leadership has emerged, had valuable training, and developed a base for action, while previously discounted segments of the population have made themselves heard or obtained jobs and contracts. In effect, the political issue has had to be settled and the service question has inevitably been secondary. In an effort to open new doors, bring forth new leaders, and redress long-term wrongs, the issue of "who is the community" has often been answered in terms of balance of power in local confrontations, visibility, following, persistence, and similar political criteria. Increasingly and (we would hold) properly, however, the matter is being referred to the political process. Democratic societies, for all their failings, have some experience with the periodic use of the ballot box to choose leaders and to seek the consent of the governed. Where the right to speak for a community is in contention, a society can do no better than appeal to elections and seek to ensure widespread participation in the voting (local, decentralized school boards and community action agencies). Or elected officials may be called upon to designate appointees and to bear the consequences if local citizens consider them to be unrepresentative. Neither process precludes a degree of ethnic or racial or class preference at a given time and place to redress long-term wrongs and bring new voices to the table. Political leaders can and should "risk" such designation. For some purposes a given proportion of places on committees might be reserved for experienced users (welfare mothers, day care parents, public housing tenants, parents of retarded children). For state-level planning and programming, a very broad constituency should be represented. Neighborhood efforts have a variety of requirements. Where current users do not, alone, express the total public interest, they should not be regarded as the sole community spokesmen.

Consumers, in short, can and should be seen and heard in the various roles relating to the planning and administration of social services. Given contention as to who the representatives of such consumers are to be, elective and appointive procedures can be developed that are democratic and rational.

We note yet another type of consumer involvement as the use of categorical vouchers expands. For one thing, consumers with money or vouchers to pay for service may "vote with their feet." Their "control" takes the form of avoiding poor service. Also, given current interest in consumer cooperatives, it would be quite feasible for people with access to categorical vouchers or cash for day care or housing or nursing service to pool their entitlements, create a board of directors, and establish new service agencies under their own control.

Thus far the discussion has concentrated on closed-out citizens, the poor and other disadvantaged minorities, and their involvement in the governance of social services. But our overall thesis is that all social service requires renewal, that the postindustrial society must update its public social utilities and invent many new types of provision. There is therefore a case for a policy of consumer involvement of the several sorts in all kinds of services, whether or not decentralized, whether or not of special importance to the disadvantaged. New vehicles for such involvement, new rights for consumers, and new channels for participation are required wherever social services are rendered.

Renewal

While not the only possible policy, one widely held view — which has been our premise in much of the discussion — is that the purpose of a social services network is the delivery of service. Social control is a by-product. Individual and community protection are secondary tasks. In this sense, then, ultimate judgments about a network's worth should refer to the quantity, quality, significance, and accessibility of both concrete and practical facilities and resources, as well as of less visible but much needed personal guidance and counseling to help those experiencing trouble in coping with growth, relationships, and crises. The range thus includes child care arrangements, home helps, and the provision of furniture and food stamps, vacation facilities, prosthetic devices, telephones for isolated old people, scholarships to cultivate a child's special talents, and train tickets   as well as tutoring, advice, information, counseling, psychotherapy, socialization experiences, group activities, foster homes, adoptive parents, and so on.

Social agencies, like all organizations, are in constant danger of confusing supportive and maintenance activities related to the welfare of the organization with the implementation of the core service. Good access services and adequate provision for coordination and case integration are worthless unless the end product is a needed service, competently delivered, at the appropriate time. And we must also stop periodically to recall that, if social services are to carry the functions of acculturation-socialization-development as well as access, and help-therapy, the specific services designed to implement such functions must be updated from time to time. Moreover, as social policy shifts, the balance between and among such services is in need of constant review and adjustment.

The U.S. social welfare scene underwent a shift in its focus in the 1960s from therapy, guidance, and probation to education, job counseling and training, placement, and role training as prerequisite to the opening of opportunities to those previously closed out by major social institutions. Later, income maintenance and political participation took the center of the stage. Conceptually, this was a shift from emphasizing the use of social services to facilitate adjustment and conformity and strengthen motivation, to a view of services as opening opportunity and mobilizing human resources. Then services became a vehicle for monetary and power redistribution. Yet, despite the shifts in preoccupations of new programs, only the imperceptive, who believed that all poverty was "one lump" and all social problems the product of one cause, could argue for the closing out of guidance, counseling, personal help, foster care — and other "older" programs.

Those who would plan and implement personal social services — whether in a given, local agency or from an administrative base that influences a total network — must ask, then, whether the balance is correct, for their time and its policy thrusts, as between concrete, "hard" services and the guidance-relationship types of help, between access facilitation services and services expecting changes in the individual, between mobilizing people and changing them, between services premised on utilizing people's existing talents and services focused on developing capacities into new patterns, and between services that view users as patients and those that view them as clients. To concern oneself with correctness of the balance among optional modes is to understand that the matter is not one of "either-or" in a social services network with several functions. It is also to imply that within each of the service types there is need for updating to reflect knowledge, skill, user wishes, user characteristics, and institutional change.

Just as social service systems have found it difficult to change in response to need for new balance among service types, so has there been difficulty in updating methods. For, if the thesis is correct that modern urban industrial society has not yet learned to cope institutionally with the social change it has generated, then the need for social invention is considerable. If the argument is valid that among the responses should be a considerable expansion of public social utilities and a much improved pattern of case services — then the challenge for social service planners, programmers, and practitioners is clear. Somehow, there must be assembled in the major areas of need enough professional competence, knowledge, resources, organizational flexibility, user involvement, inspiration, and the motivation to ensure program "take-off." Students of the community and observers of the profession know how difficult this is — even though journals, agency reports, and media publicity give evidence that it does occur from time to time.

Each era must find its own outlets for urgent social invention, and the present day is no exception. The task has become more difficult with increased standardization and formalization — despite some widespread experimentation with community control and other variations on participatory administration. For, on the side of routinization, there are legislation, administrative hierarchy, governmental guidelines and regulations, professionalization, "United Way" fund raising, and all other accouterments of a substantial public and voluntary social welfare development. The very expansion of social services tends to formalize the allocation of resources, the content of programs, delivery, and training. Real social invention comes from outside the system, as "amateurs" develop new programs in response to felt needs; it comes from creative people within the system who periodically break out of tradition, and occasionally from the system itself, if it is a system organized to encourage diversity and change. With reference to the latter, administrative and organizational arrangements to promote diversity and some degree of decentralization or local option, and to admit into the system — at least experimentally — quite unorthodox programs are all essential. The social service history of the past decade indicates that circumstances such as these produced the movements and tendencies that are reflected in many programs today: outreach (bringing services and programs to clients who could not themselves seek or achieve access); advocacy (regarding as necessary those services that champion entitlements and insist on access); self-help (client-initiated service and policy innovation); new practice conceptualizations (the practitioner experiencing system ferment); consumer participation in policy development and service delivery; and service localization.

Careful program evaluation, insofar as it focuses on the adequacy of specific service components (foster parent–child matching; counseling sessions with adolescents) or on total programs (a particular agency dealing with drug abuse cases) may also guide program reinforcement and reform. Experiments with market-type devices (vouchers, cash), which permit potential consumers to "vote with their feet" and to select from among options, will offer clues and encourage some innovations. Consumer cooperatives or community boards may invent services meeting locally experienced need. We may anticipate important innovations in the realm of public social utilities, a much underdeveloped field, as citizens from various backgrounds and economic classes find ways together to seek to enrich the quality of life in their local communities. It is possible, too, to develop funding arrangements and policy participation so as to maximize the proposals for social invention that might come from interest groups as diverse as union members, "women's liberation," and students.

Innovation may be fostered by the acceptance of new social service "hosts." Federal legislation in 1968 permitted unions to bargain for day care as part of fringe-benefit packages, for example. Church groups, cooperative house owners, service clubs, and industries may evolve public social utilities or case services out of the needs of their unique constituencies and reflective of unique cultural milieux. The result could be significant innovation, a departure from the traditions in freestanding social services and a new challenge to weave both adjunctive and freestanding social services into a network. Or the alternative course may be pursued by creating a separate network for the particular constituency: for workers in a union or industry, for residents of a housing community, for members of a church.

A good rate of innovation cannot be expected unless there is a reasonable degree of flexibility about theory as well. Any type of conceptual orthodoxy, whether derived from Freudian psychiatry, behavior-modification psychology, welfare economics, neo-Marxist change strategies, or organizational sociology — to cite only a few possibilities — blocks out some possibilities. Where the formal system may not be able to offer hospitality to innovation based on unorthodox theory, the social service network must locate laboratories for research and development or experimentation, which are hospitable to change and invention. Ideally, many agencies should include among their staffs practitioner-scientists who, in interaction with direct practice, on the one hand, and the social policy thrusts of their time, on the other, can detect the need for and constantly seek new or revised service modalities.

Social services today are part of the standard of living. They are important "property" in a welfare state, urgent amenities in an urbanized civilization. Because program enacts policy and because social services sometimes implement policies whose consequences are unexplored, we have sought to introduce policy issues and to suggest their implications. Because programming determines the quality, availability, and effectiveness of service, we have highlighted approaches to systematic, efficient program development in the context of policy choice. Without exaggerating knowledge or skill, it is useful to note that increased rationality in social service planning and implementation may improve society's "buy" for money that is being spent and allow citizens to choose in the light of their priorities and preferences. These are reasonable preoccupations for a field whose very justification rests in the realms of the social minimum, social justice, quality of life, and the creation of social solidarity.

Notes

1. The listing that follows is derived from and elaborated in Alfred J. Kahn, et al., *Neighborhood Information Centers* (New York: Columbia University School of Social Work, 1966), pp. 112–119.

2. A survey of developments is presented in Alfred J. Kahn, Sheila B. Kamerman, and Brenda C. McGowan, *Child Advocacy: A National Baseline Study* (New York: Columbia University School of Social Work, 1972). Reprinted by U.S. Government Printing Office, 1973. Stock No. 1791-00185.

3. Elaine Cumming, *Systems of Social Regulation* (New York: Atherton, 1968).

4. From *Report of the Committee on Local Authority and Allied Social Services,* Cmnd. 3703 (London: Her Majesty's Stationery Office, 1968); or Alfred J. Kahn, *Studies in Social Policy and Planning* (New York: Russell Sage Foundation, 1969), pp. 278–290.

5. For elaboration, see Alfred J. Kahn and Sheila B. Kamerman, "The Course of Personal Social Services," *Public Welfare,* 36, 3 (Summer 1978), 29–42.

6. Edward J. O'Donnell and his collaborators, then in the Division of Intramural Research, Social and Rehabilitation Service, Department of Health, Education, and Welfare, have provided the most useful and comprehensive of the systematic reviews of general research in this field in a series of three articles in *Welfare in Review:* "Neighborhood Service Centers," October 1967; "The Neighborhood Service Center," January–February 1968; and, with Marilyn M. Sullivan, "Service Delivery and Social Action Through the Neighborhood' Center," November–December 1969. An overview of a national survey of over 3,000 centers appears under the title, "The Multiservice Neighborhood Center: Preliminary Findings from a National Survey," by Edwin O'Donnell and Otto M. Reid, *Welfare in Review,* May–June 1971, 1–8. See also "Service Integration: The Public Welfare Agency and The Multiservice Neighborhood Center," *Welfare in Review,* July–August 1971. My own assessment of multiservice centers and of service integration efforts appears in Alfred J. Kahn, "Service Delivery at the Neighborhood Level: Experience, Theory, and Fads," *Social Service Review,* 50, 1 (March 1976), 23–56. Also, see Sheila B. Kamerman and Alfred J. Kahn, *Social Services in the United States* (Philadelphia: Temple University Press, 1976), Chapter 7.

7. See the O'Donnell summaries as well as Alfred J. Kahn, *Studies in Social Policy and Planning* (New York: Russell Sage Foundation, 1969), Chapter 7 and citations.

8. Robert Perlman and David Jones, *Neighborhood Service Centers* (Washington, D.C.: Government Printing Office, 1967). A consumer view of services in a multiservice center is offered in Robert Perlman, *Consumers and Social Services* (New York: Wiley, 1975).

9. O'Donnell cites the evidence.

10. For a report on a pioneering experience, see Harold Weisman (ed.), *Community Development in the Mobilization for Youth Experience* (New York: Association Press, 1969).

11. For a history of reaching-out projects in the 1950s, see Alfred J. Kahn, *Planning Community Services for Children in Trouble* (New York: Columbia University Press, 1963), Chapter 10.

12. For background and extensive bibliography, see Frances Fox Piven and Richard A. Cloward, *Poor People's Movements* (New York: Pantheon, 1977).

13. On this, see Peter Marris and Martin Rein, *Dilemmas of Social Reform* (New York: Atherton, 1969); Martin Rein, "Poverty, Policy, and Purpose: The Dilemmas of Choice," *Social Policy: Issues of Choice and Change* (New York: Random House, 1970), Chapter 12,; Alfred J. Kahn, "The Anti-Poverty War as a Social Strategy," *Studies in Social Policy and Planning,* Chapter 2; and Sar A. Levitan, *The Great Society's Poor Law* (Baltimore: Johns Hopkins Press, 1969).

14. Charles E. Grosser, *Helping Youth — A Study of Six Community Organization Programs,* Office of Juvenile Delinquency and Youth Development, Department of Health, Education, and Welfare (Washington, D.C.: Government Printing Office, 1968), p. 57. For a full summary of experience, see O'Donnell and Sullivan, "Service Delivery and Social Action Through the Neighborhood Center"; and Perlman and Jones, *Neighborhood Service Centers.* Detailed documentation of limited service and the "pseudo-democratic" nature of many of the efforts at community control of antipoverty programs is offered in Ralph M. Kramer, *Participation of the Poor* (Englewood Cliffs, N.J.: Prentice-Hall, 1969). Kramer identifies many positives in these programs, even though they did not achieve the enunciated goals: control by the most disadvantaged poor and service improvement. More recent and comprehensive overviews appear as Chapter 9 in Sar A. Levitan and Robert Taggart III, *The Promise of Greatness* (Cambridge, Mass.: Harvard University Press, 1976); or Paul E. Peterson and J. David Greenstone, "Racial Change and Citizen Participation: The Mobilization of Low-Income Communities Through Community Action," in Robert H. Haveman (ed.), *A Decade of Federal Antipoverty Programs* (New York: Academic Press, 1977), pp. 241–278.

15. Alfred H. Katz and Eugene I. Bender (eds.), *The Strength in Us* (New York: Franklin Watts, 1975); and Alfred H. Katz, "Self-Help Groups," *Encyclopedia of Social Work, Seventeenth Issue* (Washington, D.C.: National Association of Social Workers, 1977), Vol. 2, pp. 1254–1261.

16. Norton Long, "The Local Community as an Ecology of Games," *American Journal of Sociology,* 64, 3 (November 1958), 251–261; also appears in

several "urban readers" and anthologies. For a most helpful discussion of community control, growing out of experience on New York's Lower East Side, see Bertram M. Beck, "Community Control: A Distraction, Not an Answer," *Social Work,* 14, 4 (October 1969), 14–20; also, Neil Gilbert and Joseph W. Eaton, "Who Speaks for the Poor?" and Lisa Peattie, "Community Drama and Advocacy Planning," *Journal of the American Institute of Planners,* 36, 6 (November 1970), 411–416, 405–410.

▶▶▶▶▶▶▶▶▶▶ Reading List

The following works and journals will be of special interest to both concerned citizens and students. Each contains further bibliography, as do the footnotes in the present book.

Bloedorn, Jack C., et al. *Designing Social Service Systems*. Chicago: American Public Welfare Association, 1970.

Cumming, Elaine. *Systems of Social Regulation*. New York: Atherton, 1968.

Encyclopedia of Social Work, Seventeenth Issue. New York: National Association of Social Workers, 1977.

Hall, Phoebe. *Reforming the Welfare*. London: Heinemann, 1976.

—————, et al. *Change, Choice and Conflict in Social Policy*. London: Heinemann, 1975.

Handler, Joel, and Ellen Jane Hollingsworth. *The "Deserving Poor": A Study of Welfare Administration*. Chicago: Markham Publishing Co., 1971.

Horton, Gerald. *Readings in Human Services Planning*. Atlanta, Ga.: The Research Group, 1976.

Jeffreys, Margot. *An Anatomy of Social Welfare Services*. London: Michael Joseph, 1965.

Kahn, Alfred J. *Studies in Social Policy and Planning*. New York: Russell Sage Foundation, 1969.

—————. *Theory and Practice of Social Planning*. New York: Russell Sage Foundation, 1969.

————, and Sheila B. Kamerman. *Not for the Poor Alone.* Philadelphia: Temple University Press, 1975, and New York: Harper and Row, paperback, 1977.

————. *Social Services in International Perspective.* Washington, D.C.: Government Printing Office, 1977. Stock No. 017-062-00108-1.

Kamerman, Sheila B., and Alfred J. Kahn. *Social Services in the United States.* Philadelphia : Temple University Press, 1976.

Katz, Elihu, and Brenda Danet. *Bureaucracy and the Public.* New York: Basic Books, 1973.

Kershaw, Joseph. *Government Against Poverty.* Chicago: Markham Publishing Co.: 1970.

Levitan, Sar A. *The Great Society's Poor Law.* Baltimore: Johns Hopkins Press, 1969.

————, and Robert Taggart III. *The Promise of Greatness.* Cambridge: Harvard University Press, 1976.

Maas, Henry S. (ed.). *Research in the Social Services: A Five Year Review.* New York: National Association of Social Workers, 1971.

Merriam, Ida C., and Alfred M. Skolnick. *Social Welfare Expenditures Under Public Programs in the United States, 1929–66.* Research Report no. 25, Office of Research and Statistics, Social Security Administration, Washington, D.C.: Government Printing Office, 1968.

Meyer, Carol. *Social Work Practice.* New York: Free Press, 1976.

Office of Human Development Services, U.S. Department of Health, Education, and Welfare. *Social Services U.S.A.* Washington, D.C.: Government Printing Office, 1978.

Perlman, Robert. *Consumers and Social Services.* New York: Wiley, 1975.

————, and David Jones. *Neighborhood Service Centers.* Washington, D.C.: Government Printing Office, 1967.

Rein, Martin. *Social Policy: Issues of Choice and Change.* New York: Random House, 1970.

Report of the Committee on Local Authority and Allied Social Services. Cmnd 3703. London: Her Majesty's Stationery Office, 1968.

Rivlin, Alice. *Systematic Thinking for Social Action.* Washington, D.C.: The Brookings Institution, 1971.

Robson, William A., and Bernard Crick (eds.), *The Future of the Social Services.* Baltimore: Penguin, 1970.

Rosenberg, Marvin, and Ralph Brody. *Systems Serving People.* Cleveland: Case Western Reserve University, 1976.

Rowbottom, Ralph, et al. *Social Service Departments: Developing Patterns of Work and Organization.* London: Heineman, 1976.

Schon, Donald A. "The Blindness System," *The Public Interest,* No. 18 (Winter 1970), 25–38.

Schorr, Alvin. *Explorations in Social Policy.* New York: Basic Books, 1968.

Scott, Robert A. *The Making of Blind Men.* New York: Russell Sage Foundation 1968.

Steiner, Gilbert Y. *The Children's Cause.* Washington, D.C.: The Brookings Institution, 1976.

————. *The State of Welfare.* Washington, D.C.: The Brookings Institution, 1971

Thursz, Daniel, and Joseph L. Vigilante (eds.). *Social Service Delivery Systems: An International Annual.* Beverly Hills, Calif.: Sage Publications, Vol. 1, 1973; Vol. 2, 1976; Vol. 3, 1978.

Titmuss, Richard M. *Commitment to Welfare.* New York: Pantheon, 1968.

————. *The Gift Relationship.* New York: Pantheon, 1971.

Townsend, Peter, et al. *The Fifth Social Service.* London: Fabian Society, 1970.

Williams, Alan, and Robert Anderson. *Efficiency in the Social Services.* Oxford and London: Basil Blackwell and Martin Robertson, 1975.

Journals

Aging (Administration on Aging, DHEW)

American Journal of Orthopsychiatry (American Orthopsychiatric Association)

Children Today (Administration for Children, Youth, and Families, DHEW)

Child Welfare (Child Welfare League of America)

Journal of Human Services Abstracts (Project Share, DHEW)

Policy Analysis

Public Welfare (American Public Welfare Association)

Social Casework (Family Service Association of America)

Social Services Review (University of Chicago Press)

Social Work (National Association of Social Workers)

►►►►►► Index